Culturally Specific Pedago~~gy in the~~ Mathematics Classroom

"*Culturally Specific Pedagogy in the Mathematics Classroom* offers a wide variety of conceptual and curricular resources for teachers interested in teaching mathematics in a way that challenges stratification based upon race, class, gender and other forms of oppression that students face in today's world …

With the publication of this book, all teachers will have available to them instructional strategies in mathematics for meeting the academic needs of culturally diverse students. They will have an explanation of the linkage between culture and students' mathematical cognition and problem solving.… The ease in which Leonard brings the reader along, and the caring way she tells a story about making mathematics a fun and social justice experience makes for an exciting learning opportunity for all students and teachers."

Carl A. Grant, University of Wisconsin, Madison, United States,
from the Foreword

"Mathematics educators are in a period of deep concern about our ability to educate all students in mathematics. Most students of color do not have the opportunities to fully learn mathematics. Nothing more important can be done for these students and their teachers than to publish this book addressing the miseducation of these students and offering a way to change what we are doing."

Carol E. Malloy, University of North Carolina,
Chapel Hill, United States

This compelling text advocates the use of culturally specific pedagogy to enhance the mathematics instruction of diverse students. It accomplishes this by making clear the link between research and practice and offering lesson templates that teachers can use with ethnically and culturally diverse students and with females. Specifically, the text draws on sociocultural theory and research on culture and mathematics cognition to focus on three goals: using qualitative research to extend the literature on culturally based education to African American and Latina/o children in their development of mathematical knowledge and skills; using cognition research as it applies to better understanding of minority students' goals, cognitive forms, and the interplay or transfer of out-of-school and in-school practices; and using pedagogical research to field-test new instructional methods for culturally diverse and female students.

Culturally Specific Pedagogy in the Mathematics Classroom:

- features a model of culturally specific mathematics instruction that is grounded in Critical Race Theory
- uses comprehensive analyses of both qualitative and quantitative data to make the case that culturally specific pedagogy enhances student achievement
- presents cultural representations in problem solving and problem posing
- interweaves case studies, vignettes, and specific examples to help teachers to visualize what culturally specific pedagogy is and how to use it
- includes problems and questions developed by and of significance to preservice and inservice teachers.

This clear, powerful text is intended for teacher educators, researchers, and upper-division and graduate-level courses in multicultural/diversity education, mathematics education, and curriculum and instruction.

Jacqueline Leonard, Ph.D, Temple University, Philadelphia, U.S.A.

Culturally Specific Pedagogy in the Mathematics Classroom
Strategies for Teachers and Students

Jacqueline Leonard

Temple University, Philadelphia, U.S.A.

Routledge
Taylor & Francis Group

NEW YORK AND LONDON

First published 2008
by Routledge
270 Madison Ave, New York, NY 10016

Simultaneously published in the UK
by Routledge
2 Park Square, Milton Park, Abingdon, Oxon OX14 4RN

Routledge is an imprint of the Taylor & Francis Group, an informa business

Typeset in Minion by Wearset Ltd, Boldon, Tyne and Wear, UK
Printed and bound in the United States of America on acid-free paper by Sheridan Books, Inc

Library of Congress Cataloging in Publication Data
Leonard, Jacqueline.
Culturally specific pedagogy in the mathematics classroom: strategies for teachers and students/Jacqueline Leonard.
p. cm.
Includes bibliographical references and index.
1. Mathematics–Study and teaching–United States–Social aspects. 2. Multicultural education–United States. 3. Minorities–Education–United States. 4. Critical pedagogy–United States. I. Title.
QA13.L46 2008
510.71–dc22
2007023657

ISBN10: 0-8058-6105-X (pbk)
ISBN10: 1-4106-1461-1 (ebk)

ISBN13: 978-0-8058-6105-1 (pbk)
ISBN13: 978-1-4106-1461-2 (ebk)

IN MEMORY OF
My brother:
Frederick Terence Leonard, Sr.
(1955–2005)
&
My uncle:
Odell Quinn
(1935–2000)
THIS BOOK IS DEDICATED TO
My progeny, especially my grandson:
Christopher Lashon Cloud, Jr.
Grand-nephew:
Terrence Jevon Leonard
&
First cousins once removed:
Cydnei Maya Quinn
Jacob Michael Leonard-Campbell

Contents

Illustrations

Foreword

Over the past two decades educators have argued that one of the reasons their instruction is not meeting the learning needs of students of color and other marginalized students is because they do not know how to meet these students' learning needs. In other words, they do not have the *cultural* knowledge, skills, materials, and where-with-all to teach students who are culturally different. Furthermore, teachers of mathematics instruction have argued that "math is math." The subject matter content of this *pure* academic subject, it was argued, should not be corrupted. Any thought about the inclusion of culture (e.g., cultural responsiveness, culturally relevant teaching) in math instruction was out of the question. While both of these arguments kept multiculturalists at bay for a while, they soon argued that such reasoning was an example of how power was being masked within the knowledge and language constructed to make these arguments. These arguments have no currency. Mathematic is not acultural.

Jacqueline Leonard's scholarship, as particularly expressed in her outstanding book *Culturally Specific Pedagogy in the Mathematic Classroom*, is one of the reasons that the "I don't know how to teach mathematics to culturally diverse students" and the "math is math" discourse will further lose its currency. With the publication of Leonard's book, all teachers will have available to them instructional strategies in math for meeting the academic needs of culturally diverse students. They will have an explanation of the linkage between culture and students' mathematical cognition and problem solving.

Culturally Specific Pedagogy in the Mathematic Classroom offers a wide variety of conceptual and curricular resources for teachers interested in teaching mathematics in a way that challenges stratification based upon race, class, gender, and other forms of oppression that students face in today's world. Case studies of urban teachers using culturally specific pedagogy are excellent for helping teachers and teacher candidates to better understand how to teach mathematics to all students. The case studies are *real* and easy to follow and understand. Additionally, Leonard does an excellent job of providing theoretical and practical inclusiveness as she discusses pedagogy in the mathematics classroom.

Leonard is part of a new generation of scholars, whose work integrates culture and context into the mainstream of their academic writing of subject matter content. This new generation of scholars does not separate culture and context from subject matter content. Scholars like Leonard are writing to inform teachers and other educators about how to make mathematics and other academic subjects relevant to the needs of their diverse student population and thereby better inform the field about the power of sociocultural and sociopolitical practices. Leonard argues for very high teacher expectations of culturally diverse students, explicitly and implicitly. She contends that "no child will obtain success in mathematics by simply knowing the basics. Teachers must teach children of color a variety of topics beyond the basics such as numeracy, rational numbers, integers, measurement, geometry, statistics, probability, and data analysis" and other important aspects of mathematics as well.

A very well-crafted social justice discourse transcends the book. However, social justice is not preached; instead Leonard integrates social justice ideas within the language and narrative of the content. In addition, she is mindful of the historical role mathematics served in helping to liberate and guide Black people to freedom during their days of enslavement. She is also mindful of the current role that mathematics plays as a gatekeeper of opportunities for students of color and their pursuit of academic and economic success.

What I found especially informative about *Culturally Specific Pedagogy in the Mathematic Classroom* is that you have at your fingertips literature reviews about: "culture and mathematics cognition," "studies on diverse students' achievement in mathematics," and an explanation of the different approaches teachers may use under the cultural pedagogy paradigm. In addition, Leonard provides great insights for teachers in how to include mathematics as a connecting strand to different subject areas: Chapter 5: The Underground Railroad: A context for learning mathematics and social justice; Chapter 6: Women in aviation and space: The importance of gender role models in mathematics education; and Chapter 7: Learning mathematics for empowerment in linguistically and culturally diverse classrooms, demonstrates to teachers how to integrate mathematics and social justice concepts throughout the curriculum, as well as to teach using culturally specific pedagogy. Finally, the ease in which Leonard brings the reader along, and the caring way she tells a story about making mathematics a fun and social justice experience makes for an exciting learning opportunity for all students and teachers.

Carl A. Grant, Hoefs-Bascom Professor
University Wisconsin-Madison
August 9, 2006

Preface

A great deal of attention has been given to what some consider an achievement gap (Ladson-Billings, 2006). The gap has been defined as differences in performance outcomes among Black and White students on standardized tests. Trends show, despite efforts to reform education with national and state standards, that White and Asian students continue to outperform African American and Latina/o students on these measures (Martin, 2003; Tate, 1997). Yet, very little attention has been given to differential educational opportunity (Kozol, 1991 & 2005; Ladson-Billings, 2006). Instead, for more than a decade, schools have been resegregating along lines of race, ethnicity, and socioeconomic status (Lee & Orfield as cited in Ladson-Billings, 2006). Given that urban school districts have largely abandoned desegregation efforts and parents of students of color have limited educational choice, the variable that continues to make a difference in urban schools is teachers. However, teachers of diverse students are more likely to be culturally and economically different from the students they serve (Gay, 2000). Thus, there is a need for teachers of diverse student populations to possess a pedagogy that will enable them to motivate, engage, and teach these students what they need to know to have access to higher education and economic success (Delpit, 1995; Gay, 2000; Martin, 2003; Moses & Cobb, 2001; Nieto, 2002; Sheets, 2005).

The purpose of this book is to advocate the use of culturally specific pedagogy to enhance the mathematics instruction of diverse students by making clear the link between research and practice and offering prospective teachers lesson templates that can be used with ethnically diverse students and females. Specifically, I use sociocultural theory and research on culture and mathematics cognition to focus on three goals: (1) qualitative research to extend the literature on culturally based education to African American and Latina/o children in their development of mathematical knowledge and skills; (2) cognition research as it applies to better understand minority students' goals, cognitive forms, and the interplay or transfer of out-of-school and in-school practices (Saxe, 1991); and (3) pedagogical research to field-test new instructional methods for African American, Latina/o, and female students. However, these strategies are not a panacea and should not be viewed as a bag of tricks or a recipe to undo decades of inadequate schooling in America.

The chapters in this book provide examples from the research studies I conducted, as well as my teaching experience (K–16) in different contexts to help teachers visualize what culturally specific pedagogy is and how to use it with diverse students. Case studies, vignettes, and specific examples of culturally relevant and specific teaching are interwoven throughout the text to provide context and convey meaning. Chapter 1 describes the need for culturally specific pedagogy and the rationale for using critical race theory as the theoretical framework. Chapter 2 outlines the development of culturally based education and includes a discussion of the link between cognition and culture and how culture can be used to help diverse students learn mathematics. From culturally relevant teaching to diversity pedagogy, Chapter 3 outlines the development of cultural pedagogy. Chapter 4 provides an extensive treatise on problem solving and problem posing and describes how multicultural literature and emerging technology may be used as scaffolds to support both activities. Chapters 5 through 7 offer practical examples, drawn from research findings and related bodies of literature, and present novice teachers with a number of strategies that can be used to engage even the most reticent students in authentic mathematics problems and activities. Chapter 5 presents data-driven activities and case studies about how to use Civil Rights as a forum to connect mathematics to the lives of African American and other students of color. From the Underground Railroad, which was the first Civil Rights movement, to the Civil Rights movement of the 1960s, connections are made between mathematics and social justice. In Chapter 6, lessons and activities that highlight the histories of women aviators and astronauts are presented alongside research findings obtained from conducting a space science study to advance gender equity. Chapter 7 outlines culturally based strategies that may be used to enhance the mathematics education of linguistically and culturally diverse students. Multicultural literature is used to make connections to Latina/o and Asian culture. Finally, in Chapter 8, I discuss issues related to mathematics achievement among African American students.

Since legal remedies such as *Brown* v. *Board of Education* (1954) and desegregation efforts have not resulted in equitable education for all students, the dilemma of underachievement in mathematics among African American and other minority populations must be addressed on moral and ethical grounds. "So long as there are ghetto neighborhoods and ghetto hospitals and ghetto schools, ... there will be ghetto desperation, ghetto violence, and ghetto fear because a ghetto is itself an evil and unnatural construction" (Kozol, 1995, p. 162). A nation that is founded on principles of democracy and equality must show the world that it embraces its own diversity and provides high-quality education for all children. Teaching and learning mathematics for social justice is imperative in helping marginalized students acquire the tools necessary to improve their lot in life (Gutstein, 2003; Martin, 2003). "Eliminating inequities in access, achievement, and persistence in mathematics" cannot be divorced from the broader contexts in which schools exist and students live (Martin, 2003, p. 17). Students must be able to "use mathematics in the out-of-school contexts that define their lives" (Martin, 2003, p. 17), if mathematics achievement and persistence are to have meaning. Moses and Cobb (2001) contend that schools and the educational community, at large, must commit to everyone gaining math-science literacy just as they have been committed to reading-writing literacy. Once society at large and policymakers adhere to the call for mathematics equity on moral and ethical grounds and allow high mathematics achievement to translate into real economic opportunity, then students of color will strive to achieve and persist in their education because economic parity has become reality (Martin, 2000).

Acknowledgments

No one accomplishes a task without the assistance of significant others in his/her life. This book is no exception. I am indebted to those who are mentioned in the following paragraphs and greatly appreciate their love and support.

First and foremost, I express sincerest thanks to Dr. Martin L. Johnson, Associate Dean of the College of Education at the University of Maryland at College Park, who served as my dissertation chair and mentor for this book. His mentoring and advice helped to shape my career and direction in academia. I will always be deeply grateful to him for all of his efforts to mold me into the scholar that I have become.

Moreover, I express deep gratitude to Dr. William F. Tate, the Edward Mallinckrodt Distinguished University Professor in Arts & Sciences, for his nurturing and affable character. I am most appreciative of his support in writing the book proposal and final manuscript; he provided office space at Washington University in St. Louis during the summers of 2005 and 2006. I also extend a special thanks to Dr. Kay Lovelace Taylor, who also provided mentoring and space to reflect upon this endeavor in beautiful Scottsdale, Arizona. Many thanks to Joyce Alexander, Julia Leonard, Lou Venia Campbell, and Stephanie Leonard for providing housing and transportation to support my work at Washington University in St. Louis.

Furthermore, I am truly indebted to Dr. Carl A. Grant for writing the foreword to this book. As an established scholar, he has been my role model. Another mentor and role model who has greatly influenced my research is Dr. James Earl Davis. I am grateful for his friendship and advice regarding the publication of this book.

In addition, I am most appreciative for the guidance and nurturing of my former principal, Mrs. Joy Barnhart. She helped me to develop a culturally responsive pedagogy early in my teaching career at Lisbon School in Dallas, Texas, and exposed me to Project SEED classes. As a result, I became a Project SEED instructor, which forever changed my expectations of students in mathematics. I want to thank my Project SEED trainers and mentors, Dr. Sandra Jones and Mr. William H. Glee, Jr. who helped me to become a stellar mathematics specialist. Furthermore, I am indebted to Mr. Ivan Shkurko, who has committed more than three decades to Project SEED instruction, for helping me to think critically about some of the mathematics examples provided in this book.

I also wish to acknowledge the efforts of my graduate research assistants,

Lakisha Baxter, Jason Christiansen, Vania Gulston, and James E. Oakley, for collecting and transcribing data. My daughters, Cara M. Moore and Victoria R. Cloud, also edited this book and transcribed data, respectively. I want to especially thank my daughters for their love and unwavering support of my research and career.

Furthermore, I would like to thank Dwain Leonard, President of Renaissance Micro, Inc., for his collaboration on the Banneker Project and the development of Riding the Freedom Train. I also acknowledge Francine Still Hicks for contributing some of the artwork illustrated in this book. She has a unique style that is all her own.

I would also like to thank administrators and teachers at Tidye Phillips School, Harriet Tubman Charter School, and West Oak Lane Charter School for their participation and support in data collection, especially Delphine Quinn, Michele Pierce, Anita Angram, Robert A. Bonseñor, Lisa Edmiston, Donnamarie Parker, Denise Tate, Kara Reel, and Louise Whitelaw.

Finally, I wish to thank my high-school English teacher, Mrs. S. Breaux Daniel, who taught me everything I know about writing and showed her students the world outside of the confines of Soldan High School. I would also be remiss if I did not acknowledge the Rev. Dr. Dorothy Watson Tatem for her support of my research endeavors in the Eastern Pennsylvania Annual Conference and Temple University for its generous support of my research through Grant-in-Aid, Junior Faculty Support Grant, and Sabbatical leave. Some of the research presented in this book was also supported by the National Science Foundation and Space Telescope Science Institute. The views contained in this book do not necessarily reflect the positions or policies at NSF or STScI.

Jacqueline Leonard

Biographical note

Dr. Jacqueline Leonard hails from St. Louis, Missouri. A product of the St. Louis Public Schools, she graduated from Soldan High School in 1975. Jacqueline received the Bachelor of Arts from Saint Louis University in 1981; Master of Arts in Teaching in Mathematical Sciences from the University of Texas at Dallas in 1991; Master of Theological Studies from Southern Methodist University in 1994; and Ph.D. in Mathematics Education from the University of Maryland at College Park in 1997.

Dr. Leonard was promoted to Associate Professor of Mathematics Education in the College of Education at Temple University in July 2003. She has made 40 conference presentations and authored 25 articles. Prior to her appointment at Temple, Dr. Leonard taught for 15 years as a public school teacher. She was a middle-school science teacher in University City, Missouri, from 1981 to 1983, and a kindergarten and intermediate mathematics teacher in Dallas, Texas, from 1984 to 1993. While working on her doctorate at the University of Maryland, Dr. Leonard also taught sixth grade in Bowie, Maryland, from 1994 to 1997.

Dr. Leonard's awards include: Leading African American Woman in Pennsylvania (Pennsylvania Commission for Women for Outstanding Service, 2005); Outstanding New Scholar Award (University of Maryland at College Park, 2004); Summer Research Fellow (Virginia Polytechnic Institute and State University, 1997); Patricia Roberts Harris Fellow (University of Maryland at College Park, 1994–1997).

Dr. Jacqueline Leonard has two daughters, Ms. Cara Moore (MSEd) and Mrs. Victoria Cloud (MPT), one son-in-law, Mr. Christopher L. Cloud, Sr., and one grandson, Christopher, Jr.

1
Culture, community, and mathematics achievement

Optimism is the faith that leads to achievement. Nothing can be done
without hope or confidence.

Helen Keller

Introduction

While on temporary assignment at Washington University in St. Louis to
finish writing this book, a conversation between me and an African American
male developed while waiting at a bus stop. At the outset, we discussed the
hot weather and a recent thunderstorm that knocked out electrical power to
tens of thousands of people. We also talked about how the repairs cost the life
of one employee who stepped on a live wire that was covered by brush. Then
the conversation shifted as follows:

> I am 34 years old and my brother is 32. He wants to go back to school to
> learn advanced mathematics like algebra and statistics. I don't think
> anyone needs to know mathematics beyond the basics unless you want to
> be a chemist or an astronaut or something like that. What do you think?

I responded:

> Knowing advanced mathematics is important if a person wants to be
> able to make sound decisions about mortgages and investments plans
> and things like that.

As the bus pulled up, he responded:

> Yes, knowledge of fractions and decimals is important, too, but I just
> don't see the importance of knowing algebra to get along in everyday
> life.

It was 6:00 p.m., and there was a shift change. The former bus driver greeted
him, and the man to whom I was talking settled into the driver's seat and

resumed the bus route. I pondered how someone in his position was not aware of the role mathematics plays in social stratification and economic advantages (Apple, 1995; Gutstein, 2003). He probably had insurance premiums and a pension plan. How could he think that knowledge of algebra and statistics was not important? He used math daily, estimating time and distances to maintain a schedule on his bus route.

Logical thinking obtained through study of mathematics is important in making everyday decisions. For example, in order to make financial decisions about how to finish this book, I had to use a great deal of mathematics. First, I wrote a proposal and budget to apply for a small grant from my home institution—Temple University—to complete the manuscript. Before writing the budget, I decided to fly instead of drive to St. Louis, as I had done the previous year. My decision to fly was based on the fact that the average price (rounded to nearest cents) of gasoline was $2.22 a gallon in the Midwest in July 2005 compared to $2.99 a gallon in July 2006. This was a net change of $0.77 per gallon. The number of miles that it takes to drive from my home in South Jersey to my mother's home in St. Louis, Missouri, is 915.41, which is 1,830.82 miles roundtrip. My SUV averages about 30 miles per gallon on the highway. To find the cost of driving to St. Louis, I manipulated the following formula: r (rate) $\times$ t (time) $= d$ (distance). Substituting 30 miles per gallon for r and 1,830.82 miles for d ($30\,\text{mi/gal} \times t = 1{,}830.82$), I found the number of gallons of gasoline needed to get to St. Louis and back. I needed 61.03 gallons of gas, which would cost $182.48 in 2006 compared to $135.49 in 2005, which was a difference of about $47.00. While the cost of an airline ticket on US Air from Philadelphia to St. Louis in July 2006 ($282.60) was about $100 more than the cost of driving, the cost of repairs on my vehicle ($314.07) after driving to St. Louis in 2005 negated any savings, not to mention the cost of tolls and the additional time it took to drive.

Mathematical reasoning not only helped me to make an informed decision about how to get to St. Louis, but it also informed my decision making about the mode of transportation after I arrived. Although a family car was available to me to commute to Washington University, I decided to take public transportation for a couple of reasons. First, parking at the university had increased to $5.00 per day from a rate of $3.00 per day the previous year. The daily cost of transportation on the Metro Bus was $4.00 (roundtrip), a weekly pass cost $17.00, and the monthly pass was $55.00. I worked at the university for 17 days over a period of four weeks in July 2006. The cost of parking would have been $85.00. The cost of a daily or weekly pass would have been $68.00. Purchasing a monthly pass would yield $30.00 in savings, plus the cost of gasoline, if I did not drive, and $13 in savings if I did not purchase the weekly or daily pass. Although the distance from my summer residence to the university was only 2.11 miles and seven minutes by car, I decided to take public transportation even though I had to take two buses and my travel time increased to 30 minutes. Second, I was able to use the bus pass several times in a single day (during the lunch hour) and on weekends if I needed to (Tate, 1994). When it came to transportation, mathematical power translated into economic power.

Common beliefs in some communities about the need for mathematics in everyday life are similar to those of the bus driver. Some people do not believe they need to know more than the basics, but data analysis, statistics, algebra, and multi-step problem solving were required for me to make a decision about whether to fly or drive from South Jersey to St. Louis, Missouri. Triggered by some event or circumstance in his life, the bus driver's brother realized that he needed to know more mathematics. His mathematical identity (Martin, 2000) was quite different from the bus driver's mathematical identity. However, whether the bus driver's brother follows through with his decision to learn more mathematics depends on his mathematics socialization (Martin, 2000). If the bus driver convinces him that he does not need mathematics, he may choose not to take advanced mathematics courses. Thus, community values about mathematics are just as important as individual beliefs.

Mathematics achievement in the U.S.

Mathematics achievement is important for individual and corporate success. Yet, underachievement in mathematics is a national dilemma that researchers and policymakers continue to ponder. Trends in Mathematics and Science Study (TIMSS) data continue to show lower achievement among U.S. students on the international level. U.S. fourth graders ranked eighth out of 49 countries and eighth graders ranked 15th out of 45 countries in mathematics in 2003 (NSTA, 2005). On a national scale, different levels of achievement are persistent among diverse student populations.

Comparisons among different demographic groups in the U.S. continue to be measured by the National Assessment of Educational Progress (NAEP). Data show average scaled scores in mathematics on the NAEP increased from 235 in 2003 to 241 in 2004 for nine-year-old students (NCES, 2005). However, average scores dropped to 238 in 2005 (NCES, 2006). The average scaled score for White fourth graders was 247 compared to 224 for Blacks at the same grade level in 2004, but average scores for these groups fell to 246 and 220 in 2005, respectively. NAEP results for eighth graders show 59% of Black and 50% of Hispanic eighth-grade students scored below basic in mathematics compared to 21% of Whites (NCES, 2006). Despite gains on the NAEP over the last ten years, only 1% of Black and Hispanic students scored at the advanced level in mathematics in 2005 (NCES, 2006).

When socioeconomic status is taken into consideration, 2005 data reveal that students ineligible for free or reduced lunch had an average scaled score of 248 while eligible students' average scaled score was 225 (NCES, 2006). The difference in achievement among affluent and poor students was 23 points in 2005. Statistics show that poor students are more likely to be American Indian/Alaska Native, Black and Latina/o (Child Poverty Fact Sheet, 2001). These data imply that poor American Indian/Alaska Native, Black, and Latina/o students are overrepresented in basic and below basic performance groups. As a result, these students begin to disappear from the mathematics pipeline as early as elementary school (Martin, 2000).

The difference in scores among poor students of color and White students is often interpreted to mean students of color are somehow deficient. However, demographic variables such as race, ethnicity, and/or socioeconomic status do not cause failure (Gay, 2000). Persistent achievement patterns among racial and ethnic groups in the U.S. suggest that results cannot be attributed solely to the performance of members of a particular group without examining the conditions that lead to those outcomes (Gay, 2000; Ladson-Billings, 2006; Stiff & Harvey, 1988).

Entwisle and Alexander (1992) found that achievement differences among racial groups were small in first grade but became progressively larger by sixth grade. Claiming that poor and middle-class children entered school with the same pre-mathematical ability, Entwisle and Alexander (1992) found mathematics achievement among diverse students began to diverge in second grade. They also found that summer setbacks and reteaching the previous year's mathematics content contributed to the widening of achievement scores among poor Black and affluent White students.

The problem of underachievement in mathematics is pervasive and complex, having roots in "share cropper" and "separate but unequal" schools for Black children (Du Bois, 1903/1995; Moses & Cobb, 2001). Black children in the U.S. suffer from a dual system of education: one for middle-class Whites and another for poor Black children (Du Bois, 1903/1995; Ladson-Billings, 2006; Stiff & Harvey, 1988). Ladson-Billings (2006) claims that policymakers and researchers should place less focus on the achievement gap and more on the education debt. She describes the education debt as the cumulative impact of more than two centuries of no education, separate and unequal education, and inadequate education (Ladson-Billings, 2006).

> No nation can enslave a race of people for hundreds of years, set them free bedraggled and penniless, pit them, without assistance in a hostile environment, against privileged victimizers, and then reasonably expect the gap between the heirs of the two groups to narrow. Lines, begun parallel and left alone, can never touch.
>
> (Robinson, 2000, p. 74)

Clearly, one cannot deny that there is something inherently flawed in the schooling process. From policymakers to the classroom teacher, we must find ways to ameliorate inequities in educational opportunity.

While schools are seen as a beacon of hope for poor and working-class students, they do not provide an equal starting point for everyone who wants to run the race (Apple, 1995). "Differences in race and social class often combine to place Black and other students of color at a disadvantage for learning" (Nieto, 2002, p. 53). Factors such as inadequate school funding, poor facilities, low teacher expectations, unqualified teachers, inadequate curriculum or no curriculum, influence student outcomes (Kozol, 1991; Leonard, 2002a; Martin, 2003). In essence, these students have been asked to make bricks without straw. Moreover, students of color are often subjected to instructional strategies that emphasize authoritative, didactic, and/or whole group instruction, which may not be conducive to their learning styles (Gay, 2000). Dismal achievement on standardized tests reflects the quality of the education the students receive and not their intellect or ability (Ladson-Billings, 2006).

Nearly two decades of reform rhetoric has not led to equity in education for the majority of poor students and students of color (Dixson & Rousseau, 2005; Ladson-Billings, 2006; Martin, 2003). Curricular reform and standards-based instruction have not solved the systemic problems related to the education of marginalized students (Martin, 2003). Social structures are institutional barriers that limit the opportunities of students of color. These students of color are more likely to be poor, attend large urban public schools, be overrepresented in special education classrooms, and be underrepresented in gifted programs. If current academic trends continue, another generation of students will also underachieve in mathematics and their economic status will most likely remain unchanged. We will know that equity has been achieved when demographic variables such as race, ethnicity, language, and socioeconomic status can no longer be used to identify high and low achievers in mathematics (Gutiérrez, 2002).

School demographics and educational reform

Demographic data obtained from the U.S. Census in 2000 show the school population of African American and Latina/o students is increasing in the U.S. In 2000 the student population was: 1.0% Native American, 3.9% Asian/Pacific Islander, 13.4% African American, 14.6% Hispanic and 67.1% Caucasian (U.S. Department of Commerce, n.d.). Projections for the year 2050 show the nation's schools are becoming more diverse: 1.0% Native American, 7.3% Asian/Pacific Islander, 14.0% African American, 23.3% Hispanic, and 54.4% Caucasian (U.S. Department of Commerce, n.d.). As demographics in U.S. classrooms become increasingly diverse, teachers remain predominantly White and female (Howard, 2003; Irvine, 1992; Remillard, 2000).

Women make up approximately 85–87% of the elementary teachers in the U.S. (Montecinos & Nielsen, 1997). Ninety percent of U.S. teachers are

White; the remaining 10% are members of minority groups (Cooper, 2002; Delpit, 1995). African Americans currently comprise 7% of the teaching population (Cooper, 2002). The number of African American teachers declined drastically during the desegregation era (1954–1972) after more than 39,386 Black teachers lost their jobs in 17 southern states (Fine, 2004; Irvine, 2002; Tillman, 2004). Asian and other ethnic groups make up less than 3% of the teaching force (Cooper, 2002). Yet, an increasingly heterogeneous student population and homogeneous teaching population require reconceptualizion of education reform.

In recent years, education reform has been synonymous with No Child Left Behind. The intent of the No Child Left Behind Act (NCLB, 2001) was to improve academic performance by making teachers, administrators, and school districts accountable for all students. Under NCLB, 95% of language minorities and special education students are subject to high-stakes testing. School districts, not unlike the School District of Philadelphia, were given more stringent rules for hiring teachers but no additional funding for teacher aides and resources. Rarely are administrators and teachers provided with the resources (capital, human, and material) to reach the lowest performing students. However, failure to meet Annual Yearly Progress (AYP) goals will ultimately result in sanctions such as state takeovers and reconstituted schools (Leonard et al., 2004).

Top-down approaches, such as NCLB, will not improve achievement among students of color or produce equitable schools if everyday classroom instruction in mathematics for these students remains focused primarily on rote skills and memorization instead of using mathematics as a context for social justice, liberation, and empowerment (Gutstein, 2003; Martin, 2003). The goals of educational reform in general and mathematics reform in particular cannot be met through traditional program models and curricular development that is separated from students' lives (Secada, 1992). Top-down approaches must be met with bottom-up approaches that take the students into account, provides them with incentives, and empowers them with the tools to use mathematics for goal-directed purposes (Martin, 2000).

Culturally relevant teaching is a bottom-up approach that has shown promise. It is a pedagogy that "empowers students intellectually, socially, emotionally, and politically by using cultural referents (objects, concepts, or events) to impart knowledge, skills, and attitudes" (Ladson-Billings, 1994, pp. 17–18). Engaging students in learning tasks that not only have cultural significance but exposes unjust practices and empowers students to challenge the status quo is teaching for social justice (Gutstein, 2003). Culturally specific pedagogy, then, goes further to help students to develop their identity within the learning community. In order to understand the nuances of culturally specific pedagogy, a theoretical framework that examines education from a social justice standpoint is needed.

Theoretical framework

The theoretical framework that supports the research reported here is critical race theory (CRT), and the construct is culturally specific pedagogy. CRT in education was first proposed by Gloria Ladson-Billings and William Tate as "a framework developed by legal scholars [that] could be employed to examine the role of race and racism in education" (Dixson & Rousseau, 2005, p. 8). CRT challenges the colorblind approach of a traditional liberal civil rights stance and can be traced to the legal work of Derrick Bell and Alan Freeman in the mid-1970s (Delgado, 1995). CRT begins with the premise that racism is the norm in the U.S. (Dixson & Rousseau, 2005; Ladson-Billings, 1998). The theory suggests that race has become a way of "referring to and disguising forces, events, classes, and expressions of social decay and economic division" (Morrison, 1992, p. 63). Cone (1990) believes that race is so endemic of American life that it is difficult to separate race from any aspect of social life (e.g. home, church, school, etc.).

Critical race theory (CRT) examines how citizenship and race interact (Ladson-Billings, 1998). There are systemic and institutional forces at work that continue to oppress persons of color. Based on the construct of "whiteness as property" (Dixson & Rousseau, 2005, p. 5), "whiteness as an explicit cultural product [takes] on a life of its own" (Apple, 2003, p. 113). CRT acknowledges the relationship between skin color (i.e. whiteness) and access to power, privilege, and status in society along with access to property and material goods. In response, CRT gives voice to persons of color as they tell their stories and experiences within a theoretical framework where the center of analysis is the narrative (Brayboy, 2005; Duncan, 2005). Thus, CRT "is an especially useful tool for examining how sociotemporal notions of race inform the naturalization of oppression and the normalization of racial inequality in public schools and society" (Duncan, 2005, p. 94). In other words, as beliefs about race become entrenched in society over time, systems of privilege and marginalization become institutionalized.

Critical race theory (CRT) is characterized by six themes that help to define the framework:

1. Critical race theory recognizes that racism is endemic to American life.
2. Critical race theory expresses skepticism toward dominant legal claims of neutrality, objectivity, colorblindness and meritocracy.
3. Critical race theory challenges ahistoricism and insists on a contextual/historical analysis of the law ... Critical race theorists ... adopt a stance that presumes that racism has contributed to all contemporary manifestations of group advantage and disadvantage.
4. Critical race theory insists on recognition of the experiential knowledge of people of color and our communities of origins in analyzing law and society.

5. Critical race theory is interdisciplinary.
6. Critical race theory works toward the end of eliminating racial oppression as part of the broader goal of ending all forms of oppression.

(Matsuda as cited in Dixson & Rousseau, 2005, p. 9)

CRT has been adapted and used by scholars from other minority groups as well. Latina/o Critical Race Theory (LatCrit), Asian Critical Race Theory (AsianCrit) and Tribal Critical Race Theory (TribCrit) all emerged from CRT. There are nine tenets of TribCrit; however, the following three tenets help to illuminate the issues that are common in all of these theories: (1) colonization is endemic to society; (2) U.S. policies toward Indigenous people are rooted in imperialism, White supremacy, and a desire for material gain; and (3) Indigenous people occupy a liminal space that accounts for both the political and racialized natures of our identities (Brayboy, 2005, p. 429).

CRT suggests that European domination, whether it is imperial or colonial, leads to oppression. In this system, "whiteness" is legitimized as the culture of power and becomes the norm (Apple, 2003). This norm is characterized when all persons of color are simply referred to as "non-white." Racism is the exercise of prejudice and power to institutionalize "white privilege" and support that privilege with laws and police power. Such a system empowers Whites and disenfranchises persons of color. For example, American Indians were deprived of land under laws such as Manifest Destiny and the Norman Yoke (Brayboy, 2005), and African Americans were not allowed to vote and deprived of land under Jim Crow (Apple, 2003; Duncan, 2005). While the Civil Rights Act was signed into law in 1964 to reverse discriminatory practices, it has done little to change the educational, housing, and income status of working-class persons of color (Dixson & Rousseau, 2005). Thus, the common thread among all of the critical race theories is giving voice to those who are marginalized while working to promote anti-racist practices.

CRT validates the voices of those who are marginalized and is a framework that may be used to examine both moral and social justice issues in education. Critics of CRT claim, however, that a single voice, abstract idea, or thought cannot explain the experiences of an entire group of people or community (Duncan, 2005). Furthermore, it does not give enough credence to the work of sympathetic Whites who reject racism and prejudice. While no theory is perfect, complete, and without limitations, collective voices, stories, and other forms of media are the community-oriented theories of individual and collective survival and responses to oppression and struggle (Brayboy, 2005; Duncan, 2005). However, as Dixson & Rousseau (2005) point out, one of the core values of the CRT movement that has been largely unrealized is "active struggle" (p. 22). More than 50 years post-*Brown*, poor African Americans have yet to benefit in general from Civil Rights legislation and Affirmative Action. Despite the incredibility of our stories, we must continue, as Paulo

Freire suggests, "in the incessant struggle to regain [our] humanity ... [so] that reflection will become liberation" (Freire, 1982, p. 25).

Culturally specific pedagogy provides the context for CRT to operate as one way to liberate marginalized persons of color from the "pedagogy of the oppressed" (Freire, 1982). Classrooms are microcosms of larger society. Racism, power, and privilege operate to empower some students and to disenfranchise others. Teachers who are cognizant of CRT can change classroom dynamics by using cultural pedagogy (Leonard & Hill, in press). Drawing from the tenets of culturally relevant pedagogy, culturally specific pedagogy supports the following three goals for students: (1) academic success, (2) cultural competence, and (3) the ability to critique the existing social order (Ladson-Billings, 1994). However, Gutstein et al. (1997), borrowing from Ladson-Billings, contend that capturing culturally relevant teaching is like trying to catch "lightning in a bottle" (p. 733). In other words, what aspects of students' culture might be used to engage students in authentic classroom activities? And how do we know culturally relevant teaching when we see it?

While there are common characteristics and traits among people who share the same race or ethnicity, no culture is monolithic. Within cultural groups are many subcultures. Individuals have multiple layers of identity and belong to more than one subgroup simultaneously. For example, I am an African American female who works in a large urban northeastern city and a member of the United Methodist Church. Thus, I have a generational, racial, gender, geographic, and religious identity. What is culturally relevant to my life may not be culturally relevant to a 25-year-old African American woman who lives in the rural south. The construct can be broadened by defining culturally specific pedagogy as: intentional behavior by a teacher to use gestures, language, history, literature, and other cultural aspects of a particular race, ethnic or gender group to engage students belonging to that group in authentic student-centered learning. Culturally specific pedagogy, then, empowers diverse students to develop a mathematics identity and socializes them as they learn to use mathematics for their own purposes (Martin, 2000).

For example, studies in Brazil (Carraher et al., 1987), Papua New Guinea (Saxe, 1991) and Nigeria (Oloko, 1994) show students engaged in informal mathematical activities with fluency when they conducted exchanges in the market place. These students were able to perform "street" mathematics with adequate success (Carraher et al., 1987). If students can perform mathematical calculations when they engage in real-world activities, surely they can do mathematics in the classroom. Teachers must learn to scaffold children's informal school knowledge by using cultural referents that go beyond a pedagogy that emphasizes memorization and learning a decontextualized set of skills to one that values children's use of mathematics in their lives (Guberman, 2005; Ladson-Billings, 1994; Sleeter, 1997). Tate (1995) illustrated this with an example of how African American students used their knowledge of data to challenge unfair marketing practices (e.g. excess liquor and tobacco ads) in their neighborhoods. We know culturally specific pedagogy is at work when students use mathematics to develop individual agency, sociopolitical conscientiousness, and positive sociocultural identities (Gutstein, 2003). Culturally specific pedagogy is one framework that explicitly links culture and mathematics and is useful in helping teachers to understand the power of cultural pedagogy to engage and empower students of color.

Prior research on culturally based education

Culturally based education has been used with American Indian/Alaska Native students for a number of years, but there is a dearth of experimental, quasi-experimental and comparative non-experimental research studies that examine the link between culture and teaching and learning mathematics and its effect on the mathematics achievement of African American and Latina/o students. Moreover, differences among research paradigms, such as the ethnographic research tradition and the mathematics education research tradition, have not led to ample research in culturally relevant mathematics instruction (Brenner, 1998). While ethnographic research has focused on culture, and mathematics education research has focused on cognition (e.g. Cognitively Guided Instruction and QUASAR), there is a lack of research that uses mixed methodology to examine both culture and mathematics cognition simultaneously (Brenner, 1998). Because of limited research on culturally based education, it remains to be seen whether or not it can serve as a viable option to improve student achievement.

Culturally based education emerged as a means to influence the school performance of American Indian/Alaska Native (AI/AN) and Native Hawaiian children (Demmert & Towner, 2003). The following six elements operationally define culturally based programs:

1. Recognition and use of Native American (AI/AN, Native Hawaiian) languages.
2. Pedagogy that stresses traditional (indigenous) cultural characteristics and adult–child interactions as a starting place for one's education.
3. Pedagogy in which teaching strategies are congruent with the traditional (indigenous) culture as well as contemporary (European) ways of knowing and learning.
4. Curriculum is based on traditional (indigenous) culture that recognizes the importance of Native spirituality, and places the education of young children in a contemporary context.
5. Strong Native community participation (including parents, elders, and other community resources) in educating children and in the planning and operation of school activities.

6. Knowledge and use of the social and political mores of the community.

(Demmert & Towner, 2003, pp. 9–10)

While there is a lack of research studies that examine culture as a basis for learning mathematics, Demmert & Towner's (2003) meta-analysis highlights several research studies that show promising results. Non-experimental comparative studies in mathematics include the Alaska Native Knowledge Network (as cited in Demmert & Towner, 2003), which was developed and implemented to examine pedagogical practices in science and mathematics that utilized indigenous knowledge and ways of knowing. Results show that inclusion of indigenous ways of knowing in science and mathematics curriculum fosters student achievement among Alaska Natives.

In one non-experimental study, Brenner (1998) investigated the influence of cognition and culture on the development of pedagogical practices in mathematics education for young Native Hawaiian children in the Kamehameha Early Education Project (KEEP). In this study, Brenner (1998) described how educational materials and teacher practices reflected three aspects of cultural relevance: cultural content, social content, and cognition. Two different comparative studies were conducted: one with kindergarteners and one with second graders. In kindergarten, students in rural areas who spoke Hawaiian Creole English (HCE) were compared with urban students who were more proficient in English. Children were given paper-and-pencil tests in HCE and Standard English. Results show no difference in how urban children performed on each form of the test. However, rural children performed significantly better on the HCE form of the test than the English version (chi-square = 8.612, p = 0.013). Second graders differed at the classroom level as one teacher in the treatment group used a school store throughout the school year to emphasize the kind of mathematics that took place in Hawaiian communities. Second graders improved their knowledge about money and their use of calculator skills. Moreover, their standardized scores in mathematics (83rd percentile) surpassed those of other second graders (76th percentile) in KEEP schools.

Quasi-experimental studies on the use of culturally based education in mathematics classrooms, however, have been more difficult to conduct. This type of research presents a number of challenges for those who wish to conduct culturally based research projects. Researchers simply do not have control over the research setting necessitated by experimental or quasi-experimental designs (Demmert & Towner, 2003). One of the major problems with quasi-experimental research is time. While lengthy time periods for implementation of an intervention are more desirable, teacher turnover and student attrition may present a problem if the time frame is too long. Ethics is also an issue as researchers may have to decide to exclude particular students on the basis of race, ethnicity, language, and disabilities to gather information about specific types of learners in diverse classrooms. Finally, there are issues of statistical power when researchers attempt to measure student achievement or other quantitative variables when the sample size needed to obtain rich qualitative data in cultural settings tends to be rather small. Thus, case studies on a select number of students of color may be more informative as they relate to their mathematics identity, socialization, and achievement (Martin, 2000).

One of the few quasi-experimental studies that examined culturally based pedagogy in mathematics was conducted by Lipka & Adams (2002). The aim of the study was to ascertain the effectiveness of a culturally based mathematics unit on perimeter and area. The unit was taught to urban and rural sixth graders. Two independent variables were examined in the study by randomly assigning teachers with intact classes to one of four subgroups: urban treatment, urban control, rural treatment, and rural control. The math unit for the treatment groups was infused with cultural artifacts that were representative of Yup'ik culture. A pre-post assessment that consisted of 17 multiple choice or constructive response items on perimeter and area was designed and administered to the students. After a series of t-tests were performed, the researchers found significant differences between urban control and treatment groups and rural control and treatment groups. Gain scores for the urban-treatment group exceeded those of the urban-control group, gain scores for the rural-treatment group exceeded those of the rural-control group, and gain scores for the urban-treatment group exceeded those of the rural-treatment group. The strengths of this study were the formation of comparison groups, consistency of mathematics concepts taught in treatment and control groups, validity of outcome measures, and the culturally based approaches built into the treatment condition.

The foregoing studies not only provide a foundation for future research but also provide teacher educators with an impetus to include cultural pedagogy in mathematics methods courses. Discussions about culture, race, and ethnicity are often absent from the discourse in teacher education classrooms primarily because the instructors themselves are "overwhelmingly White, monocultural, and culturally insular" (Price & Valli, 1998, p. 115). Institutional culture itself can be a barrier to or a catalyst for social change. Preparing teachers who are sensitive to diverse learners requires much more than taking a single course (Bollin & Finkel, 1995; Phuntsog, 1995; Price & Valli, 1998). "All courses need to be infused with content related to diversity" (Nieto, 2000, p. 183). In order to influence positive beliefs and attitudes among preservice teachers about cultural pedagogy, teacher educators must be proactive. Emphasis on culturally specific teaching is especially needed to encourage appropriate practices among prospective teachers of urban African American and Latina/o students who are more likely to be poor and minority.

Teachers' beliefs about culture and learning mathematics

Scholars and researchers of color have stressed the importance of culture and language in the education of diverse students for more than two decades (Boykin & Toms, 1985; Gutiérrez, 2002; Gutstein et al., 1997; Ladson-Billings, 1994; Leonard & Guha, 2002; Malloy & Malloy, 1998; Moses & Cobb, 2001; Sheets, 2005; Solano-Flores & Trumbull, 2003; Tate, 1995). Yet, researchers who connect culture and subject matter knowledge like mathematics and science remain sparse (Aikenhead, 2001; Brenner, 1998; Leonard & Hill, in press) while teachers are being asked to teach in ways they have neither experienced nor been prepared to teach (Kitchen, 2007). Therefore, it is not surprising that some preservice teachers are initially resistant to the idea of using culture as a context for learning mathematics (Leonard & Dantley, 2005; Kitchen, 2007). Regardless of teaching philosophy, it is imperative that teachers commit themselves to teaching all students meaningful and relevant mathematics (Ladson-Billings, 1995). Thus, mathematics educators play a critical role in helping preservice teachers make the cultural connection to mathematics.

Over the last four years, I have focused on the importance of culture in my mathematics methods courses. One of these courses was taught online at the graduate level with face-to-face meetings that were scheduled every three weeks. The class engaged in discussions about assigned readings in mathematics education during online chat sessions. In the fall of 2002, a discussion took place with prospective and beginning elementary teachers about using students' culture as a springboard to teach mathematics (Ladson-Billings, 1994; Malloy & Malloy, 1998). A verbatim record of individual comments was obtained from the discussion board archives. The topic created a flurry of discussion. One African American female offered:

> Students bring their culture with them in the classroom when doing math. How they perceive things and solve equations depends on their background and experience.

An Asian female said:

> We should make an effort to try to encompass activities; lessons that deal with other cultures … if not adopt pedagogies to relate to multiculturalism.

A White female commented:

> I am Jewish, yet many think this is a race and not a religion. I look Irish American. It [culture] has nothing to do with either my ability to do and learn math or how I teach it.

Another White female stated:

> As a special education teacher, I think it is important to look at students as individuals, determine "where" they are and build from that. I don't feel responsible to know more about their culture.

The comments above suggest some prospective and beginning teachers in the graduate course believed the concept of America as a melting pot minimized the need to stress group culture. One Latino male student said:

> If you talk about isolated cultures from small heterogeneous countries, I can see there is a preference, but in a country with so much intermingling of culture, I am not so sure.

A White female responded with the following:

> America is a melting pot. Each one of us lives parts of several cultures.

Another White female said:

> Since we as Americans are as multicultural as a country can get, and it [U.S.] is not defined by a race, language, or religion, we shouldn't base [culture] as a way for teaching mathematics, but understand that a student's perspective might by swayed by it.

Some of the opinions expressed above have merit. However, the concept of America as a melting pot negates the differences and unique contributions that various racial or ethnic groups have to offer. There are benefits to cultural and linguistic diversity that challenge the melting pot metaphor (Nieto, 2002). Studies of bicultural and bilingual students show that diverse students perform better on standardized tests when they can draw on knowledge from both culture and language, respectively (Brenner, 1998; Lipka *et al.*, 2005). In order to *melt* or blend into society as European immigrants have done, one must assimilate, but assimilation usually includes loss of language and cultural identity. For European immigrants assimilation was much easier because they had white skin. Students of color will never blend into White middle-class society on the basis of skin color. In a racialized society, whiteness is viewed as the norm (Duncan, 2005; Ladson-Billings, 1998). Because of the privileged status white skin holds in the U.S., CRT becomes an important intellectual and social tool for "... deconstruction of oppressive structures, reconstruction of human agency, and construction of equitable and socially just relations of power" (Ladson-Billings, 1998, p.9). The melting pot ideology is not a true reflection of a pluralistic and diverse society (Nieto, 2002).

Furthermore, America is *not* as multicultural as it is going to get. It is estimated that 30% of all school-age children are African American, Latina/o

American, Asian American, and Native American. These children comprise the majority of the student population in 23 out of 25 of the nation's largest cities (Delpit, 1995). U.S. Census projections show the nation is becoming more diverse with each passing year. While there is diversity of race, language, and religion, Americans of the dominant race and language—European Americans—continue to have the most power and privilege in the U.S. (Ladson-Billings, 1998; Rousseau & Tate, 2003).

Ideologies that only reflect White middle-class values and goals, wittingly or unwittingly, ensure the status quo is maintained and that rules and direction of power do not change (Delpit, 1995; Martin, 2003). Five aspects of power generally play out in schools:

1. Issues of power are enacted in classrooms.
2. There are codes or rules for participating in power; that is, there is a "culture of power."
3. The rules of the culture of power are a reflection of the rules of the culture of those who have power.
4. If you are not already a participant in the culture of power, being told explicitly the rules of that culture make acquiring power easier.
5. Those with power are frequently least aware of—or least willing to acknowledge—its existence. Those with less power are often most aware of its existence.

(Delpit, 1995, p. 24)

This culture of power is filtered down in textbooks and other forms of media. Mathematics representations in textbooks are immersed in the dominant culture. Moreover, mathematics is often taught in ways that give White males an advantage (Buerk, 1985; Campbell, 1995). Thus, the melting pot idea does not have currency. Imagine a melting pot whose respective components give no additional flavor to the stew. The melting pot metaphor, like the "color-blind" approach, trivializes the lives and experiences of persons of color. Culturally specific pedagogy necessitates that teachers learn about students, their culture, and their backgrounds, by becoming students of the students (Guberman, 2005; Ladson-Billings, 1997; Nieto, 2002).

Convincing some prospective and beginning teachers about the importance of connecting culture to mathematics instruction is a challenging task. Diverse students have ways of learning that are not necessarily consistent with what is viewed as mainstream learning (Brenner, 1998; Malloy & Malloy, 1998; Stiff & Harvey, 1988). Since the fall of 2003, I have required preservice teachers to write a cultural biography at the beginning and end of my math methods course in order to help them develop cultural competence and sensitivity. Throughout the course, we discuss and analyze articles about cultural practices, classroom videos of diverse students learning mathematics in unique ways, and multicultural children's literature (Leonard & Dantley,

2005). At the end of the course, students realize, in general, the political nature of cultural pedagogy. Using cultural pedagogy as a tool to engage students in social change and analyze social inequality and power relations is a profound idea. Many preservice teachers in the course grew from perceiving cultural pedagogy as a duty to understanding how it is necessary to help students develop math identity, exercise self-determination, and experience academic success (Gay, 2000).

Mathematics identity and mathematics socialization

Mathematics is the gatekeeper for access to higher education and higher paying jobs (Gutstein, 2003; Martin, 2000; NCTM, 1989). If poor students do not achieve in mathematics, they will be unable to compete for thousands of high tech jobs in the 21st century (Moses & Cobb, 2001). Without substantial growth in mathematical literacy among students of color, the pedagogy of poverty is perpetuated (Haberman, 1991; Knapp, 1995). Mathematical literacy involves knowing more than the basics. According to Moses & Cobb (2001), "the ongoing struggle for citizenship and equality for minority people is … linked to … math and science literacy" (p. 14). The major components necessary to develop mathematics literacy are "(a) constructing relationships, (b) extending and applying mathematical knowledge, (c) reflecting about experiences, (d) articulating what one knows, and (e) making mathematical knowledge one's own" (Carpenter & Lehrer, 1999, p. 20). In order to make mathematical knowledge one's own, it is important to know and understand one's mathematical identity and the process of mathematical socialization.

Martin (2000) defines the construct of mathematics identity as a person's belief about "(a) their ability to perform in a mathematics context, (b) the importance of mathematical knowledge, (c) constraints and opportunities in mathematical contexts, and (d) the resulting motivation and strategies used to obtain mathematics knowledge" (p. 19). "Mathematics socialization describes the processes and experiences by which individual and collective mathematics identities are shaped by sociohistorical, community, school, and intrapersonal contexts" (Martin, 2000, p. 19). Teachers can help students to develop mathematics identity and participate in the mathematics socialization process by embracing historical figures who used mathematics and by helping students to understand how they can and do use mathematics in their everyday lives.

African American culture can be used to promote the development of mathematics identity and mathematics socialization in a myriad of ways. First, all students should know that mathematics is a part of African American history. Benjamin Banneker, an African American who lived during the colonial period, excelled in mathematics. He used his genius to create the first wooden clock and designed plans for the nation's capital. Bessie Coleman was the first American woman to earn an international pilot's license in 1921

(Borden & Kroeger, 2001). She excelled in mathematics and used it to accomplish her lifelong dream of becoming an aviator. In 1941, John W. Greene established the first African American-owned airport in Prince George's County, Maryland (PG County Fact Sheet, n.d.). Two new members of the Space Shuttle Discovery crew are Joan Higginbotham and Robert L. Curbeam, Jr. Their recent space flight marks the first time in history that two African American astronauts have flown on the same mission (*Jet*, 2006). Certainly mathematics was important in the lives of all of these African Americans.

Mathematics is part of the social milieu and culture of diverse students' lives. Subject matter should be placed within a context that draws upon cultural knowledge (Tate, 1995) and validates different ways of *mathematizing* problems. Mathematizing is how students count, measure, classify, and infer mathematical meaning (D'Ambrosio, 1985) and can be linked with culture. Therefore, framing mathematics instruction within the context of diverse students' culture has legitimacy.

The bus driver who was described earlier in this chapter failed to understand how mathematics is related to success in life (Lave, 1988). With an ever-growing underclass in urban cities, welfare reform, school lunch program reductions, and affirmative action critics, voices for justice and equity are quiescent. Theories of meritocracy, which presuppose that cream always rises to the top, are sufficient. Raising the mathematics literacy standard requires the adequate preparation of all students for a college preparatory sequence of mathematics in high school (Moses & Cobb, 2001). Enrollment in advanced mathematics courses is critical to gaining access to higher education. Higher education provides students with broader opportunities for economic success. Knowledge is power and mathematical literacy opens the door of opportunity. Mathematics education has the potential to liberate the poor from social and economic oppression and can ultimately lead to life, liberty, and the pursuit of happiness. The entire learning community (i.e. parents, teachers, administrators, and policymakers) must take responsibility to ensure that all children develop mathematics identity and mathematics socialization.

2
Cognition and cultural pedagogy

If you can dream it, you can do it.

Walt Disney

Culture, cultural transmission, and cultural capital

Three scholars of color provide definitions of culture for consideration. Ladson-Billings (1997) defines "culture [as] deep structures of knowing, understanding, acting, and being in the world" (Ladson-Billings, 1997, p. 700). Nieto (as cited in Nieto, 2002) defines culture "as the ever-changing values, traditions, social and political relationships, and worldview created and shared by a group of people bound together by a ... common history, geographic location, language, social class, and/or religion ... and how these are transformed by those who share them" (p. 53). Hollins (1996) offers a three-part definition of culture. First, Hollins' (1996) view of culture is one that includes artifacts and behavior. Artifacts refer to visual and performing arts and culinary practices, and behavior refers to social interaction patterns, rituals, ceremonies, and dress (Hollins, 1996). Second, Hollins (1996) agrees with Nieto's notion of culture as the social and political relations and viewpoints that are shared by people bound together by a combination of factors. Third, culture is also seen as affective behavior and intellect, which guides the reasoning, emotions, and actions of a particular group of people (Hollins, 1996). Each of these definitions implies that culture is part of a socialization process where cultural knowledge is acquired from parents and significant others (Cole, 1992; Sheets, 2005).

Enculturation is the process of being socialized into a specific culture (Malloy & Malloy, 1998; Sheets, 2005). Cultural norms have tremendous power to shape beliefs and values and influence one's behavior (Irvine, 2002; Sheets, 2005). Cultural capital, which embodies the norms, ideologies, language, behavior, mores, and practices of a particular group, is transmitted to children as cultural knowledge (Bourdieu, 1973; Howard, 2003; Sheets, 2005). As a result, children develop different habits of mind and ways of doing things, which may conflict with what is expected of them in school (Howard, 2003; Sheets, 2005). However, the cultural knowledge and background experiences of marginalized students are often omitted from school curricula (Nieto, 2002).

In a study that investigated the lives of Navajo students in and out of school, Deyhle (as cited in Nieto, 2002) found that students who did not have a strong Navajo identity and who were rejected by non-Navajos, were more likely to experience school failure. On the other hand, students who attended Navajo schools experienced more success than students who attended non-Navajo schools because they were able to affirm and retain their cultural identity. So, one explanation for underachievement among students of color is the cultural incongruence between student culture and school culture (Banks, 1993; Gay, 2000; Nieto, 2002). Thus, culture and cognition are not mutually exclusive.

European American culture is the dominant culture in the U.S. It has been institutionalized and incorporated into all aspects of American life, including government, business, schools, and mass media (Sheets, 2005). If the cultural capital of the child is congruent with the dominant culture, then that child, who understands the rules, subtleties, and verbal and non-verbal nuances of that culture, is more likely to succeed in school (Gee, 1989; Irvine, 1992). Students who are part of a minority group must adapt by going through a process of acculturation (acquisition of dominant group norms as needed) or assimilation (acceptance of dominant group norms to the exclusion of their own) (Malloy & Malloy, 1998; Sheets, 2005). Yet, students of color must be enculturalized in order to have access to higher education, goods, and services (Gee, 1989). A cultural pedagogy uses the cultural capital students of color bring to school as a bridge to help them acquire dominant group norms. Knowledge and acquisition of mainstream discourse—ways of communicating verbally and nonverbally—is also needed to enhance the academic success of minority children (Delpit, 1995; Gee, 1989; Ladson-Billings, 1995).

Theories about cognition and culture

There are several theories that support the use of cultural pedagogy with students of color. According to Demmert and Towner (2003), culturally based education (CBE) is undergirded by three major theories: Cultural Compatibility Theory, Cultural–Historical–Activity Theory (CHAT) and Cognitive Theory. The basic premise of "cultural compatibility theory is that education is more efficacious when there is an increase in congruence between social–cultural dispositions of students and social–cultural expectations of the school" (Demmert & Towner, 2003, p. 8). CHAT, on the other hand, is a theory of development that "places a great deal of emphasis on community-level elements for connectivity, thereby multiplying the richness of potential associations between student experience and the academic curriculum"

(Demmert & Towner, 2003, p. 9). Thus, involving parents and community members as resources to help students develop knowledge is a key component of CHAT. Both cultural compatibility theory and CHAT are congruent in many ways to cognitive theory, which has roots in developmental psychology.

Cognitive theory

Lave (1988) contends that cognition is a multifaceted social phenomenon that is observed in daily practice and is encompassed by "mind, body, activity and culturally organized settings" (p. 1). Cognitive theory supports the view that culture plays an important role in learning mathematics (Cole, 1992; Saxe 1991; Saxe *et al.*, 1996), and mathematics activity is expressed in unique forms in different situations (Lave, 1988). For example, learning to count is influenced by culture. In Western culture, each finger is used to count by ones while in Indian culture each finger is divided into sections (Guha, 2006). Each section of the finger is used in counting. Further, results of the Adult Math Project (AMP), an observational and experimental study of everyday math practices in different environments, revealed that success in problem solving varied for the same individuals in different contexts (Lave, 1988). An excerpt from one participant in the program highlights this issue:

> There's only about three or four [apples] at home, and I have four kids, so you figure at least two apiece in the next three days. These are the kind of things I have to resupply. I only have a certain amount of storage space in the refrigerator, so I can't load it up totally ... Now that I'm home in the summertime, this is a good snack food. And I like an apple sometimes at lunchtime when I come home.
>
> (Murtaugh as cited in Lave, 1988, p. 2)

While the above supermarket problem is open-ended, the parameters of the problem were defined and a solution was devised simultaneously (Lave, 1988). Thus, the problem took on meaning in a particular setting and cultural context. However, functionalist theories of cognition assume "that children can be taught general cognitive skills if these 'skills' are disembedded from the routine contexts of their use" (Lave, 1988, p. 8). In other words, these theorists believe that if culture is stripped from mathematics, knowledge can be transferred in different situations. However, as described above, the problem and the solution are dictated by the situation itself.

On the contrary, the Vygotskian point of view supports the notion that communication and social life are central to meaning-making (Vygotsky, 1978). Social constructivism recognizes that children are part of a classroom environment in which individual and corporate meaning take place (Steffe & Kieren, 1994). In general, constructivists believe that individuals build new knowledge by connecting it to prior knowledge (Davis *et al.*, 1990). For example, fraction concepts are generally difficult for early childhood and elementary students to understand. However, connecting the concept of fractions to real-life situations such as fair sharing helps children to construct meaningful experiences that can scaffold new knowledge (Garafolo & Sharp, 2003).

Vygotsky's research draws upon the epistemological underpinnings of Marx and Hegel (Saxe, 1991). Vygotsky's work stresses the importance of children's use of cultural artifacts and scaffolds to mediate their interactions with the environment (Saxe, 1991; Vygotsky, 1978). Social interactions are critical to the teaching–learning process as "natural processes in cognitive development [are] redirected by social and historical influences" (Saxe, 1991, p. 10). Moreover, Vygotsky describes what he terms the Zone of Proximal Development (ZPD), which is the difference between what children can accomplish on their own versus what they can accomplish with an adult or with peers (Saxe, 1991, 1999; Vygotsky, 1978). In comparison to Piaget, Vygotsky's work provides a richer analysis of the types of cognitive forms individuals might structure to carry out cognitive functions that link to math activities (Saxe, 1991, 1999). Moreover, the interdependence of sociocultural and cognitive development processes is evident as individuals exhibit intellectual skills in the context of their activities (Brenner, 1998; Guberman, 2005; Saxe, 1991; Saxe et al., 1996).

Núñez, Edwards, and Matos (1999) offer yet a third view of cognitive theory that is based on a situated approach that incorporates linguistic, social, and interactional influences. In essence, this theory purports "there is no activity that is not situated" (Lave & Wenger, 1991, p. 33). However, Núñez et al. (1999) argue, in addition to environmental and social factors, that thinking and learning are also situated within biological and experiential contexts to shape our understanding of the world. Núñez et al. (1999) contend that "knowledge and cognition exist and arise within specific social settings ... and that the grounding for situatedness comes from the nature of shared human bodily experience and action, realized through basic embodied cognitive processes and conceptual systems" (p. 46). This approach, however, does not place a great deal of emphasis on culture per se.

The Saxe model of cognition

Saxe (1991) describes a constructivist approach to study both culture and cognitive development. The Saxe (1991) model is grounded in the developmental theory associated with Piaget (1972) and the constructivist theory of learning advanced by Vygotsky (1978) and emphasizes the relationship between cognition and culture. Saxe (1991) argues that individuals create new knowledge while participating in culturally influenced goal-structured activities that often occur in social settings. The model focuses on three areas: (1) goals for learning that are structured by common cultural practices; (2) particular cognitive forms and functions created and used to reach goals; and (3) identifiable characteristics involved in the interplay across learning in different cultural contexts (Saxe, 1991). Goals for learning, then, are modified and shaped by the structure of cultural activities and social interactions. Within the context of African American learners, each of these goals is described below.

First, the *goal structure* of cultural practice consists of the tasks or activities that must be carried out. In the African American community, an example of goal structure can be found in the game of dominoes (Nasir, 2005). "Games are inherently artifacts of culture through which cultural roles, values, and knowledge bases are transmitted" (Nasir, 2005, p. 6). Such artifacts serve to reflect and reproduce culture simultaneously. In dominoes, the goal is not simply to win but to make appropriate decisions to maximize the number of points one can score (Nasir, 2005).

Second, according to the Saxe model, sign forms—such as counting systems—and cultural artifacts—are needed to execute and influence goals that emerge in cultural practice. "In this model, the individual and the social context are linked in multiple ways as individuals appropriate cultural forms to solve socially situated and culturally structured problems as they actively construct both problem-solving goals and ways to accomplish those goals" (Nasir, 2005, p. 7). As players move to advanced levels in the game of dominoes, they adjust the rules of the game to fit their own purposes. Thus, there are shifting relationships between particular forms that are used in play and the functions they serve. There are shifting cognitive processes in the game as players conform to meet individual needs, social interaction, and cultural practices (Nasir, 2005).

Another example of sign forms is found in my research on the use of culturally based computer modules (Leonard *et al.*, 2005). Two African American girls were observed using joint-finger counting and hand clapping to solve a problem that involved adding two-digit numbers. Much like the handclapping rhythms performed by Celie and Nettie in *The Color Purple* (Spielberg, 1985), these girls created a system of counting that was quite unique to solve the problem.

Mathematics is embedded in other types of African American children's play as well. The game of *jacks* teaches children multiples as they gather *onezies, twozies, threezies,* and so on. Furthermore, rhymes such as "Mary Mack" and songs sung while playing *double-dutch* (jumping with two ropes) contain mathematics. For example, one version of "Mary Mack" is described below.

Mary Mack, Mack, Mack all dressed in black, black, black,
Wore silver buttons, buttons, buttons, all down her back, back, back.
She asked her mother, mother, mother, for fifty cents, cents, cents
To see the elephant, elephant, elephant jump over the fence, fence, fence.

He jumped so high, high, high, he touched the sky, sky, sky,
And he never came back, back, back, until the Fourth of July.

While playing double-dutch, to keep up with the number of jumps without stopping or tripping on the ropes, African American children often sing:

Ten, twenty, thirty, forty, fifty, sixty, seventy, eighty, ninety ... one.
Ten, twenty, thirty, forty, fifty, sixty, seventy, eighty, ninety ... two.
Ten, twenty, thirty, forty, fifty, sixty, seventy, eighty, ninety ... three.

To keep count of the jumps, children intuitively know that the number one stands for one hundred and two stands for two hundred and so on. Among the African American students I have observed as a teacher and a parent, regardless of class and geographic location, it is not unusual to hear such rhymes and counting strategies on a playground or in a park. These songs and rhymes build number sense and fluency in counting.

The interplay between learning across contexts, the third part of Saxe's (1991) model, addresses the problem of learning transfer. At this particular stage, it is important for students to transfer informal out-of-school tasks, such as trading and bartering to formal in-school tasks. Previous research studies show that Brazilian children who were proficient with everyday transactions had difficulty with written assessments (Carraher et al., 1987) and Nigerian children who worked in street trading performed worse than non-working children on timed assessments in arithmetic (Oloko, 1994). Perhaps language, written text and symbols, or the abstract nature of the assessments limited the transfer of knowledge among children who worked as street vendors. Recall that Hawaiian children performed better when teachers used Hawaiian Creole English to scaffold mathematical understanding (Brenner, 1998).

In my own research, diverse students were able to retain information when the content was anchored to cultural experiences, such as designing a city (Leonard, 2004) and using patterns on quilts and stars in the sky to learn how fugitive slaves traveled north on the Underground Railroad (Leonard et al., 2005). Additional studies are needed to investigate African American students' ability to transfer culturally based mathematics knowledge to general mathematics applications.

Children's cognition and learning in mathematics

Several research studies that contribute to knowledge of student cognition in mathematics emerged from the Cognitively Guided Instruction (CGI) (Carey et al., 1995; Carpenter et al., 1993; Fennema et al., 1993) and QUASAR projects (Silver et al., 1995). While these projects do not deal with culture explicitly, they offer teacher educators insight in regard to best practices. Two CGI studies along with results and findings are described below.

Carpenter *et al.* (1993) conducted a study of kindergarten children who spent a year solving a variety of basic word problems. The study consisted of 70 students who were enrolled in six classes at two different schools. Each school was diverse in terms of race, ethnicity, and SES. The teachers had been year-long participants in CGI, a program that encourages children to use informal or invented problem-solving strategies (Carpenter *et al.*, 1992). These young learners often used a modeling approach, that is fingers, counters, or tally marks, to solve story problems. Other strategies noted by the researchers were counting strategies (counting up, counting back, and skip counting) and derived facts (number facts). The results of the study show 46% of the kindergarten students used a valid strategy to solve 100% of the problems, and 63% were able to solve 78% of the problems using one of the strategies described above. The major finding that came out of this research study is that early childhood students are able to solve different types of word problems, including multiplication and division (Carpenter *et al.*, 1993).

The second CGI study reported here took place in a first-grade classroom. The classroom teacher, known as Ms. J, used a problem-solving approach in teaching and learning mathematics. The children in Ms. J's class were Native American, African American, Hispanic, and European American. Ms. J. was often observed interweaving knowledge about problem-solving types and solution strategies with pedagogy. Students were encouraged to explain their reasoning process when they arrived at an answer. Results show all of the children were successful at solving many types of problems including grouping and partitioning problems, which is consistent with the results of the aforementioned study by Carpenter *et al.* (1993).

However profound, results such as those described in the CGI studies above do not reveal what happens to students when they matriculate in school. Are students able to carry over the strategies they learned from one teacher to the next, even when the next teacher does not share the same philosophy of education as the previous year's teacher? McNeal (1995) conducted a case study that coordinated anthropological and cognitive perspectives to examine one student's—Jamey's—learning in mathematics during his second- and third-grade years in school. During second grade, Jamey's mathematics instruction was inquiry-based, and mathematics tasks involved the construction of relationships among real and personal objects (Cobb *et al.*, 1992). Students were not taught basic algorithms but allowed to invent their own procedures for solving addition and subtraction problems. In these inquiry-based classrooms, children were encouraged to offer conjectures, explain their thinking, and critique each other's mathematical ideas. Thus, the environment could be described as emancipatory as students validated the correctness of mathematics problems in a learner-centered community. During second grade, McNeal (1995) discovered that Jamey's "mathematical constructions were quite stable as evidenced by the use of the same strategies to solve similar tasks" (p. 211).

When Jamey matriculated to third grade, his teacher, Mrs. Rose, did not encourage student use of invented algorithms. Mrs. Rose taught the students specific procedures to solve mathematics problems and reinforced those procedures by discouraging the use of "alternative methods and original ideas" (McNeal, 1995, p. 222). As a result of being placed in this type of learning environment, Jamey lost a great deal of the mathematics confidence he had acquired in second grade. Moreover, he had difficulty remembering the steps to carry out standard algorithms in addition and subtraction and "abandoned attempts to make sense for himself of the tasks encountered in a school context in favor of trying to recall procedures discussed in class" (McNeal, 1995, p. 228). Thus, teachers' reliance on the use of algorithms rather than invented strategies or other valid strategies that make sense to the students may have a negative impact on student learning in mathematics.

An example that illustrates the dilemma of teaching algorithms in lieu of mathematical understanding is found on a video clip that complements a mathematics methods text by Cathcart *et al.* (2006). In the video, preservice teachers observe Gretchen as she attempts to solve a two-digit subtraction problem.

The transcribed interview of the dialogue that takes place between an interviewer (I) and the student (C) is presented in the vignette below.

Vignette 2.1

I: Okay. How about this one?

C: That's easy.

I: Seventy take away 23.

C: Okay.

I: Okay. And your answer is ... ?

C: Fifty-three.

I: Okay. Could you show me that problem—this problem, too, with these blocks?

C: Okay. Umm ...

I: Do you want me to just take the pen out of your way?

C: It's okay. One, 2, 3, 4, 5, 6, 7. Okay, 70. Here's 70.

I: Uh huh.

C: Okay; 23. There's 23. Okay. Umm ... okay; 1, 2, 3. And it is 1, 2, 3, 4, 5, 6.

C: Okay; 7, 8.

C: Oh, gee. Hmm ... I don't get it.

I: What did you get for your answer over there?

C:	Over here, umm, like … it's weird, because like … Okay; 1, 2, 3, 4, 5, 6, 7.
I:	Uh huh.
C:	Over here, I get 47. But on here, like … okay. Zero … zero take away 3.
I:	Uh huh.
C:	Yeah, that's 3. Okay.
C:	And then, umm, 7 take away 2 equals 5. So, umm, I put 3 there, and 5 there.
I:	Uh huh. And then over there, you got what?
C:	Forty-seven. But I don't get it.
I:	Which one do you think is right?
I:	You think that one's right?
I:	Hmm … Is there another way you could solve the problem? Do you ever use these? Do you ever use a hundreds chart?
C:	Uh huh.
I:	Do you want to try it that way?
C:	Sure.
I:	Okay. So you have 70 of something, and you're taking away—Can I just move it over here, so we can see?
C:	I usually use it with, umm …
I:	With a marker?
C:	Yeah.
I:	Oh, we have a marker. You have 70, and you're taking away 23.
C:	Seventy. Okay.
C:	Okay. There's 70.
I:	Okay.
C:	Okay. Take away … okay.
C:	Umm … 1, 2, 3 … okay. And … hmm … Oh, wait.
C:	Okay; 1, 2, 3. One, 2, 3, 4, 5, 6, 7, 8, 9, 10, 11, 12, 13, 14, 15, 16, 17, 18, 19, 20, 21, 22, 23.
I:	What'd you get this time?
C:	But then I don't get it.
I:	What'd you get this time?
C:	Forty-seven. But I don't get it.
I:	And what did you get with the orange blocks?
C:	Forty-seven.
I:	So which answer—what do you think the answer should be?
C:	I think it should be, umm … 53. Because like … see, 3 take away zero is … 3. But then like … okay; 7 take away 2: 7, 6, 5. So I put 5 there. But then I don't get it.
I:	Hmm …
C:	Forty-seven, umm, like couldn't be right. Because … like it has to be 53.

The foregoing transcript of the video clip reveals not only Gretchen's misconception about the subtraction algorithm but also her inability to resolve mathematical incongruence. The interviewer encouraged Gretchen to model the subtraction problem using base ten blocks. Using the blocks, Gretchen got an answer of 47 to the problem 70 minus 23. However, she did not have confidence in the answer because she was convinced that the algorithm she used was correct. When Gretchen solved the problem a different way using the hundreds chart and also got 47 for an answer, she became even more confused, stating "forty-seven, umm, like couldn't be right." When teachers compel students to use an algorithm that they do not understand and at the same time discourage them from using invented algorithms that make sense, students may be more prone to make errors and develop misconceptions. Such teaching practices also have the negative impact of preventing some students from resolving their misconceptions even when they are confronted with evidence that challenges those misconceptions. What evidence would have convinced Gretchen that the answer was 47 and not 53? I contend that a model or example that was culturally specific to Gretchen's life may have helped her to solve the dilemma.

Culture and children's mathematical reasoning

Malloy and Jones (1998) conducted a study that examined how African American eighth-grade students solved mathematics problems and how strategies and problem-solving plans related to their success. Twenty-four students (16 female and eight male) participated in individual talk aloud problem-solving sessions where they were observed solving five non-routine mathematics problems. The researchers used Polya's (1945) problem-solving framework, which was adapted by Lester *et al.* (1989): (1) orientation—understand the problem, (2) organization—determine a plan to solve the problem, (3) execution—carry out the plan, and (4) verification—evaluate the solution or plan. These strategies are similar to those identified by Cathcart *et al.* (2006). Paper, pencils, and calculators were available to the students who were allowed ten minutes for four problems and 15 minutes for the most difficult problem—the church problem.

Malloy and Jones (1998) used both quantitative and qualitative methods to analyze results of this study. Qualitative data sources included transcripts of problem-solving sessions and interviews with the students. Problem-solving process actions and approaches were coded and mapped to a rubric.

The rubric was used to rate the students' conceptual understanding and accuracy. A score of zero to two meant the solution was not correct and the student had no understanding or minimal understanding of the concept. A score of three or four indicated the solution was nearly correct or correct and the student had a conceptual understanding of the problem. Thus, individual scores for any particular problem could range from a low of zero to a high of four.

Results of the study show that students were marginally successful on the five problems. Analysis of problem type shows that students were most successful on the car wash problem ($M = 3.71$) and least successful on the church problem ($M = 0.088$). Both problems are embedded in culture. By eighth grade, students may have experienced a car wash and attended a church service. Both problems are presented below for further analysis:

Nakisha, Gregory, Kerstin, and Brandon had a car wash on Saturday. Nakisha washed twice as many cars as Gregory. Gregory washed 1 fewer than Kerstin. Kerstin washed 6 more than Brandon. Brandon washed 6 cars. How many cars did Nakisha wash?
(Answer: 22)

At a community church, the leader plans to place the page numbers for three different songs on the board in the front of the church. The leader must buy plastic cards to put on the board. Each card has one large digit on it. The leader wants to buy as few cards as possible. The song book has songs numbered from 1 to 632. What is the fewest number of cards that must be purchased to make sure that it is possible to display any selection of three different songs?
(Answer: 65)

Eighty percent of the students were able to use successful strategies to solve the car wash problem. The mean score for students classified as high achievers ($n = 11$) was 3.91, 3.90 for average achievers ($n = 10$), and 2.33 for low achievers ($n = 3$). Scores for high and average achievers were consistent only on the car wash problem, suggesting that this problem may have been more relevant to all of the students' experiences. Twenty-two students used the "work backward" strategy to solve the car wash problem. A second strategy used by ten students was making a list or chart, and only one student, who solved the problem incorrectly, did not use a strategy.

Surprisingly, 87.5% of the students did not solve the church hymn problem correctly. Twelve of the students in the study did not use a single strategy to solve the problem, indicating a high level of difficulty. Nine students used one or more strategies unsuccessfully. The strategies these students used were drawing a picture or diagram, making a list or chart, patterns, and logical deduction. Only three students were able to successfully use a list or chart and logical deduction to solve the church hymn problem. The researchers did not explain what errors or misconceptions the students may have had as they attempted to solve this non-routine multi-step problem. However, to solve this problem, students must understand place value and possess number sense. The student must know how many digits are needed to make any number from 1–632 three times. Then the students must identify how many cards are needed for the hundreds', tens', and ones' places. The answer of 65 is obtained by realizing the digits 1 to 5 are needed seven times ($5 \times 7 = 35$) and the digits 6 to 9 and 0 are needed six times ($5 \times 6 = 30$). One solution strategy accounts for the digits by making a drawing such as the one shown below in Figure 2.1.

One possible explanation for these students' ease with the car wash problem and their difficulty with the church hymn problem may be their lack of exposure to problems that do not depend on strategies (organization) or execution but representation—that is, understanding the relationship between the variables in the problem (Mayer & Hagerty, 1996). By its familiarity, students did not have as much trouble visualizing and making an appropriate representation of the car wash problem. However, problems like the church hymn may not be as easy to visually represent with a drawing. Problems of this nature are difficult and require additional time to solve. By allotting only 15 minutes to solve this problem, the researchers may have stifled some students' cognitive processes. It is not uncommon for teachers to spend an entire class period on a problem of this nature (Carpenter *et al.*, 1999; Fennema *et al.*, 1993; Franke & Kazemi, 2001; Villasenor & Kepler, 1993). Regardless of the cultural context, students need time and space to solve very difficult non-routine problems.

In another study, Ku & Sullivan (2001) studied the problem-solving ability of 136 fourth-grade Taiwanese students. These researchers claim that personalized word problems, such as inclusion of personal background information in the problem context, enhance student outcomes (Ku & Sullivan, 2001). Because the problem context is familiar to the students, these researchers contend that attending to fewer details reduces cognitive load and enables students to perform better. Furthermore, if students have high interest in the problem, they may be more likely to persist in problem solving. To test their hypothesis, two forms of a 12-item pre-posttest (personalized and non-personalized) were given to students. Results show that students were better at solving personalized rather than non-personalized problems. For example, in one problem, the words "soft drink" were replaced with "milk tea" in order to personalize it. Mean posttest scores by treatment improved from 55% in both groups to 86% for students in the personalized treatment group and 78% for students in the non-personalized treatment group. Moreover, students' attitudes were more positive ($M = 3.52$), on a scale of 1 to 4, when problems related to their own lives versus problems that did not ($M = 3.31$). These researchers conclude that personalized story problems lead

5	5	3
5	5	4
5	5	5

Figure 2.1 Solution strategy for church problem.

to improved performance because children are better able to identify and interpret relevant information (Ku & Sullivan, 2001).

More recently Lipka et al. (2005) conducted a study detailing the results of implementing *Math in Cultural Context* (MCC), a culturally based math curriculum designed for urban and rural Yup'ik (Native Eskimo) students. The researchers used mixed methodology to conduct the 2×2 research design of treatment and control groups in urban and rural settings. Students in the treatment groups in urban and rural settings had the MCC curriculum while those in the control groups did not. Findings show significant statistical differences when pre-post scores in treatment and control groups were compared. Furthermore, the researchers analyzed case studies of two teachers' practices with Yup'ik students.

Specifically, they analyzed teacher-student relationships, student-to-student talk, and mathematics communication. Ironically, both of the teachers used in the case studies (treatment), had been former teachers in the control group. Thus, the researchers were able to compare teachers' practices before and after intervention. In one case, the teacher was very traditional in her instruction when she participated as a teacher in the control group. Although she worked with a different group of students in another community, she taught primarily by telling students information and asking them to repeat it (Schifter & Fosnot, 1993). However, when she began using the MCC curriculum, the same teacher's pedagogical style changed. She began to use inquiry-based instruction and the activities in her classroom changed from teacher-centered to student-centered activities. In the second case, the teacher already had a student-centered teaching philosophy. However, use of MCC helped her to build stronger teacher–student relationships. Students knew they were in a "safe zone" where they could learn, have fun, and take risks (Lipka et al., 2005, p. 378). As a result, the second teacher's students outscored all of the other students who participated in the project. Other benefits of using MCC curriculum were: (1) altered social organization and communication in the classroom; (2) guided inquiry to facilitate problem solving and multiple solutions to math problems; (3) positive changes in classroom relationships among teachers and students and between the classroom and the community; (4) pride in culture and identity and ownership of knowledge; and most importantly (5) creation of the "notion of 'third space' … in which historically silenced knowledge of Indigenous peoples such as the Yup'ik is privileged alongside traditional academic discourses" (Lipka et al., 2005, p. 369).

Reform-based education and opportunities to learn

Although a great deal of evidence exists that shows positive student outcomes when reform-based pedagogies such as constructivism are used (Carpenter et al., 1993; Fennema et al., 1993; Villasenor & Kepler, 1993), getting teachers to change from traditional mathematics pedagogy to a constructivist or inquiry-based one is a daunting task. First, students may offer some resistance and express a desire for more traditional activities when it comes to the subject of mathematics (Lubienski, 2000; Martin, 2000). Lubienski (2000) found that poor females were particularly resistant to learning mathematics when a problem-solving approach was used. It may be difficult for these students to communicate their mathematical thinking because they have been unaccustomed to the inquiry approach (Martin, 2000). Instead, teachers in high-poverty schools have stressed low-level skills, which require little effort and thinking on the part of the student (Kitchen, 2007). Constructivist practices that allow students to articulate their ideas in meaningful problem-solving situations have led to more successful performance outcomes for all students regardless of demographic variables (Kitchen, 2007; Peterson et al., 1989; Villasenor & Kepler, 1993).

Peterson et al. (1989) conducted a study of 39 first-grade teachers and 710 first-grade children from three Catholic and 24 public schools in Wisconsin. Those teachers whose beliefs were consistent with a cognitively based approach used word problems as a basis for introducing addition and subtraction. Teachers whose beliefs were less cognitively based placed greater emphasis on memorizing number facts. They found that teachers differed significantly in how their pedagogical content beliefs corresponded to a cognitively based perspective. Findings also show an interrelationship between pedagogical content beliefs and pedagogical content knowledge. Furthermore, a significant correlation ($r = 0.32$, $p < 0.05$, one-tailed) was found between the teachers' scores on a belief questionnaire and students' mathematical achievement. These findings "suggest that teachers' pedagogical content beliefs and teachers' pedagogical knowledge may be significantly linked to teachers' classroom action and, ultimately, to students' classroom learning in mathematics" (Peterson et al., 1989, p. 36).

In order to expand on the importance of reform-based education in the mathematics classroom, the following discussion, which took place in my online graduate level mathematics methods course, is presented for consideration. There were 29 students enrolled in the course, but I divided them into two cohorts to encourage broader participation in the chat room. Cohort 1, which I focus on here, consisted of 12 students: ten females (seven White, two African American, and one Asian); two males (one White and one Latino). Each chat room session was one hour in length. The discussions centered on reading assignments in *Mathematics Methods for Elementary and Middle School Teachers* (Hatfield et al., 2000) as well as independent reading assignments of research articles. The dialogue that took place is presented below in Vignette 2.2. For anonymity, students are referred to by number, while I refer to myself as JL.

Vignette 2.2

1	*JL:*	What do cognitive theorists say about student culture?
2	*Student 1:*	You mean Piaget, Bruner, and Vygotsky?
3	*Student 2:*	Students are not a blank slate.
4	*Student 3:*	Use of culture needs to be constant and consistent to make further connections.
5	*Student 4:*	Stages of development.
6	*Student 5:*	We build on what we know through stages.
7	*Student 6:*	Essentially they say that students bring their own experiences and developmental stages to learning and that they create or construct knowledge on their own.
8	*Student 4:*	We need to adapt our teaching to those stages.
9	*Student 2:*	So tapping into a child's previous knowledge [whether it is] correct or incorrect is very important?
10	*Student 7:*	That is where the students start. They enter our classroom with preconceived notions, and it is our job to validate [and] guide them to new understanding.
11	*JL:*	Yes, Student 2. Every child comes with some cultural capital. It is up to us as teachers to tap into it.
12	*Student 8:*	I don't know how an elementary school teacher can teach mathematics without constructivism.
13	*Student 3:*	Also, they start [to learn] before we even realize.
14	*Student 5:*	Try children start to learn and associate long before they can talk.
15	*Student 9:*	Incorporate their knowledge and personal experience to help them achieve higher thinking.
16	*Student 10:*	I think it is important to use culture to bring relevance to a student and have them connect.
17	*Student 1:*	Piaget is a top person, but they all feel that learning is action.
18	*Student 2:*	Even agreeing with constructivism, for a new teacher, I find it very hard to do well.
19	*Student 6:*	That will only help them connect mathematics with neutral networks they have already constructed by bringing culture into the class.
20	*Student 2:*	It's much easier to slip into dictation mode even with good intentions at the outset.
21	*Student 1:*	Kids need to be more involved in the lesson, which means more use of manipulatives.
22	*JL:*	Student 8, believe me there are those who still do direct teaching. They model how it is done, and the students mimic what they do.
23	*Student 7:*	Student 2, you are probably doing more than you realize.

24	*Student 11:*	Making math hands-on as the constructivists point out makes math real.
25	*Student 10:*	I don't want to get stuck on this, but bringing in a culture to [show] relevance and [make] connection[s] is different than saying that students from certain cultures have different learning preferences.
26	*Student 6:*	Constructivism is, in some ways, quite natural—it is how we all learn when we aren't in school.
27	*Student 9:*	Use activities that students can relate to.
28	*Student 8:*	Personally, I believe that no one can teach mathematics well without a higher understanding of where it's going. Once you have that, the constructivist part comes easy.
29	*Student 5:*	Constructivists believe in hands-on and ownership. Some cultures shy away from forwardness and this has to be dealt with.
30	*JL:*	Student 2, we have to let the children tell us how they would solve a particular problem or let them explain their own thinking. It is tough to do because we are so used to teaching by telling.
31	*JL:*	Student 6, excellent point!
32	*Student 1:*	Today, I tried to integrate math and science by having students measure each other's arm span. With guidance, they did pretty well ... Next we will graph the data.
33	*Student 5:*	I agree with the ownership, it helps to bring about self-esteem as well as learning.
34	*Student 10:*	Constructivism is difficult because it takes a great deal of trust on the part of the teacher.
35	*Student 4:*	True.
36	*Student 2:*	Patience and skill and asking the right questions, too.
37	*Student 6:*	I think constructivism is like teaching someone how to change a tire. I wouldn't just tell them about it and then give them my car! Why do the same in the classroom?
38	*Student 1:*	I used to get upset when giving out materials and the kids start exploring before you tell them. But they need to touch and feel and experience.
39	*Student 3:*	Yes, guiding what the student says to where you want him to be ...
40	*Student 4:*	It is more time consuming to be a guide, instead of a lecturer ...
41	*Student 2:*	It changes the [structure] of the math classroom—students gather in groups rather than sit in rows.
42	Student 11:	Yes, patience. I believe ... one has to establish organization and plan well in the class for the hands-on activities to go smoothly.

Twelve students entered the chat room to participate in the online course. However, one student had technical difficulties, leaving only 11 to actively participate. The dialogue was analyzed using the Constant-Comparative Method (Glaser & Strauss, 1967). After coding the transcript, four themes emerged in Vignette 2.2: (1) definitions and descriptions of constructivism; (2) beliefs about the role of culture in knowledge construction; (3) beliefs about constructivist pedagogy; and (4) reflections about the challenges of constructivist-based teaching. Each of these themes is discussed below.

Definitions and descriptions of constructivism

Several comments in Vignette 2.2 center on a discussion of what constructivism is and what it is not. Seven students made 11 comments related to definitions and descriptions of constructivism. Four comments focused on theories of learning [lines 3, 13, 14, & 17]. These views are consistent with current research on brain and behavior (Bransford *et al.*, 2000). To this conversation, Student 1 added "learning is action" [line 17]. This notion is consistent with research on Cognitively Guided Instruction (Carey *et al.*, 1995; Carpenter *et al.*, 1993; Fennema *et al.*, 1993). Three comments focused on Piaget and/or his stages of cognitive development [lines 5, 6, 7, & 17]. Students 6 and 9 explicitly linked student experiences to the definition of constructivism [lines 7 & 15]. Student 6 also described constructivism as a *natural* way of learning [line 26]. Finally, Student 5 connected the use of hands-on activities with constructivist-based instruction, highlighting the importance of the student role in knowledge construction [lines 29 & 33] (Hufferd-Ackles *et al.*, 2004).

Role of culture in constructing knowledge

Four students made comments about culture and its role in knowledge construction. Students 3 and 10 believed that teachers should use culture for relevance to make mathematical connections [lines 4 & 16]. These views are consistent with the genre of current research on the use of culturally relevant teaching in mathematics classrooms (Brenner, 1998; Gutstein *et al.*, 1997; Ladson-Billings, 1995; Leonard & Campbell, 2004; Leonard & Guha, 2002; Malloy & Malloy, 1998; Tate, 1995). However, Student 6 presented an opposing view stating: "That will only help them connect mathematics with neutral networks they have already constructed by bringing culture into the class." Student 10 challenged this perspective, clarifying that use of culture for relevance and connections is not the same as looking at different cultural styles of learning [line 25]. Moreover, Student 6 failed to understand how culture can be used as a springboard to bridge children's prior knowledge developed through their cultural experiences to new knowledge (Aikenhead, 1997; Delpit, 1995; Leonard *et al.*, 2005; Leonard & Guha, 2002). However, Student 5 cautions that children from different cultural backgrounds "may shy away from forwardness" [line 29]. Therefore, teachers should be cognizant that diverse students may have different levels of classroom involvement (Nieto, 2002; Sheets, 2005).

Beliefs about constructivist pedagogy

Prospective and beginning teachers' beliefs about the use of constructivist-based teaching also emerged in Vignette 2.2. Eight students shared their views about constructivist-based pedagogy and supportive activities that may be used in mathematics classrooms. Student 8 expressed strong beliefs about the importance of constructivist teaching in the mathematics classroom [lines 12 & 28]. Student 4 believed teachers should consider Piaget's developmental stages and adapt their instructional practices according to the students' level of cognition [line 8]. Students 7 and 3 believed that teachers should *validate* children's thinking and guide them as they develop new knowledge [lines 10 & 39]. Students 1, 9, and 11 believed that teachers should motivate children by making real-world connections through the use of manipulatives in the classroom [lines 21, 24, & 27]. Student 2 expressed beliefs about the impor-tance of classroom structure, patience, and pedagogical content knowledge— that is, asking appropriate questions to get at children's thinking [lines 36 & 41]. Finally, Student 11 pointed out the importance of organization and plan-ning to implement constructivist-based activities.

Challenges of a constructivist-based teaching pedagogy

The final and perhaps most critical theme that emerged in Vignette 2.2 is the challenge that teachers face when they attempt to use constructivist-based pedagogy. Six students expressed an opinion about the challenges of constructivist-based teaching. Student 2 was the first to express her concern, raising the challenge brought about by not correcting children's misconcep-tions [line 9]. Ball (1993) pointed out this dilemma, stating it is difficult for teachers to know "when to provide an explanation, when to model, [and] when to ask the rather pointed questions" to help clarify students' thinking (p. 393). Furthermore, Student 2 explained the difficulty associated with the constructivist model and how easy it is to just lecture to students [lines 18 & 20]. While Student 7 tried to be consoling [line 23], Student 4 offered that teaching in a constructivist manner takes more time [line 40], and Student 10 shared that reform-based teaching involved having *trust* in the children [line 34]. The notion of trust has three implications: (1) teachers must trust that their students will participate and engage fully in this type of learning environment; (2) teachers must trust that constructivist-based teaching will lead to better student outcomes; and (3) teachers must trust in their efficacy to implement this type of instruction. Student 6's metaphor about teaching by telling as it relates to changing a flat tire on a car was very insightful. In order to retain information, it is crucial that children learn by doing, and in the process, teachers will learn from their own practice (Ebby, 2000; Sherin, 2002).

Finally, Student 1's experiences with constructivist-based teaching methods were perhaps the most convincing. She explained her apprehension when she tried to integrate a math and science lesson, but her urban minority students were able to perform well with guidance [line 32]. Student 1 admitted her frustration with students' excitement about using manipulatives, but she underscored the importance of using the senses in authentic learning. Students need to "touch and feel and experience" [line 42]. Ultimately, it is the students' needs that should take precedence and not the needs of the teacher. Teacher behaviors should be guided by student needs and not what is easiest for teachers to do.

Summary

Data obtained from reform-based and traditional mathematics classrooms suggest students learn different kinds of mathematics in each of these learning environments (Cobb et al., 1992). Mathematical reasoning tends to develop in classrooms where students are able to actively participate in knowledge construction characterized by classroom discourse (Wood, 1999 & 2001). In these types of classrooms, students are expected to explain the thinking that led them to use a particular strategy to get a solution to a problem (Wood, 2001). "As advocated in the reform documents, learning mathematics with understanding is thought to occur best in situations in which children are expected to problem solve, reason, and communicate their ideas and thinking to others" (Wood, 2001, p. 116). In order to foster such environments, teachers must learn to resist the inclination to teach by telling (Schifter & Fosnot, 1993; Wood, 2001) or oversimplify problem-solving tasks (Crespo, 2003; Wood, 2001). Instead teachers must allow students the freedom to use a variety of ways to represent their mathematical ideas and to use strategies that make sense to them as they develop mathematical cognition (Wood, 2001).

3
Cultural pedagogy

The future belongs to those who believe in the beauty of their dreams.

Eleanor Roosevelt

The need for cultural pedagogy

Issues of race and social class continue to pervade and influence the quality of education for students of color in U.S. schools. More than 12 million children in the U.S. live in poverty and 35% of poor children are under the age of six (National Center for Children in Poverty, 1999). The poverty rate is highest for African American (37%) and Latina/o American (31%) children (Child Poverty Fact Sheet, 2001). These data imply that there is a relationship between race and poverty (Sheets, 2005). Students of color are more likely to be poor and attend large urban schools where highly qualified teachers and adequate resources are less abundant than in suburban schools (Howard, 2003; Imazeki & Reschovsky, 2006).

When educational tools, such as computers and calculators, are available, they are often underutilized in high-poverty schools because some teachers lack technology training (Manoucherhri, 1999) and/or fail to understand the importance of using such tools, especially in mathematics (Dixson & Rousseau, 2005). Thus, students in high-poverty schools often receive a different kind of mathematics education (Martin, 2000). This differential instruction contributes to differences in achievement outcomes (Ladson-Billings, 2006).

Studies that compared the mathematical ability of early childhood students by socioeconomic status emerged in the 1990s (Jordan *et al.*, 1994; Kerkman & Siegler, 1993; Wright, 1994). Jordan *et al.* (1994) conducted a two-year longitudinal study to determine differences among students from poor and middle-class backgrounds on calculation tasks. The participants included 42 first-grade students from New Brunswick, New Jersey. Researchers observed student use of finger strategies, counting strategies, and unknown (not able to determine by observation) strategies. Findings revealed no gender differences in nonverbal calculation and only slight differences on the calculation of number facts among poor ($M = 81\%$) and middle-income ($M = 88\%$) children. Wright (1994) also assessed the mathematics knowledge of Australian kindergarten and first-grade students from poor and middle-class backgrounds. Wright found that kindergarten students had a wide range of calculation abilities regardless of SES. There was less variability, however, among first graders. The study concluded that first-grade students were able to deal with part-whole operations and understand addition and subtraction as inverse operations. Kerkman and Siegler's (1993) study examined individual differences among poor and middle-class first-grade children's retrieval and use of backup strategies on three types of tasks. When problems became difficult, students from both SES groups increased their use of backup strategies at the same rate. The Analysis of Variance (ANOVA) was used to compare students' scores on the California Achievement Test (CAT). Results revealed no significant differences among first-grade students, controlling for gender and SES: suburban ($M = 79.0$, November testing); urban ($M = 84.5$, April testing). These findings concur with the findings of Jordan et al. (1994) and Entwisle & Alexander (1992).

On the contrary, achievement differences among students of diverse economic backgrounds become evident in mathematics by fourth grade (Lesh et al., 1987; Martin, 2000; NCES, 2005 & 2006). While there is a plethora of reasons for underachievement in mathematics, what happens in the teaching–learning context in mathematics classrooms influences student failure or success (Martin, 2000; Rousseau & Tate, 2003).

Kazemi and Stipek (2001) investigated how classroom practices create conditions for conceptual learning of mathematics. The purpose of the research study was "to identify the sociomathematical norms in classrooms that promote students' engagement in conceptual mathematical thinking and conversation" (Kazemi & Stipek, 2001, p. 60). Four teachers and their fourth- and fifth-grade students participated in the study.

The case study method was used to study the role and professional development of these teachers as they enhanced student learning of fractions. In order to select cases for further study, the researchers used two composite variables: (1) press for learning and (2) positive affect. Press for learning is defined as "the degree to which teachers engaged students in mathematical thinking, specifically, how much they: (a) emphasized student effort; (b) focused on learning and understanding; (c) supported students' autonomy; and (d) de-emphasized performance" (Kazemi & Stipek, 2001, p. 61). Positive affect is defined as "the degree to which the classroom appeared as a positive social environment" (Kazemi & Stipek, 2001, pp. 61–62). Four teachers, two classified as high press and two classified as low press, were selected for further study. The cases were used to hypothesize about the kinds of discourse and interaction patterns that encourage conceptual thinking.

Teachers who exhibited high-press behaviors compelled students to provide reasoning for their mathematical decisions and focused on conceptual rather than procedural knowledge, but teachers who exhibited low-press behaviors engaged in the same social practices except that reasoning focused more on procedures and algorithms. In other words, students in low-press situations were more apt to explain *how* rather than *why* they engaged in a specific action. While teachers engaged in inquiry-based practices and students' activities consisted of open-ended problems, differences among high- and low-press exchanges in these teachers' classrooms show that differences in teaching practices impact the nature and degree of students' conceptual thinking. The results of this study reveal that simply asking students to explain their thinking is not enough. Teachers and students must engage in meaningful conversations that get at the depth of mathematical understanding in order for students to develop mathematical power (Gutstein, 2003; Hufferd-Ackles *et al.*, 2004; Kazemi & Stipek, 2001).

The studies above elucidate the importance of appropriate discourse practices in the development of mathematical cognition. Yet, teachers must not only engage in discourse but instructional practices that are culturally responsive and meaningful to children's lives (Gay, 2000; Howard, 2003; Ladson-Billings, 1994; Sheets, 2005). In other words, teachers must learn to develop a cultural pedagogy.

Types of cultural pedagogy

Cultural pedagogy, as an emerging discourse in education, has historical roots in American Indian and Native Hawaiian education (Brenner, 1998; Demmert & Towner, 2003). The impetus for culturally based education in this context was poor assimilation of Hawaiians into Western culture (Brenner, 1998). Some of the Kamehameha Early Childhood Program (KEEP) researchers believed cultural dissonance or conflict between Native Hawaiian children's culture and school culture was one of the causes of underachievement (Brenner, 1998). At the time of this study, Native Hawaiian children represented the largest group of minority children (24%) in Hawaii. These students lagged behind their peers in mathematics and other subjects, performing below other ethnic groups on standardized tests (Brenner, 1998). Brenner (1998) hypothesized that an approach that linked ethnographic and cognitive considerations in the form of cultural pedagogy could close the gap between ethnic minority children and other children in the U.S. Researchers developed culturally compatible programs to improve the academic achievement of Native Hawaiian children in reading (Tharp, 1982) and mathematics (Brenner, 1998). Results revealed that vocabulary and reading comprehension subtest scores were superior for KEEP students compared to students in a control group (Demmert & Towner, 2003). Results in mathematics, as previously discussed, favored students who were taught using a culturally based approach. Overall, findings show culturally based education adds value to a standards-based curriculum (Demmert & Towner, 2003).

Over the years, a number of terms have emerged to describe pedagogical practices that include cultural considerations. Terms such as culturally relevant teaching (Ladson-Billings, 1994), cultural brokering (Aikenhead, 1997), culturally responsive teaching (Gay, 2000), culturally specific pedagogy (Irvine, 2002), and diversity pedagogy (Sheets, 2005) have emerged to describe what effective teachers do to enhance learning opportunities for students of color. Each of these pedagogies has some similarities and differences in its approach to improving learning outcomes for students of color. While these pedagogies offer alternative means to improve learning and achievement among students of color, they also provide different ends as some focus on social and political ramifications and issues of social justice to accomplish educational goals. A brief description of each of these pedagogies is presented in the following sections along with examples from research and practice.

Culturally relevant teaching

Culturally relevant teaching in mathematics classrooms has a two-part definition: (1) the recognition that mathematics has been present in every culture since societies have had recorded histories; and (2) the effect of mathematics on any culture and its people (Hatfield *et al.*, 2000). One of the pillars of the culturally relevant teaching paradigm is the belief that poor and ethnically diverse students are capable learners (Howard, 2003; Ladson-Billings, 1994 & 1997). Culturally relevant pedagogy has been described as an effective way to meet the intellectual and social needs of students of color (Howard, 2003; Ladson-Billings, 1994). It supports the following three goals for students: (1) academic success; (2) cultural competence; and (3) the ability to critique the existing social order (Ladson-Billings, 1994). Ladson-Billings (1994) describes the following set of behaviors as those most closely associated with culturally relevant teaching:

- treat students as competent;
- provide instructional "scaffolding" in order for students to move from what they know to what they need to know;
- demonstrate instruction has high priority;
- extend students' thinking and abilities; and
- possess in-depth knowledge of both students and subject matter.

(pp. 123–125)

Moreover, culturally relevant pedagogy acknowledges the link between culture and learning and views diverse students' cultural capital as advantageous to school success (Howard, 2003). In addition, culturally relevant teachers use non-traditional means such as role-playing, skits, poems, rap, and group projects to assess what students know. Despite clear descriptors of what culturally relevant pedagogy is, how to implement culturally relevant teaching in mathematics classrooms is not always apparent to novice teachers (Albert, 2000; Ladson-Billings, 1994).

Albert's (2000) description of her dilemma with culturally relevant teaching in the mathematics classroom is one example. Albert (2000) gave her seventh-grade mathematics class an assignment that required them to write an essay about a mathematician. Albert believed the assignment was standards based as it met one of the five process standards articulated in the NCTM *Principles and Standards* (2000): communication. The goal of the lesson was for students to learn how to communicate their ideas and then clarify, refine, and consolidate their thinking (Albert, 2000; NCTM, 1989). However, Albert, an African American teacher, was surprised to learn that she had missed the mark with her African American students.

Five African American males approached her about changing the assignment to include writing a rap instead of an essay (Albert, 2000). The request caused Albert to reflect critically upon her pedagogy. She realized that her lesson projected European American middle-class values and did not reflect the interest, needs, and cultural backgrounds of her students (Albert, 2000; Howard, 2003). Unwittingly, Albert had marginalized the voices of diverse students by censoring the type of writing she expected from them. She realized her lesson, while well intended, was not culturally relevant to her students' lives. In an effort to make the lesson culturally relevant, Albert revised the assignment to allow students to write about the historical contributions women and persons of color made to the field of mathematics. Moreover, the mode of writing was expanded to include informal poems, plays, long or short essays, creative stories, and rap. Such lessons also challenge the view that mathematics is a male domain (Fennema & Sherman, 1976). Students could report on women mathematicians, such as Maria Agnesi, Hypatia, Mary Somerville, Sophie German, Ada Lovelace, and Evelyn Boyd Granville, and their roles in the history of mathematics (Albert, 2000).

By matching the assignment to students' interests and experiences, Albert (2000) found a more relevant and empowering way to teach mathematics. Teacher reflection was a major component of Albert's shift toward a culturally relevant pedagogy. Teachers must be reflective in order to practice culturally relevant pedagogy, being ever mindful of how traditional European American middle-class cultural values might shape their thinking about students and curriculum (Howard, 2003).

Cultural brokering

The concept of *cultural brokering* emerged from Aikenhead's (1997) work with secondary Native American science students in Canada. For the vast majority of students, regardless of Western or non-Western origin, science is a *foreign* or strange subject (Aikenhead, 2001; Aikenhead & Jegede, 1999). Students perceive science to be strange because there is incongruence between the real-life culture of students and culture embraced by members of the science community (Costa, 1995), the students' world view and views commonly accepted by Western scientists (Aikenhead, 1997), and the social context for learning science and context for using science knowledge (Aikenhead & Jegede, 1999; Hennessy, 1993). In order to overcome these obstacles, Aikenhead (2001) suggests that science teachers exhibit the following behaviors:

1. Recognize Western science as a cultural entity into itself.
2. Acknowledge that most students experience cultural border crossings as they move from their life-worlds into the world of school science.
3. Consider the myriad of ways students deal with cognitive conflicts arising from culture clashes.
4. Aid students as they negotiate their border crossings to reduce cultural conflicts.

(p. 181)

Aikenhead (1997) defines border crossing as the movement between cultures and microcultures. For many students, border crossing from the microculture of family and peers to the microculture of school science is tenuous, and the transition from the students' culture to school culture in the science classroom is a cross-cultural experience (Aikenhead & Jegede, 1999). Cultural brokering eases this transition as teachers help students to move fluidly between their culture and the microculture of school science by addressing conflicts that may arise in interpretation (Aikenhead, 1997). An example of cultural brokering is provided below in Vignette 3.1. In this vignette, Hannah (pseudonym), an African American preservice teacher, used cultural brokering to help African American third graders understand Earth science concepts. The purpose of the lesson was to learn about the Earth's crust and how the layers move to create folds and faults.

Vignette 3.1

21	*Hannah:*	I want you to tell me what you want to know about rocks.
22	*Student:*	Do they grow?
23	*Hannah:*	That's interesting. Do rocks grow?
24	*Student:*	Do they break?
25	*Hannah:*	Okay, good. Can rocks break? Okay, I'll take two more hands.
26	*Student:*	Can you move rocks?
27	*Hannah:*	Can you move rocks? What do you think? If you went outside and you saw a rock do you think you could move it?

28	*Student:*	Yeah.
29	*Hannah:*	So we can answer that question with yes. We can move rocks. Can we move all rocks?
30	*Student:*	No, because some are big and heavy and stuck on the ground.
31	*Hannah:*	Do you have another question about rocks?
32	*Student:*	How do rocks grow?
33	*Hannah:*	Okay, we have that question up on the board already. This is what we're going to do. Since you already know that rocks can be gray, they can be big or small, they have layers, and you want to know whether rocks can grow and can rocks break, today we're going to end up answering "Can rocks break?" when we do our activity. But since you already know that rocks have layers, I want you to put your thinking caps on real tight. What are some other things you know of that have layers?
34	*Student:*	Cake.
35	*Student:*	A sandwich.
36	*Hannah:*	Good, a sandwich. What are the layers of a sandwich?
37	*Student:*	Meat.
38	*Student:*	Pickles.
39	*Student:*	Tomatoes.
40	*Student:*	Bread.
41	*Student:*	Cheese.
42	*Hannah:*	Good, those are all different layers of a sandwich. So we have cake, a sandwich, what are other things that have layers?
43	*Student:*	Lettuce.
44	*Hannah:*	Lettuce. How do you know that it has layers?
45	*Student:*	You can keep pulling the lettuce off and there is more underneath of the other layers.
46	*Hannah:*	This is what we're going to do today. We're going to study rock layers. There is a special word for that, and it's a really big word. It is called stratigraphy. Can everybody say that?
47	*Class:*	Stratigraphy.
48	*Hannah:*	Stratigraphy is the study of rock layers. Today we're all going to be scientists. If you think that's cool then I want to see you do the silent cheer.
49		[STUDENTS RAISE THEIR FISTS IN THE AIR.]

Vignette 3.1 illustrates how Hannah helped first-grade students to build background knowledge by contextualizing Earth science vocabulary: *rocks, layers, stratigraphy,* and *scientists.* Furthermore, she used students' prior knowledge of rocks to make connections to their everyday lives. By linking the content to students' experiences, Hannah used cultural brokering to help them understand the concept of layers. She provided an opportunity for students to cross borders when she asked: "*What are some other things you know of that have layers?*" By comparing a sandwich to rock layers, the students were able to understand an important science concept. Hannah made science visible and accessible and gave students some autonomy in decision-making by using the KWL process, which is a hallmark of inquiry-based instruction (Beerer & Bodzin, 2004; Linn & Hsi, 2000). As a result of her inquiry-based instructional style, Hannah helped urban first graders cross borders into the microculture of science.

Border crossing

Building on the grounded theory of Costa (1995), Aikenhead (2001) categorizes the degrees of ease in which students cross borders into school science and describes how teachers might facilitate border crossing as cultural brokers:

1. *Potential Scientists:* smooth border crossings that lead to an in-depth understanding of science.
2. *"I Want to Know" Students:* adventurous border crossings that lead to a modest yet effective understanding of science (there are hazards but students want to know).
3. *Other Smart Kids:* easily managed border crossing but with no personal interest in pursuing science.
4. *"I Don't Know" Students:* hazardous border crossings into a superficial understanding of science (there are hazards, but students do not want "to look stupid" in the eyes of their peers or teacher).
5. *Outsiders:* impossible border crossings that lead to dropping out, physically or intellectually.
6. *Inside Outsiders:* impossible border crossings due to institutional discrimination in spite of personal interest in understanding science.

(p. 186)

Although these six categories were developed within the context of learning science, they can just as easily be applied to learning mathematics.

Mathematical knowledge is mediated by language, which is a social construct. Historically, groups of people developed different systematic ways to communicate the quantitative aspects of their lives. Mathematics is a language with rules and syntax that must be followed. According to Reisman & Kauffman (1980), children must learn the meaning of symbols and signs (arbitrary associations) in order to perform basic operations and solve word problems (higher level generalizations). The categories of *Potential Mathe-matician*, "*I Want to Know*" *Students*, *Other Smart Kids*, "*I Don't Know*" *Stu-dents*, *Outsiders*, and *Inside Outsiders* can also be used to describe different types of mathematics learners.

If teachers reflected on the different ways their students experienced science and mathematics, they could help to facilitate learning better in their classrooms (Aikenhead, 2001). For students in the *Potential Scientists* or *Mathematician* category, Aikenhead (2001) describes the teacher's role as that of a *coach*. For students in the "*I Want to Know*" category, the teacher's role might be similar to that of a *tour guide* as they nurture students' interest in an apprentice type of relationship (Aikenhead, 2001). The role of the teacher described by Aikenhead (2001) for students labeled "*Other Smart Kids*" is a *travel agent* since they require some guidance. But what role does a teacher play for students that fall into the last three categories? How can teachers broker these students' knowledge?

In the case of the "*I Don't Know*" *Student* perhaps the metaphor of a *sherpa* (porter) describes the teacher's role. The *sherpa* not only guides the students but helps them to know what pitfalls to look out for. Students who have limited science or mathematics knowledge need someone to build scaffolds that link students' cultural knowledge to official school knowledge (Banks, 1993) and walk them across the border. For students in the *Outsiders* and *Inside Outsiders* categories where border crossing is impossible, the teacher's role may be described as one of an *ambassador*. In such cases, cultural broker-ing requires taking risks such as going into the students' environment on behalf of the *Outsider*, or changing the status quo on behalf of the *Inside Out-sider*. By breaking down the barriers that prohibit these students from learn-ing science or mathematics, the stage is set for learning to occur.

Culturally responsive teaching

The concept of culturally responsive teaching emerged from the multicultural education literature of the 1970s (Gay, 2000). Banks, a proponent of multi-cultural education, contends, "Teachers should use elements of culture to help [students] attain skills which they need to live alternative lifestyles" (Banks, 1974, p. 166). Gay (2000) defines culturally responsive teaching as "using the cultural knowledge, prior experiences, frames of reference, and performance styles of ethnically diverse students to make learning encounters more relevant and effective for them" (p. 29). Some of the characteristics of culturally responsive teaching include:

1. Acknowledgment of the legitimacy of different ethnic groups' cultural heritages as worthy content to be taught in the formal curriculum.
2. Building meaningful bridges between home and school experiences as well as between academic abstractions and sociocultural realities.

3. Using a wide variety of instructional strategies that are connected to different styles of learning.
4. Teaching students to know and praise their own and others' cultural heritage.
5. Incorporating multicultural information, resources, and materials in all subjects and skills routinely taught in schools.

(Gay, 2000, p. 29)

Culturally responsive teaching is validating, comprehensive, multidimensional, empowering, transformative, and emancipatory (Gay, 2000). It is validating because it affirms and strengthens students' identity. It is comprehensive because it addresses the needs of the whole child. It is multidimensional because it encompasses the curriculum, learning environment, student–teacher relationships, instructional strategies, and formal assessments (Gay, 2000). It is empowering because it enables students to be successful learners and productive citizens (Gay, 2000; Moses & Cobb, 2001). It is transformative because it challenges the use of traditional pedagogical practices among students of color (Gay, 2000). And it is liberating in creating a *third space* where ethnic ways of knowing are valued alongside dominant canons of knowledge (Gay, 2000; Lipka *et al.*, 2005). In essence, third space "is an opening in which the classroom can become a site for social change" (Nieto, 2002, p. 66).

In sum, "culturally responsive pedagogy simultaneously develops, along with academic achievement, social consciousness and critique, cultural affirmation, competence and exchange; community building and personal connections; individual self-worth and abilities; and an ethic of caring" (Gay, 2000, p. 43). The ethic of caring is the most consistent and powerful finding of research studies related to diverse students' academic achievement (Gay, 2000; Irvine, 2002). "Students defined caring teachers as those who set limits, provided structure, had high expectations, and pushed them to achieve" (Irvine, 2002, p. 141). Care is manifested by teacher attitudes, expectations, and behaviors related to students' intellectual capacity and academic performance (Gay, 2000). When teachers truly care about students, they hold them in high esteem and view them as competent. Students, in turn, rise to the occasion by exhibiting high levels of social, ethical, cultural, and scholarly behavior (Gay, 2000; Ladson-Billings, 1994). The ethic of care is the hallmark of culturally responsive pedagogy.

Culturally specific pedagogy

Culturally specific pedagogy emerged out of Irvine's (1992) research on cultural synchronization. It acknowledges the style, language, behavior, and tradition of the students' community (Cooper, 2002) and supports the use of curriculum materials that highlight a distinct ethnic background. Diverse storylines may be used to frame historical and contemporary experiences that genuinely depict a particular aspect of an ethnic group's way of life to teach mathematics. Capitalizing on significant genres and events in African American history, such as the Underground Railroad, African American music, and Black aviation, teachers may use specific elements of the African American experience to make explicit connections and engage students in culturally specific mathematics tasks (Leonard *et al.*, 2005; Leonard & Hill, in press). To supplement reform-based mathematics curriculum, I helped to develop culturally specific multimedia, which will be described later in this book. The creative work, also known as the Benjamin Banneker Project, underscores the importance of using culturally specific materials to motivate and engage African American students in learning mathematics and science (Leonard *et al.*, 2005; Leonard & Hill, in press). The prototype multimedia module was developed to tell a story based on the Underground Railroad (Leonard & Leonard, 2003). The module was field tested with African American students in Philadelphia, New York, and Chicago with positive results.

Students were able to learn from culturally specific texts as African American children's literature was used to help students acquire the background knowledge needed to succeed on the multimedia task. Children in third- and fourth-grade classes identified with the literary characters and engaged with the text on an emotional level. Students and teachers negotiated classroom norms and attempted to develop shared meaning about what it meant to travel on the Underground Railroad. Multicultural books provided a third space where knowledge, different ways of knowing, and self-determination came together in a culturally specific context to learn mathematics and science (Leonard & Hill, in press; Lipka *et al.*, 2005). This work fits within the framework of culturally specific pedagogy outlined in Irvine's (2002) study of African American teachers in the CULTURES project. In CULTURES, African American teachers engaged in critical reflection as they examined how their ethnic identity, beliefs, and practices influenced the achievement of their African American students (Irvine, 2002).

All teachers, regardless of race, gender, or socioeconomic status can be effective teachers of African American students (Cooper, 2002; Delpit, 1995; Ladson-Billings, 1994). Cooper (2002) characterizes effective teachers of African American children as those who:

1. Commit themselves to the Black community and provide a sense of family.
2. Promote positive racial identity.
3. Help students to succeed in school endeavors, despite the racist nature of both the institution and society in general, by using alternative instructional methods when necessary.
4. Take personal responsibility for their students' learning.

5. Know their subject matter.
6. Demand excellence of students in all areas, including curriculum and discipline.

(p. 52)

In order to understand exactly how a teacher might engage in culturally specific pedagogy, consider the case of Ms. Baker (pseudonym) and her fourth-grade students in a Philadelphia charter school. Ms. Baker was a participant in the Benjamin Banneker Project. She read three African American literature books to students about the Underground Railroad. The content is culturally specific to her African American students. The following vignette describes her teaching behaviors as she read *Freedom River* (Rappaport, 2000) to her students.

Vignette 3.2

49	*Baker:*	Let's begin. *Freedom River.* Great predictions. They were all wonderful predictions. Let's begin. See where we go with this. [Reading] "Before the Civil War, Kentucky was a slave state. And Ohio, a free state. In the 1800s, the Ohio River was less than one thousand feet wide in (at) Berkeley, Ohio. Runaway slaves from Kentucky followed the (Maysville) Road to the river and then swam or rode across it to freedom."
50	*Baker:*	So, they could swim a thousand feet.
51	*Baker:*	[Reading] "Sympathetic whites and blacks in Ripley hid the fugitives and then transported them farther north."
52	*Baker:*	So *fugitive* is our new word. Yesterday we were saying *runaway* right? Today, I said, *fugitive.* So what does *fugitive* mean?
53	*Students:*	Runaway.
54	*Student:*	It's like …
55	*Baker:*	What's fugitive mean, [*Name*]?
56	*Student 1:*	Runaway.
57	*Baker:*	Well, is it—is that—? What do you think the definition of fugitive—? It means runaway. But … Did you have a definition for it? It means runaway, but if I run away from …, am I a fugitive?
58	*Students:*	Yeah.
59	*Student 2:*	Why?
60	*Baker:*	Raise your hand. [*Name*].
61	*Student 2:*	I think a runaway was, like, when you was a slave, you runaway from them, and the people_____.
62	*Baker:*	[*Name*], let's hear from you.

63	*Student 3:*	A fugitive is somebody that is one of the colonies, a part of the Underground Railroad.
64	*Baker:*	Let's try another. (Calls on another student.) *Runaway* is on the right track. Are you allowed to runaway?
65	*Student 4:*	A runaway slave? A runaway slave is not allowed to runaway.
66	*Baker:*	Alright, let's read on, class. [Reading] "John Parker was a successful businessperson and one of Berkeley's most active conductors on the Underground Railroad. He had been born a slave and earned enough money to buy his freedom. But he had never forgotten the pain of being taken from his mother's loving arms when he was eight years' old. This is the true story of one of his journeys into Kentucky to help an African-American family escape to freedom."
67	*Baker:*	Okay, class; let's talk about the word "conductor" on the Underground Railroad. [Short pause] [*Name*], what's a conductor?
68	*Student 5:*	Somebody who helps somebody escape?
69	*Baker:*	Somebody who helps somebody—.
70	*Student 6:*	Free from slavery.
71	*Student 7:*	Become free.
72	*Baker:*	Become free. So then, the Underground Railroad—.
73	*Student 8:*	It's like a freedom train. When you go to the Underground Railroad and you wait for the people to come. You sit there and then when they come, they just take you to the safe house. And you got to see if it's safe. And then you go to sleep. And then you go. And then they come looking for you. Then you got to hide. And then, if they ... come looking for me, I'm a go out the back door.
74	*Students:*	[Laughter.]
75	*Baker:*	Very good. So the conductor lives in the safe house. Maybe helps the people. Okay, let's move on, class.

The purpose of Ms. Baker's lesson was to read the text and introduce students to culturally specific vocabulary that was important to know in order to understand the context of the story. Baker slowed the reading down to help students understand words like *fugitive* [line 55] and *conductor* [line 67]. However, the dynamics of the discourse shifted as the topic became more focused on the Underground Railroad itself [line 72]. By making connections to the Underground Railroad, Baker inadvertently changed the classroom norms. This is evident by the statement: "If they ... come looking for me, I'm a go out the back door" [line 73]. The student clearly identified with John and the gravity of the situation. Yet, the remark relaxed social norms in the classroom [line 74] as students got very excited about the content. Thus, using culturally rich literature to engage students in reading activities appears to impact diverse students' motivation to participate in classroom discourse.

The text could have also been used to make connections to mathematics. At the beginning of the story, Ms. Baker made a very interesting comment: "So they could swim 1,000 feet." The actual text read: "In the *1800s*, the Ohio River was *less than one thousand feet wide* at Berkeley, Ohio." Several mathematics terms and concepts could have been explored at this juncture. The term 1800s could have been used to set the story in context. It is important for students to know how long ago the story took place. One activity that was suggested to enhance the lesson was the development of a timeline. A timeline functions to establish an event alongside other significant events of a given period while placing that event in chronological order. To get a better understanding of the time period, important people, events, and inventions could be labeled on the timeline to help students clearly understand the mode of travel and the dangers and hardships a fugitive slave would encounter on the Underground Railroad. In addition to the time period, the concept *less than*, the quantity *one thousand*, and the terms *feet* and *wide* presented the opportunity to help children learn number sense, compare distances, understand measurement, and realize the sheer tenacity and strength it would take for someone to swim across the Ohio River.

Furthermore, John Parker (the story's main character) was a successful businessman who had saved enough money to purchase his freedom. Mathematics problems dealing with how long it might take to save enough money, usually about $2,500, to purchase one's freedom could also be introduced. Problems dealing with Parker's monthly income from the foundry he owned could also be incorporated into a mathematics lesson. Although Ms. Baker's goal was to read the story and focus on vocabulary, there were opportunities to engage students in problem solving within a culturally specific context as well. Beginning teachers should be made aware of these opportunities through teacher education programs and professional development sessions. Multicultural literature and problem posing provide entry points for teachers to use culturally specific pedagogy with diverse students (Ameis, 2002; Strutchens, 2002).

Historical facts and statistical data can be used to develop culturally specific mathematics lessons. For example, on a recent visit to the Reginald F. Lewis Museum of African American History in Maryland, I learned that a $40,000 reward was offered for the capture of Harriet Tubman in 1856. A discussion about what the reward would be worth in 2006 dollars ensued between me and a friend. I estimated that the reward would be worth $1,000,000. My friend thought the reward would be worth a lot more given 150 years of inflation.

A mathematics lesson could begin with a fact sheet about Harriet Tubman and the reward. Then students could estimate what they think the reward would be worth in the current year. Background information about inflation and the Consumer Price Index (CPI) integrates the lesson with economics. An algebraic formula for comparing how much purchasing power $1 in 1856 had in 2006 (2006 Price = 1856 Price × (2006 CPI/1856 CPI) may be found at the following URL: www.minneapolisfed.org/Research/data/us/calc/hist1800.cfm. The CPI in 1856 was estimated to be 27, and the CPI in 2006 was estimated at 604.3. Substituting these values in the formula yields the following result: $40,000 × (604.3/27) = $895,200. My estimate of $1,000,000 was a bit high but not unreasonable. Students could then discuss the implication of placing such a steep reward on Harriet Tubman's head.

Many credit Harriet Tubman, who escaped from a Maryland plantation, with making more than 19 trips to the South to free more than 300 slaves from 1851 to 1858 (Public Broadcasting System, n.d.). However, this figure could be inaccurate. Harriet Tubman is quoted as saying: "I freed a thousand slaves. I could have freed a thousand more if only they knew they were slaves" (ThinkExist, 2006). Another math problem that could be calculated is the average number of fugitive slaves Harriet assisted on each trip given a minimum of 300 and a maximum of 1,000. Knowing how much of a threat Harriet was to the South's way of life will help students to understand the high price on her head. The $40,000 reward is equivalent to rewards posted for fugitives on the FBI's ten most wanted list. In 1856, Harriet Tubman was perceived to be as dangerous as someone wanted for armed robbery today.

A more contemporary example that uses statistical data can be found in the movie industry: Which movie has had the highest gross ticket sales? In order to find the number of tickets sold for a particular movie, gross box office receipts must be divided by the average ticket price (Box Office Mojo, 2007). However, movie ticket prices are also affected by inflation. In 1970, the average price of a movie ticket was $1.55. Today the average cost is $6.58. A chart listing average ticket prices from 1920 to the present day can be found at the following URL: http://boxofficemojo.com/about/adjuster.htm. In order to adjust for inflation the number of tickets sold must be multiplied by the average ticket price for the year of conversion.

A mathematics lesson could begin with students guessing which movie had the highest gross ticket sales. Students may manipulate the aforementioned formula to determine the gross ticket sales for their favorite movies. Graphs and charts can be made to compare and contrast the gross receipts for movies in a given year. This lesson can be linked to social justice issues by discussing how the number of theatres a movie plays in is related to the number of ticket sales. For example, at the 64th Annual Golden Globe Awards on January 15, 2007, Meryl Streep stated her movie, *The Devil Wears Prada*, opened at every movie theatre across the country. Later that same evening, Jamie Foxx stated that *Dreamgirls* only opened in 800 theatres across the country. Then he said,

"You do the math!" In other words, Foxx implied that the gross receipts for *Dreamgirls* were limited by the number of theatres it played in. Many factors, such as limited engagements and misprinting tickets (i.e. giving one a ticket for a movie other than the one he/she wanted to see) may underestimate ticket sales for a particular movie. Meryl Streep advocated for equity, stating theatre managers should be asked why a particular movie is not showing in a certain neighborhood. Students could take on the role of social activists and be encouraged to write letters to the CEOs of large movie chains like United Artists, AMC, and Regal. This lesson is culturally specific because it challenges racial prejudice. Social injustice occurs in the movie industry just as it does in all other aspects of American life.

Diversity pedagogy

Drawing from research on cognition (Bransford *et al.*, 2000; Cole, 1992), diversity pedagogy is an ideology that acknowledges the relationship between culture and cognition and is paramount to the teaching–learning process. Diversity pedagogy is characterized as the co-construction of new knowledge by both teachers and students (Sheets, 2005). It recognizes students' ability to select specific cultural tools for learning in different contexts from prior knowledge, skills, backgrounds, and real-life experiences that are then used to acquire new knowledge and develop new understandings (Nasir, 2005; Sheets, 2005). Thus, learning is situated within the culture of the community (Núñez *et al.*, 1999).

Diversity pedagogy has eight dimensions that describe teachers' pedagogical behavior. These dimensions along with their corresponding student displays are outlined below in Table 3.1.

Recognizing no ethnic or racial group is monolithic, "diversity refers to dissimilarities in traits, qualities, characteristics, beliefs, values, and mannerisms present in self and others" (Sheets, 2005, p. 15). Children bring multiple layers of identity into the classroom. Diversity pedagogy emphasizes cultural differences but affirms students' membership in multiple groups (Cole, 1992; Sheets, 2005). Diversity pedagogy encourages teachers to create optimal learn-

Table 3.1 Dimension of diversity pedagogy

Teacher behaviors	Student displays
1. Diversity	1. Conscious of difference
2. Identity	2. Ethnic identity development
3. Social interaction	3. Interpersonal relationships
4. Culturally safe classroom context	4. Self-regulated learning
5. Language	5. Language learning
6. Culturally inclusive content	6. Knowledge acquisition
7. Instruction	7. Reasoning skills
8. Assessment	8. Self-evaluation

Source: Sheets (2005), pp. 15–16.

ing conditions by valuing the unique qualities, strengths, and abilities children possess while eschewing the colorblind approach and one-size-fits all practices (Rousseau & Tate, 2003; Sheets, 2005). However, placing too much emphasis on culture-as-difference overlooks some of the universal characteristics that all humans possess (Cole, 1992).

To further understand diversity pedagogy, Sheets (2005) offers many examples and counterexamples of diversity pedagogy. Vignette 3.3 is a counterexample that took place in a Spanish/English bilingual classroom, and Vignette 3.4 is an example of diversity pedagogy in an urban high school.

Vignette 3.3

Hearing that their sons would be making tortillas in class, three Mexican American mothers arrived at school early in the morning to explain to the teacher that their sons are not allowed to make tortillas. Ms. Harding, a bilingual European American teacher, explained politely, "In my classroom everyone participates in group activities. That's the way we build community." Seemingly aware that the mothers were uncomfortable, she added that making tortillas is a culturally relevant learning activity designed to encourage gender equity. The mothers tried to explain that they do not object to how she teaches, but they do not want their boys to make tortillas. They explain that the children's fathers were unable to take time off from work, but that they were concerned that this may confuse their sons' idea on what it means to be male—*un hombre.* (Sheets, 2005, p. 36)

Ms. Harding attempted to implement a culturally relevant activity for her bilingual students. Although it was a great idea, she was unaware of cultural gender norms. Mexican American males did not make tortillas (Sheets, 2005). Had she gotten parent input prior to planning the activity, she might have avoided the conflict that ensued. When planning culturally relevant activities, it is important for teachers to use parents and other members of the community as resources in order to avoid cultural conflict, especially when the teacher is not a member of that community (Nieto, 2002).

Vignette 3.4

Ms. Stuart, a fourth-year teacher, works in an ethnically diverse urban high school with a majority of students from groups of color. She allows students to choose where to sit in her eleventh-grade U.S. History classes. Although most students sit in the same seats, they can change or move the individual desks to form groups. She determines the number of groups and often selects the concepts or topics under discussion for group work. Students self-select for group assignments, and there are no limitations to the number of students per group. Students received two grades for group projects, an individual grade and a group grade. They are encouraged to work collaboratively. (Sheets, 2005, p. 73)

The case of Ms. Stuart is an excellent example of diversity pedagogy. By allowing students to have choices and sit wherever they wish, Ms. Stuart allowed her students to have some autonomy. By trusting her students, Ms. Stuart encouraged them to live up to her expectations. Ms. Stuart also demonstrated the ethic of caring (Gay, 2000) and cultural competence described in culturally relevant teaching (Ladson-Billings, 1994). Teachers should acknowledge and respect the cultural capital diverse students bring to the classroom and engage in classroom practices that create learning environments that are supportive of social interaction (Delpit, 1995; Sheets, 2005).

Summary

Each of the cultural pedagogies described above explicitly and implicitly emphasizes the importance of students' culture in the learning process. Teachers should not only use students' culture as a bridge to cross borders but infuse it in the mathematics curriculum in order to diminish cultural dissonance. By situating the learning of mathematics within specific cultural contexts, students are socialized to learn mathematics and will develop a mathematics identity (Martin, 2000). Thus, they learn its usefulness in their lives and may be less likely to ask: "When am I ever going to use this?" or "Why do I need to know mathematics beyond a basic level." When teachers make mathematics connections specific to students' everyday lives, students are motivated to learn more mathematics and are empowered to use mathematics to accomplish personal goals (Albert, 2000; Martin, 2000; Nasir, 2005).

No classroom is void of cultural influence on teaching and learning. While culturally specific pedagogy utilizes elements of cultural brokering, cultural responsiveness, and cultural relevance, the purpose of this text is to highlight specific behaviors that teachers can use to support the mathematics learning of diverse students in their classrooms. Students of color continue to struggle in U.S. schools when teachers attempt to assimilate rather than acculturate them into mainstream culture (Howard, 2003; Malloy & Malloy, 1998; Sheets, 2005). These students are in need of a *coach, tour guide, travel agent, sherpa,* and/or *ambassador* to help them cross borders from the microculture of peers, family, and community to the microculture of school mathematics.

In sum, effective teachers believe diverse students can learn "despite inadequate material resources and social hostilities, claiming Du Bois' vision of schools as liberating forces" (Cooper, 2002, p. 62). This principle has been used in culturally specific contexts with Alaskan Native (Lipka & Adams, 2002; Lipka *et al.*, 2005), Hawaiian (Brenner, 1998; Tharp, 1982), Latina/o

(Gutstein, 2003; Gutstein *et al.*, 1997), and African American students (Irvine, 2002; Leonard *et al.*, 2005; Leonard & Guha, 2002). Qualitative and quasi-experimental studies provide evidence that cultural pedagogy improves student outcomes among Alaskan Native and Hawaiian students in mathematics (Brenner, 1998; Lipka *et al.*, 2005). Additional research studies are needed to show how culturally specific pedagogy can be used to improve student outcomes among African American and Latina/o populations. In the case of ethnomathematics (Ascher, 1991), the use of culturally specific pedagogy recognizes the richness of diverse mathematics practices and systems around the world (Brenner, 1998).

It is incumbent upon schools, colleges, and departments of education to critically examine the manner in which new teachers are prepared (Howard, 2003; Irvine, 2002). "In the case of teacher education, a crucial goal must be to promote fundamental shifts in the perspectives of beginning teachers" (Remillard, 2000, p. 132). Teacher educators and preservice teachers must be willing to tackle the subject of race and equity in teacher education programs. Critical reflection of one's own racial and cultural identity is prerequisite to understanding the racial and cultural identity of students and is a prelude to developing pedagogical strategies that infuse culture into the curriculum (Howard, 2003; Remillard, 2000). In short, promoting teaching as a transformative journey where teachers learn about students and learn from students affirms diversity (Nieto, 2000). After affirming students' identities by recognizing that everyone brings uniqueness to the classroom, then teachers can use cultural pedagogy to ensure that all students have opportunities to learn.

4

Problem solving, problem posing, multicultural literature, and computer scaffolding

Great works are performed not by strength, but by perseverance.

Samuel Johnson

Introduction

Multimedia in the form of texts, videos, computer programs, and posters can be used to enhance mathematics lessons and increase students' motivation and engagement in authentic mathematical tasks (Chappell & Thompson, 2000). Storytelling provides a meaningful context for teachers to motivate students to solve embedded mathematics problems as well (Ameis, 2002). Students can create and read an adventure story with routine and non-routine problems related to the character's survival or well-being (Ameis, 2002; Leonard et al., 2005). Moreover, parents and children can read multi-cultural stories and solve mathematics problems simultaneously (Chappell & Thompson, 2000; Strutchens, 2002). Anderson et al. (2004) found that parents and children shared a variety of discourses in mathematics during shared storybook reading. Children's literature can be used to support mathematical literacy and problem solving.

How children learn to solve mathematics problems

Baroody and Coslick (1998) acknowledge the difficulty that all students have with non-routine word problems. Particularly, students have more difficulty with problems that require two or more steps to solve (Geary, 1996). However, recent studies report on a variety of successful strategies that improve students' ability to solve mathematics word problems (Fuchs et al., 2004; Ku & Sullivan, 2001; van Garderen & Montague, 2003).

Fuchs et al. (2004) conducted a study that utilized schema-based instruction (SBI) with 366 third-grade students. Research assistants who received similar training delivered instruction in all groups. Building on the work of Chen (1999), Fuchs et al. (2004) hypothesized that children aged 8–10 have a greater ability to use transfer or schemas to solve problems by type. The researchers hypothesized that when students encounter a new problem, they

59

must recognize its similarity to other problem types. Thus, transfer occurs as students develop schema to solve unique problems. The study involved using three types of treatment conditions with high-, average-, and low-performing students: contrast, SBI, and SBI plus sorting. The contrast group received six lessons that addressed general problem-solving strategies. Students received explicit instruction and engaged in didactic practice, independent work with checking, and homework. SBI and SBI plus sorting groups received 24 additional lessons and two review lessons for a total of 26 lessons. SBI lessons focused on problem–solution methods and schema-enhanced methods. In the SBI plus sorting group, research assistants also incorporated guided schema-based sorting practice by asking questions such as: What kind of problem is this? Is this a transfer problem? What kind of transfer problem is it?

The researchers found that schema-based instruction improved problem solving among third-grade students of different achievement statuses and concluded that explicit instruction of sufficient duration has a dramatic impact on students' mathematics problem solving (Fuchs et al., 2004). In addition to these findings, van Garderen & Montague (2003) found that students who could draw schematic representations (diagrams or images that show relationships between objects) rather than pictorial representations (diagrams or images only) were more successful in solving non-routine problems. These findings suggest schema-based instruction and representations enhance problem-solving competence for students with low achievement profiles and disabilities (Fuchs et al., 2004). Thus, children can be taught to solve word problems.

The problem-solving process

Generally speaking, most researchers describe problem solving as a four-step process (Polya, 1945). Mayer and Hagerty (1996) offer the following four-step process for solving mathematics problems:

- Translating involves constructing a mental representation of each statement of the problem.
- Integrating involves constructing a mental representation of the situation described in the problem.
- Planning involves devising a strategy for how to solve the problem.
- Executing involves carrying out the plan, including computations.

(p. 34)

In addition to the problem-solving process, strategies include but are not limited to the following: estimation, making a list or chart, creating a pattern, drawing a picture or diagram, working backwards, guess-and-check, solving a similar problem, and acting it out (Cathcart et al., 2006). Observations of teachers in the field reveal that some primary teachers instruct children to use a keyword approach to solve problems (Leonard *et al.*, 2004). In order to explain this kind of instructional strategy, consider the following problem:

Two pigeons land on a Maple tree. Three more pigeons land on the same tree. How many pigeons land on the Maple tree altogether?

In the keyword approach, teachers tell students to focus on the number words, such as *two* and *three*, to develop a number sentence. Then students are told to focus on keywords, such as *how many* and *altogether*, to determine what mathematical operation to use. I have observed some elementary teachers telling students that *how many* and *altogether* imply addition. Without explaining the context of the sentence, a number sentence such as the following is often written on the board: *2 + 3 = [ ].* Students quickly learn to pick out the numbers and add when they encounter problems of this type. As a result, students are not conditioned to carefully read the problem and do not understand the relationship between the terms. They develop what Mayer & Hagerty (1996) call a direct translation or keyword approach, but this approach is only useful for certain types of problems (Mayer & Hagerty, 1996).

The problem illustrated above is called a *join result unknown* problem type (Carpenter *et al.*, 1999). Other problem types are *join start unknown* and *join change unknown*. These types of problems are more difficult for students to solve and using the keyword approach may result in the wrong answer. For example, consider the following problems:

Some pigeons land on a Maple tree. Three more pigeons land on the same tree. If five pigeons land on the Maple tree altogether, how many pigeons landed on the tree in the beginning?
(join start unknown)

Two pigeons land on a Maple tree. Some more pigeons land on the same tree. If five pigeons land on the Maple tree altogether, how many pigeons joined the first group of pigeons?
(join change unknown)

The keyword approach is not useful in solving the problem types above. Students taught to use keywords will simply add the numbers and get incorrect answers of eight and seven, respectively. What is needed is a problem model approach where students understand the relationship between the variables in the problem (Mayer & Hagerty, 1996). In this case, drawing a picture, working backwards, or modeling the problem with manipulatives are useful strategies. Mayer and Hagerty (1996) contend the source of difficulty with problem solving is not execution but problem representation—that is, comprehending relational statements. Once students understand how one part of the problem is related to other parts, it is much easier to solve. Successful problem solvers are those who use a problem model approach instead of the direct translation or keyword approach (Mayer & Hagerty, 1996).

The correct equations to solve the problems above are: *[ ] + 3 = 5 and 2 + [ ] = 5*. Once students understand the number sentence that is needed to solve the problem, they should practice solving problems with missing addends. Giving students the *join result unknown (x + y = [ ])* type of problem over and over again may cause them to misunderstand the meaning of the equal sign. Regardless of how the problem is written, some students may be tempted to operate on the numbers they see and put that solution in the open sentence. For example, a common error is to write *2 + [7] = 5*. To address this misconception, it is important for teachers to use mathematical representations to help students understand how to solve problems with missing addends.

The term *representation* can be described as "external embodiment of students' internal conceptualizations" (Lesh *et al.*, 1987). The five different types of representation systems associated with learning mathematics and solving problems are as follows:

- experienced-based scripts (knowledge is organized around real world events);
- manipulatives such as Cuisenaire rods and Unifix cubes;
- pictures or diagrams;
- spoken languages (including logic);
- written symbols such as variables and various types of mathematics notations ($<$, $>$, %, and $\div$).

(Lesh *et al.*, 1987, pp. 33–34)

Lesh *et al.* (1987) found that most fourth- through eighth-grade students have a deficient understanding about the models and language(s) needed to represent and manipulate mathematical ideas. These researchers suggest that successful teachers are able to simplify, concretize, and illustrate the ideas embedded in word problems in familiar situations or scripts students can understand. Students of diverse language and cultural backgrounds may use different scripts to solve problems (Solano-Flores & Trumbell, 2003). Cultural scripts are especially beneficial for low socioeconomic students who tend to apply their emotional and personal perspectives to word problems, projecting their own concerns and experiences onto the way they solve problems (Ku & Sullivan, 2001; Solano-Flores & Trumbell, 2003; Tate, 1995).

Solano-Flores and Trumbell (2003) argue that some mathematics problems may be difficult for poor and minority students because they may interpret the problem differently from middle-class students. Differences of interpretation occur when students bring a different cultural lens to the mathematics classroom. Solano-Flores and Trumbell (2003) claim that existing approaches to assess English Language Learners (ELLs) "do not ensure equitable and valid outcomes because current research and practice paradigms overlook the complex nature of language, including its interrelationship with culture" (p. 3). Tests are cultural products. Because it is impossible to construct a culture-free test, they are indubitably cultural devices (Solano-Flores & Trumbell, 2003). For example, consider the following NAEP problem:

Sam can purchase his lunch at school. Each day he wants to have juice that costs 50¢, a sandwich that costs 90¢, and fruit that costs 35¢. His mother has only $1.00 bills. What is the least number of $1.00 bills that his mother should give him so he will have enough money to buy lunch for five days?

In their analysis of student responses to this question, Solano-Flores & Trumbell (2003) found the word *only* was problematic in the sentence: "His mother has only $1.00 bills." The researchers found 84% of White, 56% of Native American, and 52% of African American students understood the sentence as it was intended. However, 10% of Native American and 18% of African American students interpreted the problem as: "His mother has only one dollar bill." None of the White students interpreted the problem this way. Furthermore, students of different socioeconomic statuses also interpreted the words in the lunch money problem differently. The question some students answered was not the intended question, but "What can Sam buy with a dollar?" Thus, the researchers contend that the error was not a result of poor reading but interpretation, claiming that "students from certain cultural groups tend to incorporate emotion and personal perspectives" into the problem-solving process (Solano-Flores & Trumbell, 2003, p. 4). The lunch money item underscores the complexity of both language and sociocultural context in problem solving (Solano-Flores & Trumbell, 2003).

Similarly, Tate (1994) found the following question on a district-wide assessment was interpreted differently by some African American children:

It costs $1.50 each way to ride the bus between home and work. A weekly pass is $16. Which is the better deal, paying the daily fare or buying the weekly pass?

The district's test developers assumed that students would choose to pay the daily fare because it was cheaper. However, that assumption was not consistent with the lives and daily experiences of a majority of African American students who thought it was better to buy the weekly pass because it could be used more than once a day and shared with other members of the family.

"For these students, choosing the weekly pass is economically appropriate and mathematically logical" (Tate, 1994, p. 480).

In a case study comparing the problem-solving abilities of predominantly White students from working-class, and middle-class backgrounds, Lubienski (2000) found that poor White females had difficulty with reform-based curriculum and open-ended and contextualized word problems. Lubienski (2000) conducted her study in a school with 500 predominantly Caucasian students with a population that was also 2% Asian, 3% Hispanic, and 11% African American in a midwestern city. Conducting a teacher-research study, Lubienski (2000) piloted the Connected Mathematics Project (CMP) in a class of 30 seventh-grade students.

During typical lessons, Lubienski allowed students to work in groups to explore and solve the problems. Then she facilitated whole-group discussion to review the students' work. Rather than teaching by telling, Lubienski encouraged the students to solve problems on their own. Data sources included interviews, surveys, student work, and teaching-journal entries. Data analysis focused on finding patterns of similarities and differences among students' experiences controlling for socioeconomic status.

The results of the study presented several interesting findings. First, Lubienski (2000) found that students from more affluent backgrounds liked the curriculum, but students from high-poverty backgrounds were ambivalent about CMP. Some students from working-class backgrounds expressed a preference for direct instruction and traditional curriculum that provided number problems instead of word problems. These students wanted the teacher to tell them the rules in order to spend less time trying to figure out what to do and more time trying to solve the problems. When it came to context, Lubienski (2000) believed poor female students' "common sense" way of solving the problems prevented them from generalizing the problem to other situations. Lubienski (2000) concluded that abstract mathematics curriculum might be better for these students and questioned the use of reform-based curriculum and open-ended, contextualized problems to narrow differences in mathematics achievement among higher and lower SES students.

The results of the foregoing studies raise tough questions about the use of culture in problem solving. There has been a paucity of studies that examine the problem-solving strategies of students from different socioeconomic groups. Thus, Lubienski's (2000), Solano-Flores & Trumbell's (2003), and Tate's (1995) research are important to the field. Moreover, there is research that suggests students of color benefit from explicit directions (Cooper, 2002; Delpit, 1995; Irvine, 2002; Kitchen, 2007). There have also been a number of studies that examined contextualized word problems among students of different ethnic and racial profiles, who were often from poor and working-class backgrounds (Ku & Sullivan, 2001; Ladson-Billings, 1995; Leonard et al.,

2005; Leonard & Guha, 2002; Lipka *et al.*, 2005; Malloy & Jones, 1998; Nasir, 2002 & 2005; Strutchens, 2002). The findings suggest that contextualized problems benefit students from poor and ethnically diverse backgrounds.

While programs like the Algebra Project (Moses & Cobb, 2001) and Project SEED (Phillips & Ebrahimi, 1993) are successful abstract-oriented programs, they are not divorced from context. Having been a Project SEED instructor in Dallas, Texas, from 1986 to 1988, I can attest that real-world examples are used to help students make links to abstract problems. Mathematics is not acultural but situated in context (Lave, 1988; Nasir, 2005; Solano-Flores & Trumbell, 2003). The findings of Lubienski (2000), Solano-Flores & Trumbell (2003), and Tate (1995) suggest that problems must be posed with care and field tested with diverse student populations. Nevertheless, additional studies that examine the variables of gender, ethnicity, and socioeconomic status in problem-solving contexts are warranted.

Culture plays a role in children's problem solving. However, the foregoing discussion elucidates the difficulty that interpretation brings to the problem-solving context. Teachers must be cognizant of cultural differences and help to bridge cultural differences by exposing poor children to problems within and outside of their cultural experiences. The previous discussion also illuminates diverse students' limited exposure to different kinds of problems. Quintero (2004) suggests that teachers pose or present students with a variety of problems to solve. Implementing a problem-posing framework that uses multicultural children's literature encourages collaboration and enhances multidirectional participatory learning (Quintero, 2004).

Teachers may use multicultural texts to bridge the culture of the school and home by providing students with authentic problems to solve (Quintero, 2004; Strutchens, 2002). Use of multicultural texts creates opportunities for teachers to use cultural pedagogy. The texts provide the context to engage students in critical literacy as they discuss and challenge the validity of the context, the portrayal of the characters, and the authenticity of the story (Quintero, 2004). Questions, such as whose story is this, what message is being sent about the characters, and is the perception correct, may be asked (Quintero, 2004). Most importantly, mathematics problems that will interest students of diverse backgrounds can be developed from rich storylines for students to solve (Leonard *et al.*, 2005; Leonard & Hill, in press). Story problems have been used to motivate students to persist and succeed in problem solving (Ameis, 2002; Leonard *et al.*, 2005; Malloy & Jones, 1998). However, developing meaningful story problems for students to solve is not a trivial task.

Learning to pose problems to students

The NCTM *Principles and Standards* (2000) call for students to engage in activities that require students to reason, communicate, represent, problem solve, and make mathematics connections. However, teachers often have difficulty presenting students with authentic mathematical tasks that require cognitively demanding skills (Crespo, 2003; Stein *et al.*, 1996). Learning to pose authentic mathematics problems that require high cognitive demand from students is a challenge since novice teachers have been more exposed to problems that require memorization and application of procedures and algorithms (Crespo, 2003; Ebby, 2000; Kahan *et al.*, 2003). However, Crespo's (2003) study of preservice teachers' ability to pose problems that require high cognitive demand from fourth-grade students is promising.

Crespo (2003) conducted a study to examine how novice teachers learned to pose mathematics problems to students, how their practices changed, and what contributed to the changes. In this study, 13 preservice teachers posed problems to students in a fourth-grade class by giving them word problems to solve weekly via pen pal letter writing over the course of the semester. In addition, they were required to reflect on students' feedback as well as their own growth and learning by writing their reflections in a journal on a weekly basis.

Early analysis revealed that preservice teachers undermined the students' opportunities to solve challenging problems by giving problems that were too easy to solve, posing problems that were too familiar, and posing problems blindly without understanding the complexity involved. After receiving various forms of feedback from the students, such as the demand for more rigorous and challenging problems, the preservice teachers began to change their expectations of students, giving them more difficult problems to solve. Crespo (2003) reported shifts in preservice teachers' views and beliefs as they gave students worthwhile mathematics tasks that required high cognitive demand (Stein *et al.*, 1996). Posing culturally specific problems may yield the same results.

Using multicultural literature as a context for problem posing

Given that classrooms are becoming increasingly diverse, multicultural children's literature provides an excellent context for learning across the curriculum (Chappell & Thompson, 2000; Strutchens, 2002). Linking literature to mathematics instruction has a number of benefits. These benefits include using mathematics in contexts that promote a positive light, making interpretations and applying mathematics to specific situations (Leonard & Campbell, 2004), engaging students in authentic activities that expand beyond everyday classroom experiences (Chappell & Thompson, 2000; Tate, 1995), and using literature as a springboard to engage students in mathematical discourse (Anderson *et al.*, 2004).

Mathematical discourse is part of a larger framework of "Discourses" and "integrates words, acts, values, beliefs, attitudes, and social identities as well as gestures, glances, body positions, and clothes" (Gee, 1989, p.7). Primary discourse is developed in the home where children learn to make sense of the world and interact with others. Literacy is the mastery of secondary discourses (Gee, 1989), which are acquired through schools, churches, businesses, and other institutions (Gee, 1989). Minority children often have difficulty using and mastering school secondary discourses because of conflicts between their primary and community-based secondary discourses (Gee, 1989). In other words, there is cultural discontinuity—a mismatch between the culture of the school and the culture of the home (Diller, 1999). Teachers can serve as cultural brokers (Aikenhead, 1997), helping urban children to acquire secondary discourses through culturally responsive teaching—empowering students to acquire secondary discourses by scaffolding on students' cultural knowledge (Gay, 2000).

Minority students may acquire mathematical literacy through "apprenticeship" in a discourse-oriented learning environment (Gee, 1989; Longo, 1993). Discourse-oriented teaching "describes the actions taken by a teacher that support the creation of mathematics knowledge through discourse among students" (Williams & Baxter, 1996, p. 22), providing them with a means of transforming individual ideas into shared knowledge (Wood, 1999). As the "Black preacher" engages in the discourse that is recognizable by its cadence, movement and speech patterns (Gee, 1989), students' engagement in mathematical discourse is recognizable by their explanations, questions, and conclusions (Campbell & Johnson, 1995).

Multicultural children's literature may be used to facilitate classroom discourse and to develop mathematical literacy and reasoning skills. Chappell and Thompson (2000) categorize multicultural literature and other media as "*culturally contextual* (culturally specific to one race or ethnic group), *culturally amenable* (not specific to a particular culture or race although the characters may be of a specific race or ethnic background) or *culturally influenced* (neither culturally contextual nor culturally amenable)" (pp. 135–136). An example of a culturally contextual text is *The Black Snowman* (Mendez, 1989). This story is about how one young African American boy's attitude is changed by learning about the African Diaspora. Money problems can be created around the recycling project presented in *The Black Snowman*. An example of a culturally amenable text is *The Three Little Javelinas* (Lowell, 1992), which is the Spanish version of the three little pigs. The story provides a context to develop problems around architecture and construction. In addition to mathematics literacy and problem solving, these texts provide students with an understanding of different cultural traditions and knowledge of vocabulary from different languages. An example of a culturally influenced text is *The Snowy Day* (Keats, 1962). Although the story is about an African American family, race has nothing to do with the story itself. The family could have just as easily been European American, Asian, or Latina/o. However, we get a glimpse of Peter's family and his life as he tries to save a snowball in his pocket. This text can be used to help students learn mathematics and science by measuring temperature, recording data, and observing differences among forms of precipitation.

In addition to texts, multicultural storylines may be presented in the form of multimedia (Leonard *et al.*, 2005; Leonard & Hill, in press). Research has shown that students are highly motivated to engage in computer simulations (Page, 2002; Wenglinsky, 1998). The main incentive for teachers to use computers in their classroom is the excitement and increased motivation they offer students (Ertmer *et al.*, 1999; Van Dusen & Worthen, 2000). The Internet may be used to foster literacy, inquiry, and the natural curiosity of elementary and middle-school children (Brown & Boshamer, 2000; Craig, 1999). Emerging technology is a tool that may be used to scaffold students' mathematics problem-solving ability (Edelson, 2001; Page, 2002).

Emerging technology and problem solving

The computer has become a powerful tool to assist student learning in the educational process (Crews *et al.*, 1997). Most of the software programs used at the early childhood and elementary levels are commercial products that offer adventure stories with verbal and visual reinforcement and animation (Ainsa, 1999). Computers and software programs are cognitive tools that can extend and strengthen learners' cognitive processes by providing information and data to collaborate, investigate, and create artifacts (Salomon *et al.*, 1991). Because of modern advances in technology, several types of learning systems have emerged that utilize text-based and digital information systems. These systems include learning-centered design (LCD) (Soloway *et al.*, 1994), computer-assisted instruction (CAI) (Ertmer *et al.*, 1999), intelligent computer-assisted instruction (ICAI) (Christmann & Badgett, 1999; Steele & Steele, 1999), open-ended learning environment (OELE) (Land & Hannifin, 1996), anchored interactive learning environment (AILE) (Crews *et al.*, 1997), and resource-based learning environment (RBLE) (Hill & Hannafin, 2001) programs.

Computer-assisted instruction

Steele and Steele (1999) studied the use of Intelligent Tutoring Systems (ITS) to teach special education students how to solve mathematics word problems. The program, known as DISCOVER, utilized a direct-teaching model to offer students different strategies, hints, and coaching as they attempted to solve a variety of word problems (Steele & Steele, 1999). Intelligent tutoring programs are able to keep track of student progress and recommend individual instruction (Steele & Steele, 1999; Van Dusen & Worthen, 2000). After field testing DISCOVER with adult GED students, researchers found the advantages of the program include "high success rates, low anxiety, motivation for using the computer, and increased confidence in solving word problems" (Steele & Steele, 1999, p. 358).

Brown and Boshamer (2000) conducted a research study on computer-assisted instruction (CAI) with approximately 100,000 elementary and middle-school students in North Carolina. The researchers used a pretest-posttest design to determine the effect of using CAI as a supplement to traditional mathematics instruction. The software program that was used in the North Carolina schools was *FUNdamentallyMATH* (Brown & Boshamer, 2000). Results show African American fourth graders who used CAI had significant pretest-posttest gains compared to African American fourth graders who did not have CAI ($p = 0.001$). Moreover, female students also improved significantly on the posttest after using CAI ($p = 0.041$). The data show posttest scores were not statistically significant for White students after they participated in CAI. Perhaps such programs may have limited impact because these students have greater access to computers at home compared to African American and Hispanic students (Swain & Pearson, 2003). CAI is a tool that can be used to inform and sustain culturally specific computer-based instruction. The study underscores that CAI is an effective tool for African American students and females. However, Vale & Leder (2004) found gender differences among middle-school students when they analyzed students' perceptions of computer-based tasks.

Most studies on using computers in the mathematics classroom have focused on cognition and achievement without regard to the affective domain (McCoy as cited in Vale & Leder, 2004). In a study that used mixed methods (both quantitative and qualitative), Vale & Leder (2004) investigated the gender attitudes of eighth- and ninth-grade students in Melbourne. A total of 49 students (17 girls and 32 boys) completed computer-based mathematics tasks using *Geometer's Sketchpad* and *Excel* software programs. *Geometer's Sketchpad* is used to help students develop geometric knowledge by constructing points, angles, lines, and figures. The program also enables students to learn about angle properties such as degrees. In the study, *Excel* was used to calculate profits and losses in a fictitious business exercise. Data sources included interviews and open-ended surveys. Chi-square was used to compare students' responses on the survey. Two-way ANOVA was used to compare the attitudes of males and females toward computer-based mathematics tasks.

The researchers found no significant differences among students' perceived achievement in mathematics and computing or student beliefs about using computers in mathematics (Vale & Leder, 2004). However, there were significant differences in attitude toward computer-based instruction ($F(1,44) = 20.35$, $p = 0.00$, partial $\eta^2 = 0.32$). Analysis of interview data reveal boys were more likely to believe that computer usage was relevant in the mathematics classroom. Boys also made positive comments about computers being enjoyable, interesting, or challenging. On the other hand, girls stated they were dissatisfied with *Geometer's Sketchpad*, but they were more favorable of the *Excel* activity. In general, girls had a less favorable view of computer-based mathematics lessons than boys did. These findings reveal that student attitudes about computer-based math tasks are associated with their views of using computers in mathematics class (Vale & Leder, 2004).

The results of the Vale & Leder (2004) study are important because few studies have examined gender equity and computer usage in mathematics. The choice of computer programs may have made a difference in girls' attitudes toward computer usage. Having used *Geometer's Sketchpad* in mathematics methods courses, I do not believe it is very user friendly. Furthermore, the mathematical tasks are not culturally specific. Gender studies on girls' attitudes toward culturally relevant mathematics software programs such as *The Oregon Trail* are sparse. During my years as a mathematics teacher, I observed genuine excitement among males and females when I allowed students to use software programs like *The Oregon Trail* to supplement mathematics instruction.

Kinard and Bitter (1997) conducted a multimedia project that blended multicultural mathematics and technology. Believing that development of innovative multicultural programs would redress the underachievement and underrepresentation of female and minority students in STEM careers, Kinard & Bitter (1997) created a bilingual, culturally based, interactive computer program known as the Hispanic Math Project to target the needs of migrant sixth-grade learners of mathematics. Video and animation were embedded in situated modules in a stand-alone tutorial program that consisted of a variety of measurement lessons. A summative evaluation was conducted to learn if the module was instructionally effective and if students enjoyed using it to learn. One of the lessons on perimeter was found to be particularly effective. Results show that students were engaged in the computer-based task for 25 to 55 minutes, which was longer than anticipated. During an interview, students reported that they liked the computer module and the concepts taught in the computer program were useful in everyday life. Teachers lauded the program, stating that "'hard-to-reach' students learned how to calculate the perimeter of a rectangle and really enjoyed themselves..." (Kinard & Bitter, 1997, p. 86). The potential of culturally specific software programs to improve African American students' performance and attitudes toward mathematics was the impetus for the Benjamin Banneker Project.

The Benjamin Banneker Project

Intelligent Computer-Assisted Instruction: The Benjamin Banneker Project was a project named for an African American mathematician and scientist who lived during the colonial period. The National Science Foundation and Temple University funded the project. The purpose of this exploratory study was to examine the level of engagement as well as the strategies of third- and fourth-grade African American students as they read culturally relevant stories and solved problems on the computer. A 30-minute computer module was developed around the theme of the Underground Railroad. A CD-ROM integrated mathematics and science concepts by asking a subset of questions that were contextualized around the storyline. Students were able to link new knowledge acquired from the storyline with existing knowledge they may have learned in the home, community, or the classroom. In addition, students were able to apply their knowledge of basic mathematics operations to solve story problems and advance the storyline.

The research methods are delineated in Appendix A. The results of the Banneker Project are presented in three parts. First, the classroom discourse is analyzed to determine how teachers used multicultural texts to help students learn mathematics. Second, students' work on the computer module is examined to explain their problem-solving strategies and overall performance in mathematics. Finally, interviews with students and teachers are analyzed to determine the influence of culturally specific multimedia on classroom norms and interactions among students and teachers.

The classroom discourse

Two third-grade teachers at Parker Charter School (pseudonym) in New York combined the students in their classrooms to discuss *Minty: The Story of Young Harriet Tubman* (Schroeder, 1996). The data reveal the teachers' creativity in establishing the contextual environment for students to understand the dangers slaves faced if they dared to travel on the Underground Railroad. The teachers concentrated on mathematics and science content that was specific to survival as well as the social aspects of the Underground Railroad. Math-

Table 4.1 Comparison of math and science terms (Parker Charter School)

Key math terms	Occurrences	Key science terms	Occurrences
Big	2	Constellation(s)	6
Full	5	Cold	3
Whole	1	Freezing	2
Half	2	Water	30
Quarter	8	Snow	9
Round	1	Star	10
Shape	1	Moon	13
Month(s)	3	Night	5
Week(s)	2	River	7
Day(s)	4	Scent	26
Hour(s)	1	Sky	4
		Rain	2
		Freezing	1
		Weather	8
Total mathematics terms	30 (19%)	Total science terms	126 (81%)

ematics and science terms that occurred during class discussion are shown in Table 4.1. The keyword list helped to pinpoint the places where the discourse related to mathematics emerged as the teachers and students discussed the text. When mathematics and science terms were compared, the data show science vocabulary emerged four times as often as mathematics vocabulary. However, as shown in the following vignettes, science vocabulary was used to help students develop mathematics concepts. In these vignettes, teachers used science concepts such as the phases of the moon to help students understand the fractions *one-half* and *one-fourth* and how freezing temperatures influenced fugitive slaves' decisions about when to escape from the plantation. Pseudonyms are used to protect the anonymity of the teachers and students.

Vignette 4.1

209	*Jordan:*	What are some of the other things that Minty had to learn how to do in order to stay alive while she was in the woods running away? Antuan.
210	*Antuan:*	So, it had to be kind of dark so [master] can't see, like when the moon is a quarter.
211	*Perez:*	Oh, okay. So she did that so she would stay alive, so she would not be seen? Is that what you're saying, Antuan?
212	*Jordan:*	It wasn't that the … He [Autuan] said the moon could be a quarter.
213	*Perez:*	A quarter?
214	*Jordan:*	And it's not that the moon is a quarter. The shape of it is in a … It's a quarter of a moon.
215	*Perez:*	Right, if you look at the …
216	*Mary:*	Constellation?
217	*Perez:*	If you look at the moon, when it's full, it's completely round. And when you look at a clock, you know what's a quarter after, right? It's half of that half, right? So the moon has to be … A quarter moon is something like this. [Goes to the board to draw a picture of the moon.]
218	*Perez:*	[Drawing at the board.] Let's say this is the moon. So a quarter would be something like this. The face would be really, really dark. Now, if it was half a moon, would it be brighter, Antuan?
219	*Antuan:*	Yeah.
220	*Perez:*	Yes, good. And if it's full … oh, that makes it even brighter. So then, that is a way that she sort of stayed alive by knowing the phases of the moon and not having anyone see her escape during the night.

Vignette 4.1 reveals how two teachers at Parker Charter School allowed the students to explain their thinking and how they used student thinking to help children understand specific aspects about the Underground Railroad. In the foregoing vignette, Antuan tried to explain to the class how Minty (young Harriet Tubman) used the moon to escape on the Underground Railroad. Antuan implied if Minty left when there was a "quarter" moon [line 210], it would be dark enough for her to escape without being seen. Mr. Perez used Antuan's thinking to explain to the students what the shape of the moon might look like if only a quarter of the moon was visible [line 218].

While Mr. Perez made reference to a clock, which is a flat (two-dimensional) object, students were able to understand the relative difference between a whole, half, and quarter (one-fourth). Ms. Jordan's use of revoicing [line 212] (O'Connor & Michaels, 1993) to restate Antuan's comment validated his thinking and created the opportunity for students to learn about fractions. Antuan hypothesized that Minty would be safer if she left when the moon was a quarter. When the moon is a sliver, it may be too dark for a fugitive slave to safely run away from the plantation. Objects like the moon can be used to help students understand fractions as part of a whole. However, it is important for teachers and students to understand what type of "whole" they are working with. An orange is a better representation of the moon (three-dimensional). Yet, students should have experiences with flat objects like clocks as well as spheres like oranges to represent fractional parts.

In addition to the moon and the night sky, the teachers tried to help the students understand the importance of the weather when it came to planning an escape from the plantation. The next vignette shows how the teachers and students used science to make connections to mathematics during a discussion about weather.

Vignette 4.2

275	*Jordan:*	How could they tell it was going to snow, David?
276	*David:*	Cuz, they look at the sky.
277	*Jordan:*	That was their news. Um, Charles.
278	*Charles:*	Well, it wouldn't be a good thing if they ran away in the snow—when it was winter or snowing—because if they ran away in the snow, if there was [sic] people trying to find the people ... Running away, they might follow their footprints.
279	*Jordan:*	Oh, that's a good point, too—their footprints being followed in the snow.
280	*Perez:*	In the snow, right. You see that here, and I'm sure they saw it then. Now, if you were a slave, would you even attempt to travel in the snow in the winter?
281	*Students:*	No!

282	*Perez:*	Would that be wise?
283	*Students:*	Nooooooo.
284	*Andrea:*	Yes.
		[Lots of talking among the students.]
285	*Perez:*	You would, Andrea? Why?
286	*Andrea:*	I would keep going in the snow because I would want to go to freedom … earlier, so I can have clothes and all that, and then if I want to stop, I'll go somewhere and find a place to sleep where they can't find me. I'd be far away.
287	*Perez:*	But it'd be really cold, Andrea. And remember, like Darneice said … Slaves didn't have any shoes to wear. Now, just think when you go out in the snow and you have shoes. But won't your feet get cold even though …
288	*Andrea:*	Yes.
289	*Perez:*	So—
290	*Andrea:*	But still, you could try to find a place to sleep in.
291	*Perez:*	But remember, they had to travel for days and—
292	*Jordan:*	Months.
293	*Perez:*	—sometimes weeks and months—
294	*Jordan:*	Months.
295	*Perez:*	—to get North—up North. Now, if it takes hours and days to travel by car from, let's say, the South to the North, imagine walking. So you would have to really think about that.
296	*Jordan:*	So, you don't want to go from one—how you say—dangerous situation, like slavery, into another dangerous situation, like hypothermia.

In Vignette 4.2, the teachers tried to help the students understand the importance of knowing the seasons of the year and weather patterns to plan an escape. In addition, they helped students to understand that the journey to freedom could take several weeks or months. In many cases, all a fugitive slave had were the clothes on his or her back. The concepts of cold and snow were easily understood, especially since the lesson took place in February, and snow was on the ground in New York when the students discussed the text. Some fugitive slaves had to travel on foot without shoes. Moreover, the concept of time in this vignette was raised as teachers mentioned the hours, days, weeks, and months it took to travel on the Underground Railroad.

Upon further analysis, the discourse in Vignette 4.2 changes from the traditional IRE (initiate, respond, evaluate) pattern (Cazden, 2001) to emergent discourse (Longo, 1993). Emergent discourse is uninhibited conversations that come about as a result of relaxed social norms (Longo, 1993). The polite turn-taking that Ms. Jordan and the students had initially ceased when

Andrea disagreed with the teachers about fugitive slaves running away in the winter. The discourse shifted from the teacher-initiate and student-response pattern to emergent discourse as a conversation and dialogue ensued. It is important to note that the teachers never said Andrea's thinking was incorrect. Adverse weather conditions are a deterrent to hostile pursuit. Mr. Perez simply suggested, "You would have to really think about that" [line 295]. Allowing students to express their opinions and own the knowledge for themselves enhances opportunities to build academic success and develop cultural competence (Gay, 2000; Ladson-Billings, 1994). Ms. Jordan and Mr. Perez provide excellent examples of cultural pedagogy as they effectively use experience-based scripts, oral traditions, and critical literacy to engage students in active learning.

The discourse in Vignette 4.2 is also characterized by active student involvement. While one student participated in the moon discussion in Vignette 4.1, six students participated in the discussion about the weather. Previous research has shown that discourse emerges more frequently when science topics draw upon students' background knowledge (Lee & Songer, 2003). Students expressed their knowledge about the negative effects of weather (e.g. cold temperature, inadequate clothing, and footprints) on a fugitive slave's escape plans. Moreover, students were highly engaged in the discussion, and they communicated their ideas in complete sentences [lines 272, 274, 278, & 286]. The average length of the students' sentences in Vignette 4.2 was 34 words (excluding chorus responses). The students were engrossed in the discussion and eager to participate because they had some background knowledge, and the topic was relevant to their lives (Leonard, 2000; Leonard & Guha, 2002). Mathematics problems about temperature and how to read thermometers are often misunderstood by elementary students (Leonard, 2000). Using weather instruments to promote problem solving and student discourse provides students with a context to gain more practice with measurement problems. Contextualizing weather problems with Underground Railroad genre creates culturally specific problems that students can use as anchors to retain important information and engage in personalized word problems (Ku & Sullivan, 2001).

The computer module

The computer module consisted of a storyboard about Sam, who was a fugitive slave, and his journey from Bucktown, Maryland, to Philadelphia, Pennsylvania, c.1848. Twelve original scenes with graphics and animation were presented to students. After each scene, students were prompted to answer two to four questions out of a total of 32. Audio and visual feedback were given each time the student entered a response to a problem. Students in three classes ($n = 66$) at Parker Charter School in New York field tested the module. The module was also field tested at one school in Chicago and

Table 4.2 Math and science scores on the computer-based task (*n* = 37)

	Mathematics	Std. dev.	Science	Std. dev.
Grade 3 (*n* = 24)	50.00	20.87	90.83	13.15
Grade 4 (*n* = 13)	67.92	15.78	93.85	8.98

Philadelphia. Due to inclement weather, all of the students did not have a chance to field test the software. Therefore, scores are only provided for those students who completed the entire computer module. Due to the small sample size, scores are shown for descriptive purposes only.

Students' scores on the computer module were disaggregated by grade and content. As shown in Table 4.2, students in both third and fourth grade did better in science than they did in mathematics. On average, third-grade students were able to answer 50% of the mathematics problems correctly, while 68% of fourth-grade students could do so. In other words, third graders solved eight out of 16 items correctly while fourth graders solved about 11 out of 16 mathematics items correctly. These scores represent an improvement over a paper-and-pencil pre-assessment on similar items two months earlier. Third-grade students scored 26.7% in mathematics and 51.4% in science on the pretest. Fourth-grade students scored 55.3% in mathematics and 72.6% in science on the same items. However, it should be noted that third graders made greater overall gains in mathematics than fourth graders, 23.30% compared to 12.62%, respectively. Third graders also made greater gains in science than fourth graders, 39.43% compared to 21.25%, respectively.

Yet, these results must be viewed with caution. Higher scores in science may be accounted for by the extensive amount of science discourse that emerged as a result of reading the texts. Recall that science terms accounted for 81% of the discourse as compared to mathematical terms, which accounted for only 19% (see Table 4.1). Observations of teachers in Philadelphia and New York reveal that they discussed science concepts in great detail. These gains could also be attributable to the teacher variable. The two third-grade teachers at Parker School in New York collaborated with one another, but there was only one fourth-grade teacher. She was observed working with her students in isolation. It is also possible that fourth graders had more background knowledge and better problem-solving ability to begin with. Conducting a controlled study that accounts for baseline data and teacher variables is needed to better interpret grade-level variations. Nevertheless, scores on the computer module show evidence of student learning that can be characterized as successful in science and marginally successful for fourth-grade students in mathematics. Fourth-grade mathematics scores at Parker (*M* = 67.92) were consistent with the scores of fourth graders in Chicago (*M* = 68.90) and Philadelphia (*M* = 73.84). A subset of the mathematics

Figure 4.1 Sam gets a ride from a Quaker (source: Image courtesy of Renaissance Macro, Inc.; original design by Edgar Flores; animated by Angela Mistretta).

problems students encountered on the computer is presented below for further analysis of mathematical thinking and problem-solving strategies.

Analysis of computer-based mathematics problems

Three different types of mathematics problems are presented for further analysis. Each of the problems presented below is followed by a brief analysis of students' solutions. The analysis includes the percentage of students who answered the problem correctly, the misconceptions they may have had, and the problem-solving strategies students used. One of the digital images the students saw prior to answering one of the problems is shown in Figure 4.1.

1   *Sam can travel about 4 miles per hour in the wagon. It is about 12 miles to the next safe house. About how many hours will it take Sam to reach the next safe house?* (measurement division)

While the numbers used in this problem are easy to work with, the success rate of students on this particular problem was lower than anticipated. This problem was presented in multiple-choice format. The items students could select for an answer were: (1) two hours; (2) three hours; (3) four hours; and (4) six hours. Seventy-one percent of the students selected the correct response of three hours on the first attempt. Three students selected the correct response after receiving two hints. However, 12 students who did not select the correct response initially did not use the scaffold to try again. Of these 12 students, three (25%) selected item 1, four (33%) selected item 2, and five (42%) selected item 4. It is difficult to determine whether these students made an error or were simply guessing. Most of the mathematics items required students to input an answer. This feature allowed for examination of children's thinking and problem-solving strategies.

Another problem that gave students some difficulty was the following:

2 *William Still helped more than 2,500 slaves to escape from the South. He was born in 1821 and died in 1902. How long did William Still live?* (separate result unknown)

This problem required the students to complete a four-digit subtraction problem. This type of problem is challenging for third graders who are accustomed to three-digit subtraction and for fourth graders who may have trouble with borrowing and regrouping. Only 48% of the students knew how to stack the problem and then regroup and subtract as shown in Figure 4.2. When data were analyzed, the researcher discovered that a couple of students simply recorded 1902 as the answer. Two students estimated the answer to be 70 years of age, which was reasonable since the average life expectancy is about 70 years for African American males. However, two students had misconceptions about the subtraction algorithm. When they encountered $0 - 2$ in the ten's place, one student ignored the position of the digits and simply subtracted the larger number from the smaller number to get *2*. Therefore, his/her answer was *121*. Such an answer is unreasonable since longer life spans are not usually much more than 100 years. Another student regrouped the hundreds place to get $10 - 2$. However, this student made an error and recorded an answer of *2* instead of *8*. Thus, the answer was *21*, which is too young of an age to have helped more than 2,500 slaves escape on the Underground Railroad. Finally, one student simply added the years together to get *3,723* years old, which is an incredible answer. Thus, examining solutions for reasonableness is another strategy that teachers should emphasize.

This problem type is difficult for many elementary students for a number of reasons. First, students need to remember to stack the larger number on

Figure 4.2 Regrouping strategy.

top before subtracting. Second, students need to have number sense. Third, students often have difficulty with the subtraction algorithm. Teachers can help students with problems of this nature by teaching them to estimate; *1902* could be rounded to *1900* and *1821* to *1820*. The difference between these two numbers is 80, which could be determined by skip counting or counting up. Students could then easily determine the solution by subtracting the digits in the one's place to obtain the exact answer.

The problem on the computer module that gave students the most difficulty was the following:

3 *After Sam had been in Philadelphia for a year working as a tailor, he decided to return to Bucktown to help his parents escape. How long will it take Sam to go and return if it takes 14 days to travel each way and 3 days to find his parents?* (part-part-whole)

Only 29% of the students solved the problem above correctly. Twenty-eight percent of the children stated the solution was *17*, which was the most common error. Seventeen was obtained by simply adding the two numbers in the problem together. Some students did not read or understand the meaning of the words *each way*. Two students doubled the number of days Sam needed to find his parents to obtain an answer of *20*. Three students multiplied the numbers to get 42. Most likely, these students focused on the word *each* as a cue to multiply. However, students must understand what each number represents (relationship) in story problems (Mayer & Hagerty, 1996). Problems of this nature could easily be modeled with manipulatives or acted out.

All of the problems above provide teachers and researchers with useful information about children's errors, misconceptions, and solution strategies during problem solving. While the problems are culturally specific to motivate students and the computer format is engaging, students still need proper instruction and practice and opportunities to discuss their solutions (Fuchs *et al.*, 2004; Kazemi & Stipek, 2001). Focusing on the problem model approach and children's thinking prior to engaging them in any kind of problem-solving task, culturally based or computer-based, is essential. Teachers should use students' thinking to help students confront their errors and misconceptions as well as to learn from the strategies and invented algorithms of their peers (Campbell & Johnson, 1995; Fennema *et al.*, 1993; Franke & Kazemi, 2001; Villasenor & Kepler, 1993).

To gain further insight about student perceptions of the computer module and their problem-solving ability, 11 students (six male and five female) were randomly selected to be interviewed by one of the research assistants. Students were asked ten questions related to working on the computer, the difficulty of the content, feelings about computer usage, the storyline and content, and overall performance on the task. The interview protocol may be found in

Appendix B. Every student did not answer every question, and some students had multiple answers to the same question. A synopsis of the student interviews is presented below.

Student interviews

- *How easy did you find it to work on the computer today?*
  Four students stated the computer task was hard and two specifically stated the math problems were difficult. One student said: "It was medium." Six students thought working on the computer was easy: "It was very easy, and I only got two questions wrong."
- *How was working on the computer today different than usual?*
  Seven students replied they had not used the computer at school before, but five said they had access to computers at home. Two other students commented: "We played a different kind of game so it was not boring"; "I had more fun today."
- *What did you like most about working with computers at school today?*
  Two students referred to the computer keyboard: "I liked using the keyboard, because I like typing." "I liked typing because I like to write and typing is just another way of writing." Four students referred to different aspects of the software program: "I liked the sound effects …" "I liked the music." "I liked the clapping sound." "When the boy was running away, he was very fast." Two mentioned their feelings about the software: "It was fun." Four students mentioned the information they gained from doing computer tasks: "You get a lot of knowledge from them. You can look up a lot of information." "I got to answer some really interesting questions." "The computer was helping us learn more about the Underground Railroad." However, one student replied: "I don't know."
- *Was there anything you did not like about working with computers?*
  Five students stated that there was nothing they disliked about the computer program: "No, I liked it a lot." However, two stated that the sound effects were too loud. One student did not like having a limited number of chances to answer the questions: "You only get three tries to answer one question." One student mentioned that the storyline was uncomfortable: "In the story when they took away the little seven-year-old from his parents." One student mentioned a problem with the mouse: "When you have to pick up the mouse and put it back down to make it work." One student mentioned becoming disinterested in the content: "Yes, I was a little bored at the end."
- *What did you learn about the Underground Railroad?*
  Three students mentioned learning about the North Star, and one student mentioned learning about the Big Dipper. One student said, "Slaves who were escaping, could use the Sun to tell what time it

was." Two students mentioned learning about the Ohio River: "I learned that there was the Ohio River. They could go to Ohio for freedom." Three students mentioned learning about Harriet Tubman and how she helped slaves to escape: "I learned about Harriet Tubman. She died. She was a slave that ran away once, and she got hit in the head once and had sleeping spells." One mentioned learning about the concept of the Underground Railroad itself: "There were conductors who helped slaves run away. The slaves would use a secret passage and sometimes get there safely." One student mentioned learning about "… the different animals that lived in the woods. Some animals warned the slaves if things were OK and some animals tried to attack the slaves." One student mentioned how slave owners tried to catch the slaves: "They sent out dogs after you escaped. They sent out a bloodhound. The bloodhound could smell your scent, but if you went through water they would not be able to track you down." Three students mentioned learning that Philadelphia was a stop on the Underground Railroad: "I learned that it takes a lot of miles to get to Philadelphia." Three students mentioned learning about the character in the storyline: "I learned about Sam. He was a slave, and he escaped. And after he escaped, they had a celebration. He decided to go back and save the rest of his family. It would take him 31 days to do that." Only one student stated, "I basically knew everything!"

Analysis of student interviews

The data above show students had a variety of opinions and retained different kinds of information after completing the computer module. First, students' responses regarding the computer module were mixed. Fifty-four percent thought the computer task was easy. One student thought it was "medium" which could be interpreted as an average level of difficulty. However, four of the students interviewed thought the program was hard. Two students mentioned the difficulty of the mathematics problems.

There was more evidence of consensus when students responded to the second interview question: *How was working on the computer today different than usual?* None of the students had used the computer at Parker Charter School prior to the study. However, the school was only in its second year of operation, and computers had only recently been installed. Two students' remarks reveal the affective nature of the computer simulation. Students liked various aspects of the computer activity, including the sound effects, animation, and the storyline. While two students mentioned that the sound effects were too loud, their dislike had to do with the sound level on the computer and presumably not the sound effects themselves.

Third, students' comments about the Underground Railroad theme inform the educational community about the power of culture to make connections to content. In addition to mentioning Harriet Tubman as a prominent figure in Underground Railroad genre, 45% of the students interviewed made many connections to science. They specifically mentioned learning about the North Star, the Big Dipper, and the Sun. Students also learned that Ohio and Pennsylvania were states where slaves could escape to freedom. Two students specifically referred to mathematics problems dealing with miles to Philadelphia and the number of days Sam needed to return and help his family escape. Surprisingly, one student remembered his answer to the mathematics problem about Sam finding his family. Therefore, connecting content to culturally specific storylines may promote greater student retention.

Teacher interviews

After assisting their children in the computer lab, the three teachers at Parker School who participated in the study were interviewed by the same research assistant. Recall that Mr. Perez and Ms. Jordan taught third grade, and Ms. Clark taught fourth grade. Comments from each of the teachers follow:

MR. PEREZ

The software they used ... was very user-friendly. The program addressed the math and science standards pretty well. The software was very creative, the coloring, the pictures, and all that. It reminded them [students] a lot about the books we read. I would like to use similar software in the classroom for testing and other purposes. We just have one computer in the classroom, a laptop that we all use. Hopefully, we will be getting more computers in the classroom soon. In terms of the particular problems in math, the software was targeted toward the *Standards*. They [students] had to think about the problems and break them down. Before we started the Banneker Project, we were talking about constellations so it was great; it flowed with our third-grade curriculum. After this week, we are going to continue talking about the constellations and creating freedom quilts similar to the book they read. This sort of project connected the students with their heritage considering that the majority of students are African American. It really hits home. They hear it from their grandparents and now in school.

MS. JORDAN

At times it [computer program] appeared to be user-friendly, and there were times that I observed my students were having problems. I think it [software] needed some directions for the students to read prior to going forth with the program. The students liked the sound effects. Whenever they heard the different sound effects, they would press the buttons to hear them again. I am the English/language arts teacher. This was the only math and science lesson I have done. It [software] appears to address the math and science curriculum and the standards would be for third grade. The theme naturally fit into the things we already teach. We learned a lot about Benjamin Banneker. While it was not part of the curriculum, it was significant for them to learn about him. Some of my students did some research about him over the holiday. So it heightened their awareness about Benjamin Banneker and his inventions and contributions.

MS. CLARK

I thought it [computer program] was very user-friendly. It was easy to tell the students what steps to take and what to do. I thought it [curriculum] was great. I have students on various levels. For 80% of the students, it was just right. It was good practice for all my students. In reading story problems some of them struggled with what strategies to use. I think that it [computer simulation] was wonderful. I would be interested in seeing more of this. I loved it, and it was inspiring ... being able to tie the Underground Railroad into math and science.

Analysis of teacher interviews

For the most part, all of the teachers thought the computer simulation was user-friendly and met the *Standards* (NCTM, 2000). Mr. Perez mentioned connections to literature and science content as a positive aspect of the study. Ms. Jordan's students were intrigued with the sound effects. Ms. Clark believed her students gained a great deal from the extra practice the computer module provided for problem solving. She learned that her students struggled with problem-solving strategies. However, these teachers' comments also reveal the importance of professional development to help teachers learn how to pose authentic problems (Crespo, 2003) to help students develop good problem-solving strategies (Malloy & Jones, 1998). All of the teachers thought the computer simulation was culturally relevant and inspired the children to learn. In fact, some students conducted independent research over the holidays to learn more about Banneker and other prominent figures in Black History. However, limited access to computers in the school was problematic. The benefit of computer scaffolding is limited if there are not enough computers to go around. Finally, Mr. Perez's comment about how to extend the Underground Railroad concept to help students learn about constellations and freedom quilts provides an example of one teacher's willingness to use cultural pedagogy as a springboard to help students learn science and mathematics content. These three teachers and their students created a large freedom quilt and learned mathematics concepts in the process. Specific details about the political nature of the activity are described in Chapter 5.

Discussion

The findings of this exploratory study are: (1) cultural contexts engage students of color in mathematics and science content at high levels; (2)

computer-assisted instruction supports student learning once important conceptual foundations have been established; (3) culturally specific contexts help students retain information for later retrieval; and (4) culturally specific contexts motivated students to learn more about key Black figures. Additional studies with control groups are needed to substantiate these preliminary findings.

In this exploratory study, teachers used the concept of the Underground Railroad as an impetus for students to solve mathematics problems. Teachers facilitated classroom discourse to engage students in limited problem solving. However, the students who participated in the study needed more opportunities to develop deeper understanding about various types of mathematics problems and which strategies might be used to solve them (Carpenter et al., 1999; Mayer & Hagerty, 1996). Problem-solving activities that allow students to work in pairs or small groups to confront their misconceptions and explain their strategies tend to improve student outcomes (Leonard, 2001b; Mulryan, 1995; Villasenor & Kepler, 1993).

Summary

Given the climate of accountability that has taken the U.S. by storm, it is important to supplement and enrich mathematics curriculum. Teachers are not always able to give every student the attention he or she needs. Computer-assisted instruction (CAI) has been shown to improve the mathematics performance of fourth-grade African American students (Brown & Boshamer, 2000) and time on task (Wenglinsky, 1998). In order to improve teacher expertise with CAI, teacher education and professional development should place more emphasis on problem solving within computer-based contexts. While computer-assisted instruction is no panacea, the research reported here shows that it holds promise.

In this chapter, I have described how culturally rich problems, both traditional and computer-based, can be used by teachers to increase student engagement and learning outcomes. Culturally specific pedagogy has been used to actively engage students in problem solving and to support the learning that takes place in everyday classrooms (Brenner, 1998; Leonard, 2004; Lipka et al., 2005). Culturally based pedagogy has been shown to build relationships among teachers and students as well as their parents (Leonard, 2004; Lipka et al., 2005; Strutchens, 2002). Chapters 5, 6, and 7 further examine the construct of cultural pedagogy and how it may be used to teach students of diverse ethnic, gender, and language backgrounds mathematics within a context of social justice.

5
The Underground Railroad
A context for learning mathematics and social justice

Dismantling the master's house can only be done with the master's tools.

Audre Lorde

On the socialization of African American children

The literature on the school socialization of African American students remains sparse (Boykin & Toms, 1985; Martin, 2000; Stiff & Harvey, 1988). Socialization involves the preparation of children to assume adult roles and responsibilities in society (Baldwin as cited in Boykin & Toms, 1985). This process occurs through the transmission of culture—that is, the teaching and learning of traditional beliefs, values, and behavior patterns (Boykin & Toms, 1985). In the U.S., child socialization has primarily focused upon children from mainstream backgrounds, and the socialization process for African Americans and other students of color is largely ignored (Boykin & Toms, 1985; Kitchen, 2007). "Interplay among three competing contexts for socialization: socialization in the mainstream of American society, socialization informed by oppressed minority status, and socialization linked to a proximal Black cultural context that … dictates … mainstream American life" continues to be a triple quandary (Boykin & Toms, 1985, p. 46). A framework for Black child socialization must capture the bicultural nature of African American life while encapsulating its uniformity, diversity, complexity, and richness (Boykin & Toms, 1985).

The mis-education of African American students in mathematics

In addition to limited research on Black children's socialization, there is a dearth of research on African American students' mathematics education (Kitchen, 2007; Martin, 2000; Stiff & Harvey, 1988). In fact, it appears that a negative relationship exists between African American students and mathematics (Kitchen, 2007; Stiff & Harvey, 1988). African American students are underrepresented in advanced mathematics courses and overrepresented in special education classes (Oakes, 1990). Mathematics has been used to sort and track students into remedial, regular, and advanced coursework (D'Ambrosio, 1985; Kitchen, 2007). Thus, it should not be surprising that African Americans are underrepresented in science, technology, engineering, and mathematics (STEM) related careers. In order to change this trend, we must first dispel the belief that African Americans are "not the appropriate type of math student" (Stiff & Harvey, 1988, p. 198). Second, serious efforts must be made to help African American students develop mathematics socialization and identity (Martin, 2000; Stiff & Harvey, 1988).

In order to develop mathematics socialization and identity among African American students, mathematics must be developed at deeper levels and connected to social justice. For this type of learning to occur, three things must happen: (1) students must be motivated to do more rigorous mathematics (Mathematics Curriculum Principle); (2) students must be able to see themselves in the curriculum (Equity Principle); and (3) teachers must be able to connect mathematics content to the lives of students (Teaching Principle) (NCTM, 2000). The Mathematics Curriculum Principle lines up with the ideology of cultural pedagogy, which emphasizes academic success (Gay, 2000; Ladson-Billings, 1994).

Yet, to be successful in mathematics, students of color must be able to do more than compute (Stiff & Harvey, 1988). Preservice teachers in my mathematics methods course often ask, "Shouldn't we concentrate on the basics?" I contend that no child will obtain success in mathematics by simply knowing the basics. Teachers must teach children of color a variety of topics beyond the basics, such as numeracy, rational numbers, integers, measurement, geometry, statistics, probability, and data analysis. Moreover, problem solving is an integral part of doing mathematics and is needed to make decisions in everyday life.

Equity in mathematics education has been defined as follows:

> Equity in mathematics education requires: (a) equitable distribution of resources to schools, students, and teachers, (b) equitable quality of instruction, and (c) equitable outcomes for students. Equity is achieved when differences among these three areas are disappearing.
>
> (Allexsaht-Snider & Hart, 2001, p. 93)

According to the above definition, equity in mathematics education has yet to be achieved in the U.S. (Martin, 2003). Kozol (1991) informed the educational community about the disparities of resources between poor and affluent school districts 25 years ago. Yet, little has been done to remedy the plight of poor children in America's schools (Kitchen, 2007).

Nowhere is this disparity more evident than the city of New Orleans, Louisiana. According to Census Bureau statistics, the number of Americans living in poverty rose to 12.7% in 2004, but the rate of poverty in New

Orleans before Hurricane Katrina was almost double the national rate with 40% of the city's predominantly African American children living in poverty (*USA Today*, 2005). When NAEP achievement data for students in Louisiana pre-Hurricane Katrina are examined, we find fourth graders' average mathematics score in 2003 was 226 compared to a national average of 234. Twenty-one percent scored at or above proficiency while only 2% scored at the advanced level (NCES, 2006). At the eighth-grade level, the average NAEP score in mathematics during the same period was 266 compared to a national average of 276 (NCES, 2006). Seventeen percent of eighth graders scored at or above proficiency, and only 2% scored at the advanced level. The scores in 2005 were just as dismal: Grade 4 ($M = 230$, Louisiana; $M = 237$ (National Average)); Grade 8 ($M = 268$, Louisiana; $M = 278$ (National Average)) (NCES, 2006). Post-Hurricane Katrina, even international and national exposure of the high poverty in Louisiana has done little to change the circumstances of the nation's poorest students.

Accountability measures such as No Child Left Behind legislation (NCLB, 2001) have resulted in even more disparity as parents of students from underachieving schools are left with few options when schools are closed or reconstituted (Leonard *et al.*, 2004). Moreover, the National Council of Teachers of Mathematics (NCTM) is silent about how to accommodate the needs of students who live in poverty (Kitchen, 2007). Reform rhetoric that addresses standards without giving serious attention to structural barriers will continue to be ineffective (Martin, 2000). Sincere efforts that result in action must be made at local, state, and national levels in order to make a difference in these students' lives and to level the playing field.

An important variable to consider in the equity conversation is teacher quality (Kitchen, 2007). Teachers can and do make a difference in the lives of children. Specifically, the use of cultural pedagogy is critical when it comes to improving learning outcomes in mathematics among students of color (Chappell & Thompson, 2000; Ladson-Billings, 1994; Lee, 2001; Leonard & Guha, 2002; Malloy & Malloy, 1998; Tate, 1995). Yet, examples of how culture can be connected to mathematics pedagogy are scarce in the literature.

Linking mathematics with culture

The purpose of this chapter is to share specific ideas about how teachers can connect mathematics lessons to the culture of African American students. One context for making these connections is the Underground Railroad. The theme of the Underground Railroad not only provides an interesting context for students to learn mathematics, but it also provides a forum for all students to understand equality and the importance of social justice in dismantling racism.

The Underground Railroad was an active system of civil disobedience consisting of conductors and fugitive slaves who embarked on a trek to freedom in the North from plantations in the South. The Underground Railroad theme can be used to help students understand the life and work of African American heroes such as Harriet Tubman, John Parker, and Sojourner Truth. Children learn that the Underground Railroad was a loosely organized but successful "Civil Rights" movement that involved a coalition of Blacks, Whites, and Native Americans who put their lives on the line to help fugitive slaves escape to freedom (Mensher, 1994). Furthermore, this theme encourages students to learn about social justice, ethics, symbols, and signs. Symbols and signs, such as candles and quilts, helped determine whether a house would welcome fugitive slaves. Mathematics was important in the journey on the Underground Railroad since fugitive slaves had to estimate how far they had to travel to a safe house (problem solving), how much food and water they had to carry (problem solving), how to find and maintain their journey north (mapping), and how to protect themselves during adverse weather conditions (measurement of temperature and wind chill).

A thematic unit about the Underground Railroad (see Appendix C) was created to provide background knowledge for students who participated in the Banneker Project. Recall that the Banneker Project was an exploratory study where third- and fourth-grade students field tested culturally specific multimedia. The Underground Railroad unit consists of lessons in language arts (literacy), mathematics, science, and social studies. Students are able to acquire background knowledge by reading relevant texts and watching videos. One of the recommended videos is *The Underground Railroad* (Michaels, 1998), which is narrated by Alfre Woodard. The video tells about the history of the Underground Railroad, the saga of incredible journeys on the Underground Railroad, and important figures such as Henry "Box" Brown and William Still. Students also learn about the Underground Railroad by using a computer module called Riding the Freedom Train (Leonard & Leonard, 2003). Through this multimedia, students are able to develop literacy and learn cross-curricular content.

Using stars and constellations as a context for learning mathematics

Two teachers, Ms. Baker and Ms. Cho taught a two-week unit on the Underground Railroad. Ms. Cho was an Asian teacher, and Ms. Baker was White. Each of them taught a class of 26 fourth-grade students at the Northside School in Philadelphia, making the total number of student participants 56. Cases of Ms. Cho and Ms. Baker are presented throughout the remainder of this chapter as examples of cross-curricular and culturally specific teaching.

The case of Ms. Cho

The story that Ms. Cho read to her students when the research team videotaped her class was *Minty: The Story of Young Harriet Tubman* (Schroeder, 1996). In one part of the text, Minty threatens to run away from the plantation. Her father, Old Ben, explains to her how she needs to use the North Star to help her find her way North to freedom. After reading about half of the text, Cho stopped to explain the integrated mathematics and science task the students would be doing that day. As a culminating activity they would make a star gazer out of a tin can and construction paper (see lesson in Appendix C). This activity engages students in mathematics as they used compasses to construct circles large enough to fit over the opening of a tin can and create a pattern of stars in the shape of the Big Dipper. An excerpt of the lesson is presented below in Vignette 5.1. Pseudonyms are used for anonymity.

Vignette 5.1

127   *Cho:*   Here is the Drinking Gourd and the Little Dipper. What is another name for the Drinking Gourd? Devon.

128   *Devon:*   The um ... [Pause]. The Big Dipper?

129   *Cho:*   The Big Dipper. If you look up at the night sky, in fall and wintertime, it's really a good time to look up at the night sky because it's the clearest. The Drinking Gourd or the Big Dipper will be low in the sky. Now, [referring to the drawings on the board] here's the handle. Here is the dipper part where you dip it into the water or wherever you're trying to dip up. If you go right to this top, right-hand corner of the dipper and you go straight up a lot farther up than what's on the board, but straight up, you will come to the brightest star in the sky. And that brightest star is called Polaris. And it's simply just another name for the North Star. So you just follow the handles, come around, come to the tip of the dipper part, go straight up north, and you'll see the brightest star in the sky. Try it tonight. Because gets dark around 6 p.m., so you'll be able to go outside and look for this. You'll see Polaris. What do you notice about the star, Polaris? What is it attached [to]. Or what is Polaris a part of? Nora.

130   *Nora:*   The Little Dipper?

131   *Cho:*   The Little Dipper! If you go straight up, you'll see Polaris. It is the tip of the handle of the Little Dipper. So it's sometimes hard to find the Little Dipper in the sky because it's a lot smaller than the Big Dipper. If you follow this, look the Big Dipper. Go to this point of the Big Dipper part, look up, find the North Star. You'll be right at the handle of the Little Dipper. And that's how you'll see it in the sky on a much larger scale. It won't be this small in the sky. Questions about this? Devon.

132	*Devon:*	Is there another word for the Little Dipper?
133	*Cho:*	I don't think so. I don't know. There could be though. There could.
134	*Sherri:*	Maybe the teaspoon.
135	*Cho:*	Maybe. That's a good idea. *The teaspoon.* I only know the *Drinking Gourd* is another name for the Big Dipper. Good question, Devon. Lakisha.
136	*Lakisha:*	How would you know if it's the Drinking Gourd or the Little Dipper?
137	*Cho:*	How do you know?
138	*Lakisha:*	Uh huh. What if you forgot how it was?
139	*Cho:*	Well, hopefully, you won't. It's right here, and you can study it and when you do what you're going to do next, that'll help you keep it in your head what it look likes, what you need to do to find the North Star. Jada.
140	*Jada:*	What if …? Is it in a certain part of the sky? Like say you live in the southeast region, could you see it from there?
141	*Cho:*	Mm hmm. The only time it might be a little bit harder to see is if … Do you notice that the earth—if you look on the map up there—it's divided into different hemispheres.
142	*Jada:*	So, Ms. Cho. But, can you see it from anywhere, like you can see it from any region that you're standing in?
143	*Cho:*	Mm hmm. Any one of the United States. If you go past the equator south into Australia, South America, south in Africa, you would see that it would look different. Elliot.
144	*Elliot:*	So if you went home, right, after school. And you know it's a little dark. It start getting dark at like five o'clock. If you go outside and try to look for it, you would see it?
145	*Cho:*	Yes. Try to find it tonight. Okay. Kenneth. Sherri, you had a turn.
146	*Sherri:*	Okay.
147	*Cho:*	Kenneth.
148	*Kenneth:*	Okay. Like when I wake up at five o'clock in the morning, when I look over to this side of my porch, I can see like a smiley face or something. I don't get it.
149	*Cho:*	Okay. Sometimes stars make different patterns. And it's not going to be as easy to see the Big Dipper and the Little Dipper as it is easy to see here because there's a whole bunch of stars all the way in the sky. So you have to try to find the stars that you're looking for between all those other stars that are up in the sky. So it's difficult. Sherri.
150	*Sherri:*	Um, when you said that this would be in the sky. Last time

when I saw one of those, they didn't look like this. No, I
don't mean ...

151	*Cho:*	It's not going to look exactly like that. That's my drawing.
152	*Sherri:*	No, I'm not talking about your drawing or nothing. No, when you look at, is it like a North, a South, East or West star?
153	*Cho:*	It would be in the north. To find the North Star, it's in the northern part of the sky.
154	*Sherri:*	No, I'm saying, do they have a East, and a South, and a West star?
155	*Cho:*	Probably. Because in the southern part of the hemisphere there is a star and a constellation called the Southern Cross. And that works just the same as the North Star, but ... it points south.
156	*Student:*	So it has to be in a certain direction?
157	*Cho:*	Mm hmm.

Upon analysis of the discourse in Vignette 5.1, it is immediately apparent that the classroom is a supportive environment in which the students have a high level of comfort [lines 145 & 146]. Unlike traditional classrooms where the teacher initiates the questions and students respond and receive feedback, the discourse pattern in this classroom was emergent (Longo, 1993). In this particular teaching episode, Ms. Cho asked two main questions: "What is another name for the Drinking Gourd?" [line 127]; "What do you notice about the star, Polaris?" [line 129]. Aside from asking one question for clarification [line 129], making a request for more information [line 131], and repeating a student's question [line 137], students' queries outnumbered Ms. Cho's. Moreover, this was not an isolated event but a regular occurrence in Ms. Cho's class (Leonard & Hill, in press). The students engaged in a great deal of discourse, unafraid to ask questions and actively participate. Aside from repeating a question [line 154], five students (three girls and two boys) asked a total of eight questions [lines 132, 136, 138, 140, 142, 144, 150, 152, & 156]. Moreover, the discourse was richer and more elaborate when students asked their own questions. Compared to the responses to Ms. Cho's initial queries, students' responses went from three-word phrases [lines 128, 130, & 134] to an average of 22.36 words per response.

Student questions revealed an understanding of scientific concepts and vocabulary. For example, motivated by the scientific names of constellations, Devon was curious about another name for the Little Dipper [line 132]. Sherri's *teaspoon* response [line 134] was excellent. It not only related to measurement, but it demonstrated her ability to complete an analogy— Bigger Dipper: Drinking Gourd as Little Dipper: [teaspoon]. Moreover, students' questions led Ms. Cho to present them with even more vocabulary as she used a map to explain how being near the equator and in the southern hemisphere affected one's view of the night sky [lines 141 & 143]. Sherri's question prompted Ms. Cho to provide the students with the name of another constellation known as the Southern Cross [line 155]. Without the students' discourse, Ms. Cho would not have been able to scaffold students' learning about constellations and stars in depth. Moreover, Ms. Cho made science accessible by letting the students know they could see the constellations more clearly in the winter night sky and encouraged the science process skill of observation [lines 129 & 145].

However, the teacher is the primary source of knowledge in this teaching episode, although she was comfortable in admitting she did not know the answer to Devon's question [line 133]. Instead of simply answering all of the students' questions directly, Ms. Cho could have assigned several students the task of researching the information for themselves and bringing it back to the class. Nevertheless, Ms. Cho did an exemplary job of helping students cross borders from their cultural knowledge of the Underground Railroad to the microculture of science (Aikenhead, 2001).

The case of Ms. Baker

One multicultural text that is culturally amenable (Chappell & Thompson, 2000) and can be used to help diverse students understand mathematics and science concepts is *How Many Stars in the Sky?* (Hort, 1991). Chappell and Thompson (2000) contend the book can be used to help children think about rational counting ideas and concepts as they relate to large numbers. The book also introduces the notion of infinity as the main character discovers that it is impossible to count all of the stars in the sky. Additional activities with constellations are found in the text, *Find the Constellations* (Rey, 1982). Ms. Baker used *Find the Constellations* to develop an activity for her students. The discourse that emerged around this lesson is presented in Vignette 5.2 below. During this part of the activity, it was too difficult to determine which student was speaking. Therefore, no student is referred to by pseudonym in this vignette.

Vignette 5.2

243   *Baker:*   Okay, before we start our project, I just wanted you to take a look at these constellations. And, what we talked about yesterday was that constellations have … We talked about this yesterday a little bit but a couple [of] people weren't here. So if you look at these, the star formations actually have animals' names. So if you look … here at number one, the Charioteer, and number two is the Herdsman; number three is the Twins; number four is the Big Dog. Can you see the Big Dog in number four?

244	*Students:*	Yes.
245	*Baker:*	Can you see number five? It looks like a skinny (lion). We were talking about this yesterday. Number six is Orion. Now, I want you to turn your attention up here. [On the board is a drawing of the Big Dipper done in red marker.] I just wanted you to see those because you know some of them look like what they're supposed to and some of them don't. We started with the Big Dipper, the Drinking Gourd, and the astronomy name is *Ursula Major.* How many stars did I say?
246	*Student:*	[Calls out.] Eighteen.
247	*Baker:*	In the Big Dipper?
248	*Student:*	[Calls out.] Seven.
249	*Baker:*	Seven. [Counts the number of points on the drawing of the Big Dipper on the board.] One, two, three, four, five, six, seven. Okay. What you're going to do in your little projects that you're going to start right now is you're going to take your black paper. Now pay attention everyone because these are going to be informative. I want to hang these up outside. Okay, focus on me. I want these to hang up outside. So these are going to be informative for the whole school. Are (you) with me?
250	*Student:*	Yeah.
251	*Baker:*	Okay, you're going to take your paper. And I want these to first reflect the Big Dipper. Okay? So how many stars is this going to have when it's done?
252	*Students:*	Seven.
253	*Baker:*	Thank you. Seven stars. It's going to be a constellation. So, what does *constellation* mean? What's a constellation? Is a constellation one star?
254	*Students:*	Nooooo.
255	*Baker:*	Raise your hands. [Points to a student.]
256	*Student:*	It's like a group of many.
257	*Baker:*	Group of stars. Good. And sometimes what we do, we identify a group of stars. We might give it an animal name. We'll say [referring to the diagram of the Big Dipper on the board], "Look, you know, this looks like a big dipper. I think I'm going to name it Big Dipper. It looks like a little scooper. I'm going to name that one Big Dipper because it looks like" … We try to identify it by something that it might look like, (like the) picture. In these cases, some of these look like animals. When you connect them, they look like animals. Now, in the case of Harriet Tubman and the

		Freedom Train, who can tell me why the Big Dipper was also known as the Drinking Gourd? [Points to a student raising his/her hand.]
258	*Student:*	Because the North Star ... slaves to the ... And then you go north. And then on the north side, it's free; and on the south, or whatever that side, it's not.
259	*Baker:*	Okay. So, you want to be looking for ... You're telling me that you want to be looking for the Drinking Gourd.
260	*Student:*	The North Star.
261	*Baker:*	You want to be looking northward. Okay, good. So, um. Okay, that's good. And the drinking gourd is something that you would drink out of, just like the Big Dipper. Okay, and then if you followed the Drinking Gourd, we said, you would be headed northward, right?
262	*Student:*	Yes.
263	*Baker:*	Okay. Class, what I want you to do is take this piece of paper. I want you to listen to the directions first. Take the piece of paper. You're going to get glue ... marshmallows. You're going to make a drinking gourd out of marshmallows. Those are your stars, right?
264	*Students:*	Yes.
265	*Baker:*	You're going to glue them on and make a drinking gourd. I want to see all three of these names ...

Ms. Baker did a very nice job of connecting her lesson on the Big Dipper with the previous day's activities. The day before, the students learned the names of several constellations. She reminded them that the constellations were named by the shapes they made. Native Americans named many of these constellations after animals. Students created a representation of the Big Dipper out of black construction paper, glue, and marshmallows. While the activity allowed children to subitize the number of stars needed to make a representation of the Big Dipper, they also learned its cultural name (Drinking Gourd) and its scientific name (Ursula Major). Moreover, Ms. Baker anchored the students' knowledge of the Big Dipper to Underground Railroad genre [line 257]. When she did this, the discourse dynamics in the classroom changed from one-word answers [lines 244, 246, 248, 250, 252, & 253] to a 30-word response [line 258]. Clearly, multicultural texts allowed the students to synthesize their knowledge about stars and constellations.

Multicultural literature, mathematics literacy, and social consciousness

Multicultural literature—loosely defined as stories about diverse ethnic groups—taps into the readers' prior knowledge while building on their vocabulary and conceptual understanding. Because group discussions about the literature will occur, multicultural texts may be used as a springboard to facilitate the development of classroom discourse. As part of the Banneker Project, Ms. Baker and Ms. Cho were observed during a read aloud. Stories about the Underground Railroad constituted the text-based part of the intervention. I examined teachers' pedagogy and how they incorporated multicultural texts and cross-curricular activities to help children learn mathematics and develop an understanding of social justice.

During the study, the teachers read books to the class, discussed related vocabulary and themes, and then connected subject matter content to the day's reading. For example, on the first day, they read *Barefoot: Escape on the Underground Railroad* (Edwards, 1997). The main character in the text followed the North Star to escape from slavery. Another book that teachers read to the class was *Freedom River* (Rappaport, 2000). After discussing the text, students wrote in their journals about what life might have been like as a fugitive slave. Students also read *Sweet Clara and the Freedom Quilt* (Hopkinson, 1993). The class learned from this book that Clara, the main character in the text, designed a freedom quilt. After she planned and executed her own escape from the plantation, she left the quilt for those who she reluctantly left behind to use as a map. Other texts that can be used to tell the story of the Underground Railroad are *Minty: The Story of Young Harriet Tubman* (Schroeder, 1996) and *Under the Quilt of Night* (Hopkinson, 2002). Ms. Cho and Ms. Baker used the texts to help students learn about the Underground Railroad and social justice.

Sweet Clara and the freedom quilt

Both Ms. Cho and Ms. Baker used the text about Clara to introduce a lesson about quilting. Quilting provides students with opportunities to learn about history, culture, and economics; mathematics connections may include learning about fractions, ratios, symmetry, and tessellations (Paznokas, 2003). Terms and concepts introduced or reviewed in Ms. Cho's and Ms. Baker's classes included area, perimeter, symmetry, congruence, measurement, and geometric shapes. The students were told to make a single quilt patch. They were given a felt patch, scissors, and a glue stick. Students were told to design a patch that contained an Underground Railroad sign or symbol. Using one or more felt pieces of different colors, students designed an object, cut the object, and glued it to the square piece of felt. The quilt was to contain important information such as where a boat was hidden near the river and the location of streams, pathways, and the North Star to guide slaves toward freedom. Ms. Baker explained how she carried out this lesson with her students:

> I told them that an exact measurement of quilt patches was an important part of this activity. Therefore, a lesson on perimeter and area took

place first. The concept of perimeter was developed by measuring the distance around the outside of the quilt patch or how much was cut from the original material. Then area was defined as how much space students could fill up with decoration on the patch. To help students retain the information, during the lesson I asked students, "What is the perimeter and area of your patch?" In addition, students were given the formulas for both area and perimeter. The students were accountable for a completed quilt patch and a written description of their patch along with the area and perimeter of the patch. Examples of some of the descriptions are: (1) "My quilt patch is a picture of the North Star hanging down from the sky because slaves followed it"; (2) "My quilt patch is a picture of the Drinking Gourd; I drew it because it helped slaves get to freedom"; and (3) "I put a safe house because if I was a slave, I would stay in a safe house so the slave hunters wouldn't get me." The resulting quilt patches were incredibly creative. They included the Big Dipper, rivers with hidden boats nearby, the North Star, cotton fields, plantation houses, safe houses with quilts out front, and in the woods. The imagery came from the literature, but the children had a lot of success with area and perimeter as well. The result was a wonderful final product for the class to enjoy.

All of the patches were eventually placed on a large piece of felt to make a freedom quilt in each class. The students were very excited about the prospect of making a class freedom quilt. Specific lesson plans about quilting are written by Paznokas (2003) and Talbot (2004). These lessons may be found in *Teaching Children Mathematics* and at the following URL: http://teacher.scholastic.com/products/instructor/jan04_quiltmath.htm. The quilts made by students in Ms. Cho's and Ms. Baker's classes are shown in Figures 5.1 and 5.2, respectively.

Figure 5.1 Ms. Cho's students' freedom quilt.

Figure 5.2 Ms. Baker's students' freedom quilt.

Because of the students' high interest in quilting, several follow-up activities were scheduled for this fourth-grade class. Ms. Baker describes these activities below:

First, the school's art teacher showed a video biography about Faith Ringgold's life and artwork in quilting, and I bought them a book featuring Faith Ringgold's quilts (Ringgold, 2002). At this point, the class could entertain the notion that "quilts can tell a story" or can be used as a social voice. The class also saw that quilts were a tradition that had been handed down through the generations. Students were asked to make a story quilt about their own lives. Then students were given one piece of construction paper to divide into eight equal parts by making a series of folds. Then they unfolded the paper and made lines on the folds to show divisions of the quilt. Next students were asked to measure the perimeter and area and to record the measurements in pencil on the paper. Each student made his/her own paper quilt with eight patches describing his/her own life. One student who had recently become sullen in the classroom made his entire quilt of patches about his grandfather who had recently passed away, and I remembered that his mother cried when I showed it to her. The caption read: "R.I.P. Chief" and had an illustration of the grandfather on the quilt, and in the corner of the quilt was a little gun with an "X" marked through it. I was happy to see that many students had created one or more patches with the school or an image of him/her learning in the classroom. I saw that the quilts were another way that students could be expressive about their own lives, learn about their culture and history, and learn important content such as mathematics simultaneously. The children's story quilts were presented to a guest speaker who was part of a quilting bee that met at the school in the evenings. Finally, the guest showed quilts made by the quilting bee to the class, including a military quilt from the Vietnam War.

Analysis of quilting lesson

The quilting lesson not only provided students with a context to learn mathematics, but it helped them to make connections to social justice. After making a quilt patch about the Underground Railroad, students were able to tell personal stories, one of which was the tragic loss of a loved one due to gun violence. Ms. Baker was moved by the children's stories and touched by the tragic events in their lives. Throughout the quilting lesson, Ms. Baker's pedagogy and expectations of the children changed. As she became more acquainted with the children and their culture, she demonstrated cultural responsiveness, which was evidenced by the amount of time she spent on the unit, how she allowed the students to speak freely, how she shared student work with parents, and her willingness to invite guest speakers from the community into the classroom. Culturally responsive teachers foster a learning environment that is more likely to increase trust and cooperation among students and parents (Gay, 2000). In such environments, students are more likely to have high interest in subject matter and spend more time on task (Gutstein, 2003; Leonard *et al.*, 2005), which is correlated to high achievement (Wenglinsky, 1998). Connecting issues of social justice to mathematics not only provides students with knowledge of social, political, and cultural issues but shows them how *knowing* and *doing* mathematics empowers them to advocate change (Gutstein, 2003; Ladson-Billings, 1994; Tate, 1994).

Making connections to issues of social justice

During the two-week unit on the Underground Railroad, students at the school kept a journal. They pretended to be fugitive slaves traveling on the Underground Railroad. The students were very engaged because the theme was anchored to their lives on an emotional level. One of the poignant scenes presented to students in an original storyline on the Riding the Freedom Train computer module is shown in Figure 5.3. Scenes such as this helped the

Figure 5.3 Sam separated from parents for slave auction (source: Image courtesy of Renaissance Macro, Inc.; original design by Edgar Flores; animated by Angela Mistretta).

students to identify with characters and historical figures like Harriet Tubman and John Parker. Students learned literacy, science, geography, and social studies, and solved mathematical problems within a cultural context as they completed the computer module. They learned how mathematics applies to survival skills as they pretended to be runaway slaves. However, given the intense emotional nature of Figure 5.3, no problems were presented with this particular scene.

Students can also learn history and mathematics simultaneously by creating word problems out of the historical markers that can be found in their community (Leonard & Guha, 2002). Figures 5.4 and 5.5 show two historical markers that depict information about the contributions of two famous abolitionists: William Still and Absalom Jones. Children may conduct research to report on these individuals' lives as well as create their own story problems. Students' problems can then be bound in a book and shared with parents and peers.

Linking social justice to literacy

The students expressed their creativity and understanding of social justice in their journal writings. Examples of six students' writings are presented below and are followed by an analysis of the data. Pseudonyms are used for anonymity. Notations about person and tense are made after each essay.

Figure 5.4 William Still marker.

Figure 5.5 Absalom Jones marker.

TRAY: The night sky looks like ... I can see the Big Dipper from here. I hear dogs and leaves moving. I feel scared. I smell that enemy. I smell something that stinks. Oh, no. Now I know the slave master is coming. I determine it's safe. The safe house is only a couple of miles. I think I'll rest there. In the morning, I'll start a fresh day. Okay, it's morning. I have to ... I know I'll be ready for them when they come. I'll have to ... Then it will be my time to get my family. [First person narrative that begins in present tense and then changes to future tense.]

ALIM: I am following the Big Dipper. The night sky looked good. It's a full moon. I heard gun shots, people getting lashed. I'm sick of it. I'm going back for my people. I'll never let go. I have a ... He'll lead me back. It's humid out, but I can do it. I feel mad, so mad, no one can stop me. I smell the blood of the people. I can't touch anything. I can determine the safe house because the quilt is on it. [First person narrative with mixture of present and future tenses.]

DANDA: Once upon a time, there was a girl named Moses, and she was scared. She had two braids, and she was only nine years old. But she had run away from the plantation. She was a runaway slave. She was following the North Star when she heard a gunshot, and her [sic] and her mother cried with fear. I sat down, and I cried. I was seeing things such as people digging holes in the ground and putting people down in the hole. I mean, putting bodies in the hole. But my mom told me to think positive. But I had heard a gunshot—boom-boom—at the plantation. And I knew that it was coming from the planta-tion. But I saw a river, and it had a sign that said "Freedom River." I heard that my grandmother visit [sic] the river, but my grandmom saw constellations. But it was one that she liked the best. It was the Drinking Gourd. She had followed it, and it led her to a safe house. And she saw lightning bolts that made a sign that said, "welcome." [Begins in third person but shifts to first person but writes in past tense.]

TASHIRA: I feel really, really scared and very brave because I might get shot or hurt because I am a runaway slave. I see very tall grass and a lot of people behind me. I would smell a lot of tall grass. I would touch animals. I can tell where the safe house is because there is a small quilt hanging outside the house. The night sky will look real dark but not that dark because of the moon. [First person narrative but uses present and future tenses.]

MICHELE: I was so happy and sad at the same time. In a couple of days, I will go back and get my sisters, brothers, mom, and dad. I will come back and get my sisters. I like my people so much that I don't care about being a runaway slave. I will save my people. I can smell food from the house and eat blueberries. I can taste the water to drink. I will feel scared from hearing all of my owners' boots. I will feel the blood of my people getting beat. The night looks dark blue, and I still will follow the North Star to go to a safe house. The safe house will have a quilt, flag, or a red broom. The safe house will have a light on. The light will be yellow, blue, red, or green. I will not be happy if I got caught by my owner. [First person narrative but uses past and future tenses.]

TERRENCE: If I was a runaway slave, I would be sad, homesick, and scared. I'd see birds, crops, and maybe other slaves. I'd smell the scent of the corn. Also crops for me to take and eat on the run. I'd taste the soily spit in my mouth as dry as a leaf. And I'd touch my heart with sorrow. The sky is as dark as a black crayon filled with stars and a moon. I hear the moaning and crying of other slaves working. Also the whips against the back of a helpless slave. There are animals like birds, dogs, and snakes. Also the natural sounds like howling, crowing, and slithering. I feel scared and surrounded in sorrow. I smelled the crops. I kept my back in pain. The safe house is only a few miles away with an American flag on it. I determined tomorrow I shall follow the North Star to find it, and then I will go get my family. And nothing can stop me now. [First person narrative with use of present and past tenses.]

Analysis of student journals

The six students' journal entries reflect a variety of positions and interests generated by pretending to be a fugitive slave traveling on the Underground Railroad. While students brought some prior knowledge and background about African American history and culture to bear on their essays, the stories *Freedom River* (Rappaport, 2000), *Minty* (Schroeder, 1996), and *Barefoot* (Edwards, 1997) clearly left an impression on these young students. The text *Freedom River* was mentioned by name in Danda's essay, and she referenced *Minty* at the outset. Tashira and Terrence referenced animals and all of the students mentioned the safe house, which were key elements in *Barefoot*. However, it is important to point out that the students' journals differed in style and content.

All students wrote in character and described what it was like to travel on the Underground Railroad. Five of the six students wrote exclusively in the first person, which shows how strongly they identified with fugitive slaves. However, it should be noted that Danda shifted from third person ("... her mother cried with fear.") to first person ("I sat down, and I cried.") when she described emotions of fear and dread. Intense emotions and personal connections to fugitive slaves were clearly exhibited in all of the students' journals. Terms such as "scared" (Tray *et al.*), "mad" (Alim), and "sad" (Michele & Terrence) expressed the gravity of a fugitive slave's plight.

In addition to affective terms, the students used a number of vocabulary terms learned in class as well. For science, the students mentioned the night sky (5), North Star (3), Big Dipper (2), moon (2), Drinking Gourd (1), constellations (1), or stars (1). Alim also mentioned weather conditions as he stated, "It's humid out." Moreover, all of the students accessed their science background knowledge by referring to their senses throughout their essays: sight (7), hearing (5), smell (7), taste (2), and touch (2). In mathematics, examples of time and distance are evident in Tray's, Michele's, and Terrence's essays: *couple of miles, couple of days,* and *few miles away.* Examples of subitizing are evident in Danda's description of a girl named Moses who had *two* braids and was *nine* years old. Mathematics attributes such as size are also depicted as Tashira described *tall grass* and a *small quilt.* Students could then easily use these mathematics concepts to develop story problems out of their essays.

After initially coding the essays for affective and cognitive terminology, the data were coded again for themes and patterns. Excerpts of the six students' writings about the Underground Railroad are clustered around three themes: violence and fear, freedom for self and family, and determination and hope.

Violence and fear

The students wrote vividly about the violence experienced or avoided by fugitive slaves. Students' sense of violence and the risk of danger for fugitive slaves were captured by references to guns and gunshots. Alim and Danda wrote: "I heard [a]gun shot[s]." Alim and Michele wrote, respectively: "I smell the blood of my people; I will feel the blood of my people getting beat." Alim and Terrence wrote about *lashes* or *whips* being used on the slaves. Tashira captured a deep sense of fear when she explained in her journal: "I feel really, really scared and very brave because I might get shot or hurt because I am a runaway slave." While the use of guns to capture escaped slaves was common in the multicultural texts, students' preconceptions about guns and violence were also informed by crime in many of the urban neighborhoods where they lived.

Freedom for self and family

As students pretended to live the life of a runaway slave vicariously in their journals, they revealed their ability to understand the quest for freedom, not only as an individual quest, but also in terms of family. This was a critical point made by four students. In their journals, students went from envisioning themselves as free to desiring that their family members obtained freedom as well. After traveling north to freedom, Alim writes, "I'm going back for my people." Tray and Terrence comment, respectively, "… Then it will be my time to get my family" and "Then I will go get my family." These statements reveal a sacrificial choice to purposefully journey back, regardless of the danger of re-enslavement or death, to ensure that another family member enjoys the taste of freedom. For many students, the thought of being separated from their family was unbearable. In the following statement, Michele clearly articulates that the road to freedom is not an individual path, but one where family members share in the realization of liberation. "In a couple of days, I will go back and get my sisters, brothers, mom and dad. I will come back and get my sisters. I love my people so much that I don't care about being a runaway slave."

Determination and hope

In the foregoing excerpts, we can see the power that a sense of mission—to escape slavery and see a better day—has given to these student writers. From these students' writings, we know they understood the consequences of being a conductor on the Underground Railroad. Despite serious obstacles like the threat of recapture and death, fugitive slaves took tremendous risks. Their personal freedom and that of their family were worth the dangerous journey on the Underground Railroad. The adversities they encountered were captured as students wrote about the fugitive slaves' determination and will to survive and live as free people.

This hope for a better life seemed to propel slaves to the path on the Underground Railroad. Alim expressed their determination and persistence as follows: "I can do it. I feel mad, so mad, no one can stop me." Terrence echoes the sentiment, "… nothing can stop me now." The desire to persevere in spite of vicissitudes is at the core of these students' essays and is clearly articulated in most of their narratives. These narratives can be used as a springboard to help African American students understand that they must also persevere when faced with difficult and sometimes life-threatening challenges. Education is the key to success, and African American students can learn and succeed even in difficult subjects like mathematics and science.

Another context teachers may use to connect mathematics with social justice is African American music. Mathematics topics related to music are numbers, fractions, decimals, and percents. These mathematics topics may be infused with music as participants learn about whole notes, half-notes, and quarter-notes and how many beats are needed to create a measure. A metronome may be used to scaffold learning. Participants could also conduct research to learn about music moguls like Berry Gordy and Kenny Gamble as well as the history of Blues and Jazz. The careers of notable singers and musicians such as Muddy Waters, Bessie Smith, Buddy Guy, Duke Ellington, Miles Davis, and Marian Anderson could be used as storylines to create word problems.

Multicultural literature about the lives of Bessie Smith, Duke Ellington, and Marian Anderson may be used to enhance literacy in reading and mathematics. *Bessie Smith and the Night Riders* (Stauffacher, 2006) tells the story of Bessie's encounter with the Ku Klux Klan. Based on a true event, the story is an empowering account of courage and resilience at a time when racism and prejudice went unchecked. A picture book that helps emergent readers understand the influence of Duke Ellington is *ellington was not a street* (Shange, 2004). Another compelling text that makes a strong connection to social justice is *When Marian Sang* (Ryan, 2002). The text summarizes Marian's life from childhood to adulthood. It describes the racism she faced when she tried to perform at Constitution Hall in Washington, DC, and highlights her performances at the Lincoln Memorial and the Metropolitan Opera. Mathematics is embedded throughout this text as it provides a timeline of Marian's musical career and the number of people in the audiences. Finally, a fiction book entitled *Jazzy Miz Mozetta* (Roberts, 2004) describes an evening of dancing the jitterbug in the Blue Pearl Ballroom. Young readers will be delighted by the illustrations, rhyme, and alliteration in the text. All of the foregoing texts are culturally specific and can be used as scaffolds to help students cross borders to learn mathematics in a social justice context.

Moreover, social protest songs such as those produced by Motown and sung by Marvin Gaye and others could be incorporated in a unit plan (see Appendix C). In this context, mathematics may be applied in business simulations that show the impact of record sales and profit margins as students pretend to own a recording company. Students decide how much to pay musicians, artists, producers, and determine unit costs for each CD sold. Professionals may also be brought into the classroom in order for radio sales staff and program managers to explain the cost of airtime and how royalties are disbursed. Students can also learn the science, mathematics, and engineering needed to produce a music CD.

Another contemporary theme that explores the issue of social justice and racial equality is hurricanes. This topic lends itself nicely to event-based science and mathematics integration (Leonard, 2002b). Students can track hurricanes that develop during a current hurricane season and graph their maximum speed in stem-and-leaf plots. More advanced students may write an algebraic equation to locate the eye of a storm and use graphing calculators to check their answers (Celedón-Pattichis, 2007). Specifically, students can research and compare the cost of damages incurred after Hurricane Katrina to the cost of constructing the original levee system. As a culminating activity, participants might record songs on a CD, write a poem, participate in a skit or play, or make a presentation in a slide show to document what they learned as a result of investigating life in the Delta region before and after Hurricane Katrina.

Summary

Engaging African American elementary students in rich and meaningful mathematics learning activities is a major priority for many schools. Innovative and culturally specific instructional materials, strategies, and pedagogy are related to students' motivation and learning outcomes. In this chapter, I have demonstrated how to move the history and culture of African American students from the margins of the curriculum to the center of learning in the classroom. This alignment of culture and context encourages the modeling of teachers' practices within classrooms that make explicit the connections between students' cultural knowledge and learning mathematics (Lee, 2001). Illuminating the historical experiences of African Americans are worthwhile tasks. The social interactions of students with the teacher and each other, use of culturally based materials, and effective pedagogical practices provide knowledge about how students can be motivated in classrooms they often find boring and non-relevant to them. The quilt activity was motivational for teachers and students, allowing them to use their own creativity rather than only participate in prescribed programs that have a tendency to deskill (Fullan, 2000). Motivating marginalized students and providing an opportunity to access critical learning materials and skills in mathematics are essential to addressing disparities in mathematics achievement.

The teachers at Northside Charter School used the Mathematics Curriculum Principle to engage students in mathematics through lessons on constellations and quilting. They addressed the Equity Principle by allowing their students the chance to express themselves through artwork and writing. Moreover, Ms. Baker allowed her students the opportunity to read their journal entries aloud, which not only affirmed their identities but allowed students to learn from their peers as well. Ms. Baker grew from using culture in a superficial way at the outset to truly becoming culturally sensitive and responsive by listening to and learning from the students near the end of the unit. Most importantly, the classroom teachers used the Teaching Principle to make mathematical connections to the students' lives. The theme of the Underground Railroad provided opportunities for teachers to make links with scientific and mathematical terms and concepts that were relevant to Black history.

The Banneker Project demonstrates how student learning and teacher practices may be improved upon by using culturally specific activities. History and culture may be used as conceptual lenses to capture a shared legacy that students bring to content-related curriculum tasks (Mensher, 1994). To the extent that the educational community takes increased accountability related to student achievement seriously, the implications for using culturally specific approaches go beyond improving mathematics achievement to the very heart of learning and educational opportunities for African American and other students of color.

6

Women in aviation and space
The importance of gender role models in mathematics education

I want to do it because I want to do it. Women must try to do things as men have tried. When they fail, their failure must be but a challenge to others.

Amelia Earhart

Introduction

The stories of Elizabeth "Bessie" Coleman, the first American woman to receive an international pilot's license, and Amelia Earhart, the first woman to fly solo across the Atlantic Ocean, are awe inspiring. These women persevered despite gender barriers, and in the case of Bessie Coleman, racial barriers, to accomplish their dreams of becoming pilots. They stand as icons and role models who indubitably inspired contemporary women like Christa McAuliffe, the first teacher in space, and Mae Jemison, the first female African American to enter space, to become astronauts. Such notable achievements should inspire girls and women of all backgrounds to believe, like one of the descendants of Elizabeth Cady Stanton, an advocate of women's suffrage, that "anything's possible for anyone" (Bumiller, 1998, B6). However, when it comes to mathematics, women continue to have less participation than men "across all domains that require mathematical expertise" (Nosek *et al.*, 2002, p. 45).

In elementary and secondary schools in the U.S., Hanna (2003) claims that girls and boys have equal participation in mathematics and science. Nevertheless, at the college level women are still underrepresented in mathematics and math-related fields like engineering (16%), math/computer science (35%), and physical science (34%) (National Science Foundation, 1996; Nosek *et al.*, 2002). In fact, women hold "only 28% of the jobs in engineering, law, medicine, natural science, computer science, and college and university teaching" (Hanna, 2003, p. 212). Social and cultural factors continue to play a critical role in the underrepresentation of women in mathematics and science (Hanna, 2003; Nosek *et al.*, 2002).

Gender equity in mathematics and science

Hanna (2003) categorizes gender research into two distinct waves. During the first wave in the 1970s, researchers attributed the low participation and achievement of women in mathematics and science to differences in spatial ability and other cognitive factors (Fennema, 1974; Hanna, 2003; Leder, 1992; Tartre & Fennema, 1995). In general, the commonly held belief was that science and mathematics were male domains (Hanna, 2003). Therefore, it was accepted that men excelled in mathematics and science while women did well in language arts and writing (Hanna, 2003; Nosek *et al.*, 2002; Parker & Rennie, 2002). If women performed poorly in mathematics, they often interpreted their failure as poor ability, but men were more likely to place blame on teachers or lack of effort (Fennema, 1974; Hanna, 2003). On the contrary, women considered themselves lucky if they were successful in mathematics, but men attributed their success to high ability (Fennema, 1974; Hanna, 2003).

The second wave of research on gender differences in mathematics and science in the 1990s marked a major departure from innate biological factors (Hanna, 2003). Gender-based researchers suggested that the sociocultural context of learning mathematics was problematic (Buerk, 1985; Campbell, 1989 & 1995). The view that mathematics is an absolute body of knowledge with one correct method, answer, and exact symbols causes some women to avoid learning mathematics (Buerk, 1985; Campbell, 1989). In order to attain gender equity in mathematics classrooms, Ambrose *et al.* (1997) claim that teachers must "attend to it directly in their classrooms" (p. 236). They found certain standards-based strategies, such as facilitating discourse, created dilemmas for some female students. Yet, girls are more likely to lack assurance in their mathematics ability and to be skeptical of their competence in mathematics (Campbell, 1995). As a result, some girls may have low participation in mathematics because they lack confidence in their understanding and are ambivalent about explaining their thinking (Ambrose *et al.*, 1997; Celedón-Pattichis, 2007). Others girls are uncomfortable when debate or disagreement occurs during classroom discussions (Ambrose *et al.*, 1997). Rather than focus on whole-group discussion, a feminist pedagogy of teaching mathematics is suggested (Buerk, 1985; Jacobs & Becker, 1997).

The feminist pedagogy stresses four principles to foster gender-equitable, multicultural learning environments in mathematics classrooms: (1) using students' experiences, (2) writing, (3) cooperative learning, and (4) developing a community of learners (Jacobs & Becker, 1997). Furthermore, Campbell (1995) suggests the following teacher behaviors to enhance gender equity in mathematics classrooms: (1) hold similar expectations for students regardless of gender or race; (2) involve students as active learners; (3) provide students with hands-on activities; (4) identify and correct academic deficiencies; and

(5) allow students to have fun (Campbell, 1995). On the contrary, extensive use of lecture, seat-work, homework, and tests has been associated with females dropping out or discontinuing their study of mathematics (Fey as cited in Campbell, 1995). Specific strategies to enhance the learning of mathematics include the following:

- Provide time to experience and clarify a problem (situation) before focusing on a solution.
- Include the historical perspective to help students become aware of the person-made quality of mathematics.
- Acknowledge and encourage alternative methods and approaches, approximation, guessing, estimation, partial solutions, and the use of intuition.
- Answer questions with questions that both clarify the students' questions and help the students realize their own potential as problem solvers and problem posers.
- Encourage students to share ideas, partial solutions, and different interpretations of problems with each other.
- Encourage the asking of new questions and create an atmosphere where both teacher and student are free to wonder out loud.
- Make a concerted effort to avoid absolute language.
- Set as a goal the development of each student's internal sense of power, of confidence, and of control over the material.
- Offer opportunities for students to reflect on paper about their ideas and feelings about mathematics.
- Don't rush to closure.

(Buerk, 1985, p. 69)

Current views on gender differences in mathematics suggest physical and intellectual barriers do not impede the participation of women in science, technology, engineering, and mathematics (STEM) (Campbell, 1995; Nosek et al., 2002). The prevailing view explains that the underrepresentation of women in STEM careers is the influence of cultural and social barriers such as curriculum, learning environments, differential treatment by teachers and parents, and stereotypical sex-role identification (Hanna, 2003). In a longitudinal study of gender differences among 60 students (32 female and 28 male) at sixth, eighth tenth, and twelfth grade, Tartre & Fennema (1995) found no significant differences between males' and females' mathematics scores except at eighth-grade. When affective variables were compared, the only significant gender difference was male domain; that is males stereotyped mathematics as a male domain to a greater extent than females did (Tartre & Fennema, 1995). Furthermore, Nosek et al. (2002) found the constructs of math attitude, math identity, math-gender stereotypes, and gender identity were factors that influenced women's achievement and participation in mathematics. These findings help to change prior assumptions about females' achievement in mathematics.

Gender and academic achievement in mathematics

International and national assessments have been analyzed to measure gaps in achievement. On the international level, the International Association for the Evaluation of Educational Achievement (IEA) conducted studies known as the First (FIMS) in 1964, Second (SIMS) in 1980–1982, and Third International Mathematics Study in 1995 (now simply referred to as Trends in International Mathematics and Science Study) (TIMSS) (Hanna, 2003). Initial results on the FIMS revealed differences showing boys outscored girls in ten out of 12 countries at age 13 and in ten out of 12 countries at age 17 (Hanna, 2003). Results of the SIMS for 13-year-olds show no gender differences between boys and girls in five out of 20 countries on all mathematics subtests (Hanna, 2003). However, in ten countries, there were differences favoring boys on two of five subtests, and in five countries there were differences favoring girls on two of five subtests (Hanna, 2003). Among 17-year-olds, there were no gender differences between males and females in three out of 15 countries on six of seven subtests, but there were differences favoring boys in 12 countries on two out of six subtests (Hanna, 2003). On the 1995 TIMSS, there was no gender difference noted among 13-year-olds in overall achievement in 37 out of 39 countries. However, eighth-grade girls scored slightly higher in 12 countries in algebra (Hanna, 2003). When 17-year-olds were compared, no differences were found in five out of 16 countries. However, boys scored higher in four countries in two content areas and in seven countries in three content areas (Hanna, 2003). Thus, it appears that the gender gap is decreasing in mathematics on the international level. On the contrary, in the U.S., progress continues to be quite bleak for 17-year-old females.

The SAT, which is used as a predictor of college success, has one of the largest observed gender gaps in mathematics (Nosek *et al.*, 2002). The difference in SAT scores between males and females in 1995 was 41 points on the math section of the SAT: ($M = 500$, SD = 100; girls, $M = 478$; boys, $M = 519$) (College Board, 2005). Although SAT scores in mathematics have improved over the past ten years, there was still a 35-point difference between males and females in 2005: ($M = 520$, SD = 100; girls, $M = 504$; boys, $M = 539$). However, gender differences among fourth and eighth graders in mathematics are narrower than it is at the high-school level. On the 1995 NAEP, there was a two-point gender difference in mathematics between male and female fourth graders ($M = 238$, SD = 35; boys, $M = 239$; girls, $M = 237$) and eighth graders ($M = 279$; SD = 35; boys, $M = 280$; girls, $M = 278$). However, given smaller sample sizes, these differences though small may be significant

Table 6.1 Mean MFMT-I[a] posttest by gender controlling for race (*n* = 177)

Participants	*n*	*Pretest*		*Posttest*	
		M	*SD*	*M*	*SD*
African Americans					
Females	26	297.42	17.60	326.19	27.99
Males	16	296.94	14.54	332.13	33.00
Total	42	297.24	16.32	328.45	29.74
Whites					
Females	65	310.03	14.89	354.25	28.82
Males	70	312.86	23.84	347.03	29.89
Total	135	311.50	20.01	350.50	29.49

Source: Maryland State Department of Education, 1982.

Note
a Maryland Functional Mathematics Test, Level 1.

(Strutchens *et al.*, 2006). For example, when mathematics achievement data are disaggregated by race and gender, differences among males and females in different racial/ethnic groups are significant (Leonard, 2001b; Strutchens *et al.*, 2006). Such differences were confirmed in a teacher-research study of my sixth-grade students in 1997 (Leonard, 2001b). Standardized test scores on the Maryland Functional Mathematics test (MFMT-I) were analyzed by race and gender. As shown in Table 6.1, there was a significant interaction among these variables on the MFMT-I, $F(1, 153) = 7.685$, $p < 0.05$. African American females' scores on the MFMT-I were slightly higher than African American males' scores, but White males outperformed White females. These results concur with the findings of Strutchens *et al.* (2006).

Perhaps these achievement differences are linked to teacher practices, especially at the high-school level. Two female preservice teachers in my mathematics methods course, Myrtle and Julia (pseudonyms), shared some of their high-school experiences in their reflection papers.

I was in an advanced math class in my senior year of high school. I had a teacher who was new to the building and was used to teaching in an all male private school. He was always choosing the males in the classroom to answer questions and calling on me when he saw I was puzzled and unsure. Some teachers would take an initiative to clear up confusion in a math class, but this teacher took me out of the classroom, reminded me that this was an advanced class and suggested that I drop to a lower level. Being a stubborn young lady, I politely told him that I have been in advanced classes my whole high school career and was always successful. I told him I'll stick it out and I'll finish with a good grade. I did not appreciate his negativity towards females, especially because there were males in the class that were doing as poorly as I was. I could not help but observe that the majority of the students were struggling in the class. This obviously reflected the quality of teaching that was happening in the class.

(Myrtle, fall 2006)

Not one math teacher ever told me that I can do it if I tried, or encouraged me to ask or answer questions in math class. I have always felt "stupid" when it came to these classes and felt I couldn't relate or understand. In addition to being split up according to academic level in high school, girls were not expected to do exceedingly well in math and science. I always received Cs and Ds in math and was always placed in the average track classes. In addition to this, I had all male math teachers every year until my freshman year of college. However, in my senior year of high school, I had a male teacher who sat with me one-on-one so that I could understand. This was the first time that I received a B in math since fourth grade.

(Julia, fall 2006)

These excerpts reveal that mathematics is still viewed by some teachers as a male domain, and that some females continue to be intimidated or ignored by male teachers. On the contrary, Julia's essay reinforces the importance of caring, nurturing and supportive teacher characteristics in mathematics class. Gender-inclusive teaching strategies aimed at fostering equity in mathematics class help to narrow gender differences (Buerk, 1985; Hanna, 2003; Parker & Rennie, 2002). However, the representation of women in physical science and other math-intensive fields remains low (NSF, 1996).

To understand how social and cultural factors impact women's preferences to study mathematics over the arts, Nosek et al. (2002) conducted a study to examine how implicit identity with the group *female* related to preferences for math. Four types of implicit associations were of particular interest in the study: (a) association between the concept of math and evaluation (math attitude), (b) association between math and self (math identity), (c) association between math and gender (math-gender stereotype), and (d) association between self and gender (gender identity) (Nosek et al., 2002). Researchers used the Implicit Association Test (IAT) to measure implicit attitudes, identity, and stereotypes. A Latin-square research design was used to present students with four IATs in a counterbalanced fashion. Analyses included 79 participants (39 male, 40 female) enrolled in an introductory psychology course at Yale University (Nosek et al., 2002).

Results of this study show both males and females held negative implicit attitudes toward math and science: $t(38) = -5.09$, $p = 10^{-5}$, $d = -0.83$, men; $t(39) = -11.95$, $p = 10^{-14}$, $d = -1.91$, women. However, females held stronger negative evaluations of mathematics and science than males did. Furthermore, correlations between implicit attitude and identity for men ranged from 0.56 to 0.61 compared to 0.59 to 0.67 for women, indicating attitudes and identity were associated. These results show that strong implicit favor toward mathematics indicates strong implicit identification with mathematics.

In a second but related study, the researchers used the continuous variable of gender identity to examine the strength of the identity between the self and attributes associated with group membership. Their hypothesis was women who identified strongly with the female gender would have stronger negative attitudes toward mathematics and weaker identity with mathematics than women who had identified less with female gender. Ninety-one introductory psychology students (45 male, 46 female) at Yale University were included in the analysis.

Results of the second study show both males and females evaluated mathematics more negatively than the arts: $t(44) = -5.97$, $p = 10^{-7}$, $d = -0.90$, men; $t(45) = -11.60$, $p = 10^{-15}$, $d = -1.73$, women. However, females held a more negative evaluation of mathematics than males did. Moreover, both men and women held equal math-gender stereotypes: $t(89) = 0.41$, $p = 0.68$. Thus, social and cultural factors appeared to influence men's and women's perceptions of math-gender stereotypes in this study equally, while their preferences for mathematics differed. Results for women in the sample show the stronger their association with the male-math stereotype the weaker their preference for mathematics. Furthermore, the lower a woman's identity was with mathematics, the worse her performance was on the SAT in mathematics.

These results concur with the findings of Meringolo (2006) who examined math attitude as a male domain (Fennema & Sherman, 1976) and mathematics achievement on the PSAT among 300 high-school students in southern New Jersey. The 2 × 2 factorial design was used to analyze data among female athletes, male athletes, male non-athletes, and female non-athletes. While results show no significant differences on the PSAT when males and females were compared by athletic participation: ($M = 535$, SD $= 100$; $M = 537$ (male athletes); $M = 552$ (male non-athlete); $M = 537$ (female athlete); $M = 514$ (female non-athlete), there were significant differences between female non-athletes and female athletes ($t = 2.80$, $p = 0.007$) and female non-athletes and male non-athletes ($t = 2.47$, $p = 0.017$) on math attitude.

In addition to these results, Meringolo (2006) reported subscores on the male domain section of the Fennema-Sherman Math Attitude Survey (FSMAS) for the four subgroups as follows: female non-athletes ($M = 81.36$); male non-athletes ($M = 95.64$); female athletes ($M = 94.55$); male athletes ($M = 90.46$). Results of a paired t-test revealed no differences among male athletes and male non-athletes and male athletes and female athletes However, differences between female non-athletes and female athletes ($t = 2.80$, $p = 0.007$) and female non-athletes and male non-athletes ($t = 2.47$, $p = 0.017$)

were significant. There was also a significant correlation between attitude as a male domain and being female ($r = 0.285$). The results of this study show females who did not participate in varsity athletics were more likely to view mathematics as a male domain and score lowest on the PSAT in mathematics.

Since the results merely show the relationship between the individual and social groups and cognitive-affective factors, both the Nosek *et al.* (2002) and Meringolo (2006) studies are non-causal. Yet they imply that sociocultural factors, which have an impact on mathematics achievement, continue to influence women's attitudes toward mathematics. From my own teaching experience, I have observed that females with poor attitudes toward mathematics are politely disengaged from the learning process. To address underachievement in mathematics and science, some researchers advocate single-sex education (Celedón-Pattichis, 2007; Parker & Rennie, 2002).

Single-sex education

Because research indicates that girls aged nine to 15 suffer from lower interest and self-esteem in mathematics and science than males, single-sex education is deemed efficacious for girls (AAUW, 1992; Ambrose *et al.*, 1997; Campbell, 1989 & 1995). In addition, research also shows that girls who attend single-sex schools tend to hold less stereotypical views about women's roles in society and are more focused on academics (Celedón-Pattichis, 2007). These young women also tend to view mathematics and science as less of a male domain than their co-ed counterparts (Haag as cited in Celedón-Pattichis, 2007) and are more likely to develop greater confidence in *doing* mathematics (Leder & Fosgasz, 1997). The literature is replete with examples of successful single-sex schools (Celedón-Pattichis, 2007; Singh *et al.* as cited in Parker & Rennie, 2002). Thus, it appears that single-sex education has a positive impact on female minority students (Celedón-Pattichis, 2007).

Celedón-Pattichis (2007) conducted a case study of seventh- through twelfth-grade girls from working-class backgrounds who attended The Young Women's Leadership School (TYWLS). The school population of 360 young women was 63% Latina and 37% African American. Preliminary results of the study reveal the emergence of four themes relative to the success of single-sex schools: (1) creating a culture of success; (2) constructing a collaborative and supportive learning environment; (3) expecting girls to become leaders; and (4) establishing a sense of belonging.

These themes were evident in a number of ways. First, all girls were expected to complete pre-Calculus prior to graduation and apply for college (100% of the students were accepted to college in 2001 and 2002). Second, girls had the freedom to do board work at any time during instruction, debate with their peers and the teacher, and collaborate with their peers on mathematics assignments. Third, older girls mentored younger girls, and all students completed 60 hours in a community service project. Finally, the girls viewed the school as a home away from home as teachers enacted the ethic of care and took on the role of "other mothers" (Gay, 2000; Irvine, 2002). As a result of these practices and adequate resources, TYWLS is a highly successful single-sex school for girls (Celedón-Pattichis, 2007; Kitchen, 2007).

While some studies have shown that female participation in mathematics and science courses is greater in single-sex classrooms (Celedón-Pattichis, 2007; Parker & Rennie, 2002), gender-inclusive strategies are also effective in mixed-gender classrooms (Parker & Rennie, 2002). Strategies that encourage female participation in mathematics include cooperative group work and collaborative problem solving (Campbell, 1995; Leonard, 2001b; Parker & Rennie, 2002). Other strategies include curriculum and activities that are culturally specific to women.

Gender-inclusive culturally specific practices

In addition to cooperative learning and collaborative problem solving, multicultural curriculum that is specific to women has the potential to engage females in mathematics at higher levels. Drawn from the tenets of culturally relevant pedagogy (Ladson-Billings, 1994), culturally specific means the curriculum focuses on components from a distinct ethnic or gender background that are framed by historical and contemporary experiences that genuinely depict a particular way of life among members of the group. To address gender issues, I proposed the Bessie Coleman Project, a hypermedia module, which depicts the lives of African American and European American women in aviation and space flight.

The Bessie Coleman Project

The primary goal of the Bessie Coleman Project is to develop, implement, and study the potential benefits of an intervention that fosters female and African American students' achievement and positive attitudes toward mathematics. Second, it explores the strategies and mathematical discourse students learn and/or use to complete word problems. During the intervention, the stories of Bessie Coleman, Amelia Earhart, Mae Jemison, and Christa McAuliffe are used to frame problems within a context that is gender specific. The lessons are unique in that they rely on African American and European American women to present storylines that evoke various types of mathematical problem solving and scientific inquiry. While the storylines are about women, the content of aviation and space are male-dominated fields. Thus, the lessons expose females to STEM careers where they remain underrepresented.

The supplemental curriculum that includes the use of multicultural literature to teach the mathematics concepts may be found in Appendix C. The multicultural literature—loosely defined as stories about diverse groups of people—taps into the readers' prior knowledge while building on their vocabulary and conceptual understandings about aviation and space as well as the lives of four women. Some of the texts are: *Nobody Owns the Sky* (Lindbergh, 1998),

Talkin' about Bessie: The Story of Aviator Elizabeth Coleman (Grimes, 2002), *Amelia and Eleanor Go for a Ride* (Ryan, 1999), *Mae Jemison* (Braun, 2005), and *Christa McAuliffe: A Space Biography* (Jeffrey, 1998). After reading and responding to the stories, teachers and students may pose a mixture of routine single-step and non-routine multi-step mathematics word problems that derive from the literature. Examples of culturally specific problems drawn from the story of Bessie Coleman are shown below in Figures 6.1 and 6.2.

Figure 6.1 shows Bessie selling cotton when she was a child. Bessie was a shrewd negotiator and sold her family's cotton at top dollar. Examples of single-step and open-ended multi-step problems are presented below the figure.

- The average price of cotton at the Cotton Exchange was 11.6 cents a pound in June 1904, 14.5 cents a pound in June 1930, and 33.8 cents a pound in June 1950? How much did the average price of cotton increase per pound from June 1904 to June 1930? June 1904 to June 1950? June 1930 to June 1950?
- Bessie and her brother helped the family earn a living by picking cotton. On average, Bessie could pick 200 pounds of cotton per day. Her brother could pick 400 pounds. A bale was needed to sell cotton at the market. There are 1,400 pounds of cotton in a bale. How many days do Bessie and her brother have to pick cotton in order to make a bale? Explain your strategy.
- Search the Internet to find what the average price of cotton is today and its uses in society. Report your findings and create and solve your own mathematics problems.

Figure 6.2 shows Bessie watching planes fly in the airfield when she was a student at a Paris flight school.

Examples of multi-step problems and an example that uses the Internet are as follows:

Figure 6.1 Bessie as a child (source: Illustration by Francine Still Hicks).

Figure 6.2 Bessie at flight school (source: Illustration by Francine Still Hicks).

- Bessie watched an airplane climb to 9,000 feet. The pilot decides to do a flip. In order to do the flip, the pilot has to drop his/her altitude. If she drops 100 feet every minute, how many minutes will it take her to drop to 6,000 feet? Now decide how far the pilot will drop. Determine the distance the plane dropped from its original altitude.
- Bessie has been watching a plane fly for one half-hour. Her flying lesson begins in one hour. If Bessie decides to watch the plane for 15 more minutes, what fraction of an hour does she watch the plane?
- Bessie went to Paris, France, to learn how to fly. Search the Internet to find out how much it costs to travel to Paris from New York by plane and by cruise ship. Determine which mode of transportation is the most economical.

In addition to the aforementioned problems, story problems about Amelia Earhart, Mae Jemison, and Christa McAuliffe may be posed as well. Multicultural books provide a third space where knowledge, different ways of knowing, and self-determination can come together with mathematics and science in a culturally specific context (Leonard & Hill, in press; Lipka *et al.*, 2005). However, Lubienski (2000) found that female students of low SES backgrounds preferred explicit instruction prior to engaging in problem-solving activities. In such contexts, teachers should also help diverse students learn schema to solve different types of word problems (Fuchs *et al.*, 2004). Word problems at the elementary school level can be generally classified as join, separate, or comparison problem types (Carpenter *et al.*, 1999). Furthermore, word problems that require use of all four basic operations may ask students to find solutions based on an unknown result, unknown change, or unknown start (Carpenter *et al.*, 1999). Teachers can help children to identify these kinds of problems and use appropriate problem-solving strategies, which should transfer to other types of problem-solving situations (Anderson *et al.*, 2000), including standardized test items such as those found on the NAEP.

Moreover, activities that are student-centered, hands-on, and problem-centered are recommended by NCTM for the mathematics classroom. These activities should be gender-inclusive, allowing girls to work cooperatively or collaboratively on authentic tasks (Campbell, 1995). In the Bessie Coleman Project, lessons derive from *Mission Mathematics* (NCTM, 1997). For example, students may make model airplanes when they participate in the Bessie Coleman or Amelia Earhart modules and Alka rockets when they participate in the Mae Jemison or Christa McAuliffe modules (see Appendix C). Data may be collected on flight times and distance or height, as appropriate, to enhance student learning in mathematics and science. However, aviation and space science are not generally topics that most teachers are familiar with. In order to enhance prospective teachers' opportunity to learn space science so that the knowledge could be passed on to students, I submitted a proposal and obtained funding to conduct the Space Links Project. Its impact on preservice teachers and students is described below.

Space Links: integrating space science and mathematics

Space Links came about as a result of my experience as a classroom teacher in Maryland. I applied and was accepted into the Maryland Governor's Academy in 1995. The Academy was a three-week summer program housed at Towson State University. The program provided middle-school mathematics and science teachers with opportunities to network with one another and to develop innovative lesson plans to implement in their classrooms. The Academy was also my entrée into the Lockheed Martin Graduate Fellows Program (LMGFP). As a participant in the LMGFP, I was afforded the opportunity to work at the NASA Goddard Space Flight Center (GSFC) in Greenbelt, Maryland, for eight weeks during the summer of 1996 as a teacher intern. While at NASA, I established long-term relationships with my mentors, who were astrophysicists. The major outcomes of the internship were learning how to conduct research and the development of an integrated science and mathematics unit called "All Around the Sun," which I implemented with sixth-grade students during the 1996–1997 academic year. Because of my NASA experience, I sought to expose preservice teachers at Temple University to a similar experience.

Funded by the Space Telescope Science Institute (STScI) from 2002 to 2004, the Space Links program targeted female and minority preservice teachers. A major component of the program was to provide preservice teachers with an opportunity to work alongside a NASA scientist to learn firsthand what scientists do. Professional scientists can inspire students to set new goals and explore new vistas for career choices. Fostering an enthusiasm for science and mathematics is essential in encouraging students to investigate careers in these fields.

Research shows that poor preparation in mathematics and science during elementary and secondary school is one of the main reasons for the underrepresentation of female and minority students in STEM fields (Campbell, 1989). Thus, studies that examine preservice teachers' self-efficacy and instruction in science and mathematics are warranted. In the Space Links program, we used the case study method to examine the self-efficacy, pedagogy, and beliefs of women and minorities. The case study design is useful in studying "special people, particular problems, or unique situations in great depth, and where one can identify cases rich in information" (Patton, 1990, p. 54). The research methods may be found in Appendix D.

Participants in the Space Links project were exposed to exciting curriculum materials and professionals committed to building the social and intellectual capital of students (Pre-K–16) and to increasing the number of females and minorities choosing careers in science and mathematics. Interventions included professional development workshops, a community-based internship, curriculum support during student teaching, and a NASA externship. The results of the study are presented in two parts. First, descriptive quantitative data are presented to share the study's influence on the preservice teachers' efficacy and space science teaching. Second, qualitative interview data are presented to determine how the interventions influenced the efficacy, pedagogy, and beliefs of target participants.

Lillie, Melva, Cecilia, and Summer (pseudonyms) were selected by project staff to participate in the ongoing SUNBEAMS (Students United Becoming Enthusiastic about Mathematics and Science) program at NASA GSFC. The SUNBEAMS program allowed these preservice teachers to work firsthand with a scientist or engineer at NASA GSFC from July to mid-August 2003. The preservice teachers were among 15 teachers selected to participate in SUNBEAMS. Ten teachers from the District of Columbia Public Schools and one new-hire from Prince George's County Public Schools also participated in the program. Linking teachers and mentors with expertise in various fields of space science provided an extremely valuable learning experience.

The Space Links preservice teachers immersed themselves in the research that each scientist or engineer was working on and then developed an innovative science curriculum to use with students. Lillie spent time with a scientist who worked on the Earth Observing System Satellite-Aura Project, which measures atmospheric levels of carbon dioxide and ozone. Melva worked with a physicist on the Mars Exploration Rover Mission (MERM), a robotic vehicle designed to detect water, soil, and rock on the surface of Mars. Cecilia worked with an electrical engineer on the Messenger Mercury Laser Autometer project. An astrophysicist working on the Multi-Wavelength Milky Way Project mentored Summer. Because they participated in the NASA externship, these participants were selected for further study.

Teacher efficacy

Participants in the Space Links study completed the *Science Teaching Efficacy Belief Instrument* (STEBI-B) (Enochs & Riggs, 1990), which was administered on a pre-post basis to learn how preservice teachers' self-efficacy in science teaching changed during the study. The STEBI-B consists of a 23-item survey that contains two subscales: Personal Science Teaching Efficacy Belief Scale (PSTE) and Science Teaching Outcome Expectancy Scale (STOE). Alpha coefficients for the PSTE and the STOE scales are 0.90 and 0.76, respectively. The survey uses a five-point Likert scale to measure responses—13 positively written and ten negatively written. In the case of positively written items, the point values are: Strongly Agree (SA) = 5, Agree (A) = 4, Uncertain (UN) = 3, Disagree (D) = 4, and Strongly Disagree (SD) = 1. In the case of negatively written items, the point values are reversed. Scores on the PSTE range from 13 to 65 and indicate belief in one's ability to teach science. Scores on the STOE range from ten to 50 and indicate expectations for students as an outcome of science teaching. Comparative data show that four of seven pre-service teachers' self-efficacy increased after participating in Space Links for one year (see Table 6.2). Average PSTE scores did not change, but average STOE scores increased slightly from 37 to 38. While these results were not what we expected, Melva and Cecilia improved on both the PSTE and STOE subscales.

Science instruction

In order to evaluate Space Links participants' instruction, they were observed during student teaching. Cecilia and Summer were observed during the spring semester of 2003, and Lillie and Melva were observed during the spring semester of 2004. Each of their lessons is briefly described below.

Cecilia taught the "Air Show" lesson from the *Mission Mathematics* curriculum (NCTM, 1997) to a class of 25 linguistically and ethnically diverse third-grade students. In this lesson, students designed their own airplane and then conducted four trials to collect and analyze data. The trials consisted of obtaining the following data for each plane: (1) distance (measuring how far the airplane flies); (2) accuracy (how well the airplane lands on a target); (3) acrobatics (how many times the airplane flips during flight); and (4) duration (how long the plane stays in the air). The mathematical connection was data analysis and statistics.

Summer implemented a project-based lesson with a class of 19 urban seventh graders who were told to investigate one of the nine planets of the solar system. Mathematical connections in the lesson included number sense, estimation, geometry, and spatial sense. Students found each planet's distance from the sun, average temperature, patterns of rotation and revolution and discussed its shape. Since the teaching of this lesson, Pluto, discovered by

Table 6.2 Comparison of pre- and post-STEBI-B scores: ($n = 7$)

Participant ID	Pre-PSTE scores	Post-PSTE scores	Net change (PSTE)	Pre-STOE scores	Post-STOE scores	Net change (STOE)
4761	56	57	+1	46	47	+1
1761	56	53	−3	35	34	−1
Melva	36	39	+3	27	32	+5
Cecilia	51	54	+3	35	39	+4
1616	57	52	−5	42	42	0
0345	44	44	0	37	42	+5
9931	43	44	+1	35	33	−2
Mean (Std. Dev.)	$M = 49.00$ ($SD = 8.12$)	$M = 49.00$ ($SD = 6.63$)		$M = 36.71$ ($SD = 14.08$)	$M = 38.43$ ($SD = 5.62$)	

Tombaugh in 1930, has been reclassified as a dwarf planet and is no longer recognized by scientists as part of our solar system (Flam, 2006). Clearer definitions of what constitutes a planet have emerged. According to the International Astronomical Union (IAU), "a 'planet' is a celestial body that: (a) is in orbit around the sun; (b) has sufficient mass for its self-gravity ...; and (c) has cleared the neighborhood around its orbit" (Flam, 2006, A10).

Lillie developed her own lesson on galaxies and implemented it with 21 eighth graders attending a suburban middle school. Lillie downloaded several images of galaxies from the Internet and copied and laminated them to make sets for the students to work with. Students worked in pairs and discussed the characteristics of each galaxy in order to classify it by type. Students learned that galaxies were categorized by their shape: elliptical, spiral, or irregular (see Appendix E). The mathematical connection was geometry and spatial sense.

Melva taught the "Scrumptious Veggie Shuttle" lesson, which also came from the *Mission Mathematics* curriculum (NCTM, 1997), to 25 kindergarten students in an urban classroom. Materials needed to teach this lesson included bread (Orbiter), carrots (external fuel tank), and celery (solid rocket boosters). Cheese spread can be used for the glue to stick the parts of the shuttle onto the Orbiter. Prior to making the shuttle, Melva read a book about rockets to the students. Then students worked in small groups with parent helpers to make the shuttle. After making the shuttle, Melva and the students simulated a countdown. Thus, the mathematical connection was counting.

All of the lessons described above have been incorporated in the Bessie Coleman Project that was previously described. The "Air Show" may be done after students have read multicultural literature about Bessie Coleman and Amelia Earhart. The "Scrumptious Veggie Shuttle" and lessons about planets and galaxies can be interwoven with multicultural literature about Christa McAuliffe and Mae Jemison. In addition, the contributions of the Tuskegee Airmen (African American Pilots during World War II) and Ronald McNair (African American male astronaut) should be emphasized along with the contributions of other crew members on board the Challenger and Columbia shuttles.

The Science Teacher Inquiry Rubric was used to rate seven female participants' inquiry-based space science lessons. The STIR ratings were based on a student/teacher-centered continuum. The rubric was modified to rate lessons as follows: 0 = no evidence of scientific inquiry, 1 = highly teacher-centered, 2 = moderately teacher-centered, 3 = moderately learner-centered, or 4 = highly student-centered. Each of the videotapes and transcripts was evaluated to rate the preservice teachers across six categories. Four of the preservice teachers taught in 2003 (Year 1), and three taught science lessons in 2004 (Year 2). However, only Lillie and Melva had the benefit of participating in the NASA externship prior to teaching their lessons. Thus, the other five preservice teachers function as a type of control. Results are shown in Table 6.3.

Data were analyzed for patterns by ranking individual mean scores and comparing individual scores with the group mean scores within each category. Lillie had the second highest rank, and Melva tied for the second lowest rank, which is consistent with her low STEBI-B score. As shown in Table 6.3, the overall average STIR score across all categories was 2.38, indicating that most of the instruction among this cohort was moderately teacher-centered. Space Links participants were strongest in Category 4: "Learners formulate conclusions and explanations" but were weakest in Category 5: "Learners evaluate their explanations in light of alternative explanations." The Space Links cohort engaged students in activities that led them to understand scientific meaning and explanation, but in several instances these teachers did not provide students with multiple resources to draw alternative conclusions.

When the scores of the two preservice teachers who were exposed to the externship—Lillie and Melva—were compared with those who were not or taught before the externship, we find some interesting results. Lillie's mean score of 3.00 was above the mean, indicating that she was a moderately student-centered teacher. On the contrary, Melva's mean score of 2.00 was below the mean, indicating that she was moderately teacher-centered in her instruction. However, it should be noted that the two highest scores occurred with teachers of middle-school students, and Melva was the only teacher of early childhood students (K—2). It is quite possible that the STIR is a more appropriate instrument for middle- and high-school science teachers. It is not surprising that early childhood teachers provide more structure and direction during science instruction. There was a similar finding in the Earth Links study, when a kindergarten teacher focused on language arts rather than science inquiry during an observation (Leonard *et al.*, 2005). Younger students are limited in their ability to hypothesize and explore their own research questions (Piaget, 1965). Teachers of very young children may be more likely to use direct rather than inquiry-based instruction. Additional research is needed to validate this assumption.

Analysis of individual categories reveals some interesting patterns. Both Lillie and Melva have scores below the group mean of 1.71 in Category 1: "Learners engage in scientifically oriented questions." This implies their experience working with scientists during the externship may have encouraged them to focus on specific questions to explore rather than allow inquiry to shift or diverge into different directions. Indeed, one criticism of inquiry-based instruction has been its tendency to lead classroom discourse down unknown and sometimes unproductive paths (Ball, 1993; Jegede & Olajide, 1995; Lo & Wheatley, 1994). Lillie and Melva took risks by engaging students in hands-on activities that required some interaction and group work.

Another interesting pattern is that Lillie and Melva's individual scores (3.00) were higher than the group mean (1.57) in Category 5: "Learners evaluate their explanation in light of alternative explanations." Lillie and Melva's

Table 6.3 Comparison of STIR data

Preservice teacher ID* (grade taught)	Learners engage in scientifically oriented questions	Learners plan/ investigate to gather evidence	Learners give priority to evidence to draw conclusions and evaluate explanations	Learners formulate conclusions and/ or explanations	Learners evaluate their explanations in light of alternative explanations	Learners communicate and justify their explanations	Average
Summer[a] **(7th)**	2	3	4	4	2	4	3.17
Lillie[b] **(8th)**	1	3	3	4	3	4	3.00
Cecilia[a] **(3rd)**	1	4	3	4	2	1	2.50
Nia[c] **(5th)**	2	2	3	4	1	2	2.33
Diane[c] **(4th)**	2	2	3	4	0	1	2.00
Melva[b] **(K)**	1	2	2	2	3	2	2.00
Wilma [c] **(3rd)**	3	2	3	1	0	1	1.67
Average	1.71	2.57	3.00	3.29	1.57	2.14	2.38

*Notes
a NASA participant and student taught before externship.
b NASA participant and student taught after externship.
c did not participate in externship.

work with scientists allowed them to provide learners with multiple resources that included NASA materials. Posters of galaxies and nebula were on the walls in Lillie's class. Melva read a storybook about rockets to help young children understand what rockets were and how they were used to fly into outer space. These data suggest that preservice teachers' work with scientists may influence them to provide students with a preponderance of evidence in order to draw conclusions. Additional research is needed to validate this claim.

Nevertheless, the results of the STIR are inconclusive. It appears that teachers of older students fare better on the instrument than teachers of younger students. Early childhood teachers may be more concerned about classroom management than teachers of students at higher levels of cognitive, social, emotional, and psychological development. Findings also reveal that these prospective female teachers were much less structured and more willing to engage students in inquiry in informal settings (Leonard *et al.*, 2005). Further study is needed with larger sample sizes and a control group to compare inquiry-based instruction in formal and informal school settings.

Preservice teacher reflections

Cecilia and Melva, along with four other participants, were interviewed by project staff at the end of the second year of the study. Portions of their interviews provide additional insight about how these teachers' pedagogy developed as a result of the Space Links program. Four of the ten questions (see Appendix F for interview protocol) asked during the interview along with the responses are presented below:

- *What were your personal attitudes about math and science, and how did your attitude change over time?*
  Initially math was always my favorite subject, but science was something that I wasn't familiar with, so I wasn't very confident in teaching it, until I was able to see and integrate it. So now, after, you know, going through, you know, the math ... *Mission Mathematics* book, and seeing the integration, it was a lot easier to incorporate them (math and science) together, instead of looking at them as separate entities. (Cecilia)
     At first, I was a bit apprehensive because math and science are not my strong suits, but as I worked with my team members, I found myself becoming more and more confident. (Melva)

- *How do you feel that your knowledge of the subject has changed?*
  Um, I'm a lot more confident in my teaching in math and science. I don't see science as, you know, the forsaken zone that most teachers don't want to enter when they come to the classroom. Now that I really feel that it is an integration with mathematics, I don't see it as

a separate entity. So I feel that, right there, makes me more confident in teaching it. Knowing, you know, the content as well … I think preparation and reading up on the content beforehand makes me more confident in my teaching as well. (Cecilia)

I think that I know more, and I definitely have more to work with when I finally teach. As far as my knowledge for instance, just telling you what I know, I'll be honest. I can't just tell you this is this and that is that, but I am more comfortable in working with the resources that I have, more so than I did before I entered the program. And I know more [because of] doing more teaching in those areas. (Melva)

- *How did the space science curriculum fit into your school curriculum?*
Um, "The Air Show" combines so much, um … It combined the vocabulary that we learned in math and that we did in the previous lesson, "Rescue Mission Game." It had to do with symmetry when they created their airplanes as far as the line of symmetry. We measured the time, um, … they had a chance to, um, measure as far as the accuracy. They had a chance to [write a] hypothesis and collect data and create averages with, you know, the data. (Cecilia)

It was very interesting because at the school that I was at they already have different subject preps. So they have science prep. I really didn't have to worry about doing a whole big unit, but I wanted to do it because I have no idea about the kind of school that I am going to be entering into. So I wanted to have experience in actually creating my own unit. Like I said before, I don't like to teach one subject. I like to integrate all subjects in my teaching. So I'll probably do language arts and fit in there a lesson where I would read a science book. Then I would add on different things from there. (Melva)

- *What are specific examples that you used in your student teaching experience to highlight earth or space science in your classroom?*
I had the posters, of course, in the classroom. And with each lesson, "Rescue Mission" and "The Air Show" and, you know, the Alka-Seltzer rockets … it was not just something that we did that day, it was, you know, a build up. I tried to make it a great big unit of all the space things we were going to do. And because the lessons were so in-depth and detailed, you know, we spent more than one afternoon on any given lesson. And um, it was before I actually did my NASA Goddard experience, actually the month before we spent that time. So I didn't have the resources that I have now to incorporate it, so I think in my own teaching experience, I'll be able to do a lot more because I have a lot more resources and a lot more experience from

the NASA experience than I did when I [was] student teaching. (Cecilia)

I just actually finished my [last] week of [student] teaching. We talked about the life cycle of plants. We talked about the different parts of plants and how plants grow. As far as the rocket lesson, definitely rockets do not move by themselves. They use fuel. Fuel comes from the ground. It comes from the earth. (Melva)

Analysis of reflections

Four themes emerged about science teaching in the teacher reflections. The first theme is integration of subject matter. Both Melva and Cecilia mentioned the importance of integration as opposed to teaching science content in isolation. The major problem with teaching subjects in isolation is limited time allotted to teaching all subject matter, which leads to some subjects being squeezed out (Weiss *et al.*, 2001). Furthermore, isolation of content causes a huge disconnect for students. Science and mathematics standards call for connections to be made to the real world. In the real world, science and mathematics are not disconnected but operate together to create phenomena that we interpret to be scientific or mathematical. For Cecilia, integration led to sense making. Therefore, it was "easier to incorporate them (math and science) together." Integration led to increased efficacy in teaching science (Lehman, 1994). The second theme to emerge from the reflections was the importance of additional field experience. Melva became "more and more confident" as she worked with team members to deliver space science instruction when she taught informal science in the community-based setting. Third, both Cecilia and Melva were comfortable with the *Mission Mathematics* curriculum (NCTM, 1997), resources and ideas that were provided. The curriculum was user friendly. Cecilia specifically mentioned how she prepared more than she could actually teach and how she carried science over to additional days. Fourth, Cecilia and Melva saw how space science fitted into the school curriculum. Cecilia incorporated science vocabulary during reading time, and Melva read books about science during language arts. Both Cecilia and Melva mentioned creating space science units and not simply teaching space science lessons once just to impress the researchers. Melva did not have to do a science unit at her school, but she chose to do one anyway because she believed it would benefit her later on when she became a teacher. Overall, these teachers' reflections positively depicted several aspects of the Space Links program that helped build their self-efficacy and enhance their science instruction.

Discussion

Because the data are limited to such a small number of cases, all of the data were triangulated (STEBI-B scores, STIR ratings, and interviews) to learn how the Space Links program and the NASA externship impacted the self-efficacy and science instruction of female preservice teachers. While STIR data are inconclusive, it appears that teacher externships, where beginning teachers work with scientists, have a positive impact on their science lessons. Cecilia, Lillie, and Melva extended themselves by gathering data or materials outside of the classroom to implement innovative lessons with students. Cecilia gathered materials needed for students to make model airplanes and conduct different types of trials. Lillie took extra time to download and laminate photographs of different galaxies. Melva purchased a book about rockets and grocery items for students to make veggie shuttles. These behaviors match those of individuals categorized as high efficacy teachers (Czerniak & Schriver, 1994; Mellado, 1998). Many beginning teachers have difficulty deviating from the textbook and prescribed curriculum (Fullan, 2000). These novice teachers made science accessible and thinking visible while helping students to learn from each other and develop autonomous learning skills (Linn & Hsi, 2000).

Implications

The lessons learned from the project findings have important implications for teacher educators. One clear implication is that more and different kinds of experiences better prepare, improve, and facilitate preservice teachers' science and mathematics instruction with diverse students and communities. This implication leads me to believe that with more intensive and thoughtful planning and collaboration with community-based sites, student-teaching officials, scientists, and preservice teachers, Space Links and similar programs can be an important addition to the array of teacher-training approaches aimed at increasing the underrepresentation of females and minorities in STEM careers. Finally, the nexus of culturally specific pedagogy in science and mathematics instruction potentially offers a ray of hope for teachers, schools, parents, and communities responsible for raising the test scores of underachieving students since anchoring culture to mathematics and science instruction has the potential to increase student knowledge and retention in both subjects.

7

Learning mathematics for empowerment in linguistically and culturally diverse classrooms

Knowledge speaks, but wisdom listens.

Jimmy Hendrix

Introduction

Nieto (2002) claims that schools and colleges of education have failed to prepare prospective teachers to teach linguistically diverse students. She challenges teacher educators to: (1) advocate language diversity; (2) bring bilingual education up from the basement; and (3) promote teaching as a lifelong process of transformation (Nieto, 2002). Delpit (1995), Gay (2000), and Nieto (2002) recommend reconceptualizing teacher education so that prospective teachers develop critical perspectives about their identities and use their own cultural awareness and reflection to raise consciousness and impart knowledge, skills, and values that will result in equitable classroom practices for all children. Since mathematical knowledge provides students with passports to obtain higher education and high status jobs, as a mathematics educator I incorporate readings and activities that address issues of language and cultural diversity in my mathematics methods courses. Students read articles about culturally relevant teaching in Mexican American classrooms (Gutstein *et al.*, 1997) and assessment pieces about how English Language Learners solved mathematics problems (Solano-Flores & Trumbull, 2003). They examined multicultural children's literature books such as *Grandfather Tang's Story* (Tompert, 1997), *One Grain of Rice* (Demi, 1997), *The Spider Weaver* (Musgrove, 2001), and *The Three Little Javelinas* (Lowell, 1992).

Grandfather Tang's Story is a folktale about two foxes that are able to transform themselves into different animals as they play a game of hide and seek. Teachers can reinforce students' spatial and visual skills by allowing them to use Tangrams to create the animals while the story is being read. *One Grain of Rice* tells the story of a peasant girl, Rani, who gains favor with a Raja. The Raja promised to deliver rice to Rani for 30 days, beginning with one grain of rice and doubling the amount each day. The story helps children to learn about another culture as well as the rapid growth of exponential functions.

ise the spread of communicable diseases to engage students in
ulator activities (Dossey *et al.*, 2002). *The Spider Weaver* is a
t two men from the Ashanti village of Bonwire in Ghana who
ricate designs made by a spider. Using designs found in the
), the men get the idea to weave Kente cloth for the people in the
village. ⌐⌐ ⌐ws and string or yarn may be used to create web-like geometric
designs to connect this text to mathematics. *The Three Little Javelinas* is the
Spanish version of the three little pigs. The pigs have to use critical thinking to
outsmart the wolf who wants to consume them. This text can be used to
create story problems for students to solve.

After engaging graduate students in discussing the aforementioned articles
and texts, words spoken by two White males in my graduate mathematics
methods course still reverberate in my psyche:

Below average performance equates to below average ability.
(fall 2002)

They just need to learn English!
(summer 2005)

Both remarks reveal deep-seated beliefs about underachieving students,
who are most likely to be urban students of color and language minorities.
The first comment is false on premise because performance does not equate
to intelligence. Many factors contribute to students' academic performance in
school, including teacher expectations. Students who are perceived positively
by the teacher have advantages over those who are perceived negatively (Gay,
2000; Rist, 1970). Teacher beliefs about their students influence how they
treat students, which impacts how they will teach and how much students will
learn (Gay, 2000). This phenomenon is known as the self-fulfilling prophecy
and has six attributes:

1. The teacher expects specific achievement from specific students.
2. The teacher behaves toward students according to those expectations.
3. The teachers' behaviors convey to the students what is expected of
   them and are consistent over time.
4. Students internalize teachers' expectations, and these effect their self-
   concepts, achievement motivations, levels of aspiration, classroom
   conduct, and interactions with teachers.
5. Over time, students' behavior becomes more and more attuned to
   what the teacher expects.
6. Ultimately, students' academic achievement and other outcome
   measures are affected.

(Good & Brophy as cited in Gay, 2000, p. 58)

The second comment is viewed by some as culturally insensitive, but it is representative of prevalent views regarding the language debate. However, the use of the word "they" is indicative of elitism and prejudice toward those who have a different linguistic background than the speaker. It is a term that is often used as code to refer to outsiders, foreigners, illegal aliens, and all others one considers to be inferior. The comment internalizes the view that those who speak a language associated with low prestige and low power are deficient (Nieto, 2002). Both comments reveal that changing prospective teachers' values and beliefs about linguistically and culturally diverse students is very difficult. Yet, the growing diversity of our nation's schools necessitates that reform at the teacher education level is crucial to the development of culturally competent teachers (Gay, 2000; Howard, 2003; Nieto, 2002).

Recent trends show that the Latina/o population in the U.S. has grown substantially since the 2000 Census (U.S. Department of Commerce, n.d.). Hispanics represent the largest minority group (14.4%) with an estimated population of 42.7 million, which is up 3.3% from mid-2004 to mid-2005 (El Nasser, 2006). While language minority students may be found in large urban school districts, their numbers are also increasing in small urban cities, towns, and suburban school districts (Nieto, 2002). More than 20% of children attending U.S. schools are from households that speak languages other than English (Sheets, 2005). English Language Learners (ELLs) account for 5% of all public school students; among them are 31% Native American, Asian American, and Latina/o American students (Sheets, 2005). Thus, if we take the education of ELLs seriously, language diversity should be viewed "using the lens of educational equity" (Nieto, 2002, p. 83).

In the United States, English is the language of power (Delpit, 1995; Nieto, 2002; Sheets, 2005). In order to be successful in American society, it is necessary to learn the English language. However, the ability to speak more than one language should be viewed as an asset and not a liability (Nieto, 2002; Sheets, 2005). The same approach can also be applied to African American students who come to school speaking Black English dialect. While it is important to recognize the importance of teaching and using Standard English to help African American students utilize the language of power effectively to succeed economically, it does not have to be done in a manner that is demeaning to the child and his/her culture (Delpit, 1995). If a teacher constantly corrects a student's grammar, the student is more likely to become passive, disengaged from the learning process, and resentful of the teacher (Delpit, 1995). "Teaching language minority students successfully means, above all, changing one's attitude toward the students, their languages, and cultures, and their communities" (Nieto, 2002, p. 93).

In order to empower linguistically diverse students to achieve in any classroom, especially mathematics, Nieto (2002) purports that teachers need to: (1) understand how language is learned; (2) develop an additive perspective about bilingualism; and (3) consciously foster native language literacy. In this chapter, I will address each of these points within the context of the mathematics classroom, identifying culturally specific connections that can be made with multicultural children's literature and social and political movements, like *Viva La Causa*. In addition, I suggest strategies and activities that teachers of mathematics may use to empower linguistically and culturally diverse students to learn mathematics within the context of social justice (Gutstein, 2003; Gutstein *et al.*, 1997; Ladson-Billings, 1994; Tate, 1995). Finally, I reflect upon my own pedagogy and the power that I hold to change preservice teachers' perspectives about empowering all students, especially linguistically diverse students, to learn and achieve in mathematics.

Understanding language acquisition

According to Cole (1992), no issue in culture and human development has received more scholarly attention than the interrelationship of culture, language, and development. In order for children to acquire language, "they must not only hear language but they must also participate in the activities that language helps to create" (Cole, 1992, p. 762). "The language or languages students speak categorizes them as members of distinctive linguistic, social, cultural, and ethnic groups" (Sheets, 2005, p. 108). Thus, language and culture are inextricably linked as language is used to communicate and pass down cultural values and beliefs (Nieto, 2002; Sheets, 2005). Moreover, language is the medium to express thought and is crucial to students' cognitive development (Vygotsky, 1986). In order to implement meaningful classroom practices to support ELLs communication in English, teachers must have knowledge of second-language pedagogy (Sheets, 2005).

Two main types of language instruction have been prevalent in U.S. schools: English as a Second Language (ESL) and bilingual education programs (Nieto, 2002; Sheets, 2005). ESL teachers are trained to provide instruction in the content areas in English by using specific vocabulary and low-level reading strategies (Sheets, 2005). The goal of this type of program is to encourage assimilation among ELLs. Bilingual programs include transitional bilingual programs, which function to teach students English at a fast pace. Some bilingual programs have been criticized for transitioning ELLs too quickly into mainstream programs (Nieto, 2002; Sheets, 2005). In the maintenance bilingual program, students' home languages and culture are valued as students are allowed five to seven years to become literate in English (Sheets, 2005). In the two-way bilingual program, native English speakers are immersed alongside ELLs from kindergarten through sixth grade. In this context, more time is devoted to English over the years. However, the two-way bilingual program serves a dual purpose, giving both ELLs and native English-speaking children access to social and cultural advantages as they learn to speak, read, and write in two languages (Nieto, 2002; Sheets, 2005).

Two studies relating mathematics and bilingual education are important to note. First, a study by Bacon *et al.* (as cited in Demmert & Towner, 2003) examined whether or not eighth-grade American Indian students who received bilingual instruction (English & Cherokee) differed in reading and mathematics achievement when compared to a control group who did not have bilingual education. Analysis of Covariance (ANCOVA) reveal children who received bilingual instruction scored higher on reading and mathematics subtests compared to a control group. In a second study, Rosier & Holm (as cited in Demmert & Towner, 2003) examined the effects of initial arithmetic instruction in Navajo and later in English compared to a cohort who received arithmetic instruction in English much earlier. Findings show that students in grades four and above, who did not begin reading English until mid-second grade, scored significantly higher than a control group on two standardized tests.

These studies highlight the difficulties of second-language learners (L2) in reading and mathematics. "Second-language learning, unlike first-language learning, takes place for different social, economic, political, and educational reasons and under different conditions" (Sheets, 2005, p. 114). Moreover, second-language acquisition is not an easy process but generally takes five to seven years to develop fluency (Nieto, 2002). While more expensive, the maintenance bilingual program and two-way bilingual programs are certainly more beneficial for ELLs than ESL. However, recent challenges to bilingual education and preferences for ESL programs create additional structural barriers for ELLs to actually learn English. Language-rich environments that value students' first language as well as English provide optimal conditions for children to practice speaking, listening, reading, and writing (Sheets, 2005). Thus, it is imperative for all teachers, not just ESL and bilingual teachers, to develop common knowledge about language diversity (Nieto, 2002).

Nieto (2002) encourages teacher candidates to learn a second language and acquire the following kinds of knowledge:

- Familiarity with first- and second-language acquisition.
- Awareness of the sociocultural and sociopolitical context of education for language-minority students.
- Awareness of the history of immigration in the U.S., with particular attention to language policies and practices throughout that history.
- Knowledge of the history and experiences of specific groups of people, especially those who are residents of the city, town, and state where they will be teaching.
- Ability to adapt curriculum for students whose first language is other than English.
- Competence in pedagogical approaches suitable for culturally and linguistically heterogeneous classrooms.

- Experiences with teachers of diverse backgrounds and the ability to develop collaborative relationships with colleagues that promote learning of language-minority students.
- Ability to communicate effectively with parents of diverse language, culture, and social class backgrounds.

(Nieto, 2002, p. 208)

By acquiring a broader knowledge base about linguistically and culturally diverse students, teachers engage in the process of becoming more caring and culturally competent individuals (Gay, 2000).

Teacher educators can usher teacher candidates into discussions about language, ethnicity, race, and gender diversity by using films and books to stimulate discussion. Films such as *Lean on Me* (Avildsen, 1989), *Stand and Deliver* (Menéndez, 1988), and *Mona Lisa Smile* (Newell, 2003) are recommended. Scholarly books that may be used to engage preservice teachers in dialogue about diversity are: *Mathematics Education at Highly Effective Schools that Serve the Poor* (Kitchen *et al.*, 2007), *Savage Inequalities* (Kozol, 1991), *The Dreamkeepers* (Ladson-Billings, 1994), and *Made in America: Immigrant Students in our Public Schools* (Olsen, 1997). By incorporating critical reflection of self and cultural identity in teacher education programs, teacher educators can encourage beginning teachers to deconstruct negative beliefs and stereotypes and reconstruct positive beliefs and values about linguistically and ethnically diverse students (Gay, 2000).

Developing additive perspectives

English language learners experience a great deal of conflict when the cultural values of the home and school do not mesh (De La Cruz, 1999; Sheets, 2005). Programs such as English-Only put ELLs at risk of language loss. Sheets (2005) contends that language loss among immigrants is taking place at an alarming rate. Results of studies on bilingual students show that there are advantages to bilingual education (Bacon *et al.* as cited in Demmert & Towner, 2003; Rosier & Holm as cited in Demmert & Towner, 2003; Thomas & Collier as cited in Nieto, 2002). Language minority students who received bilingual education scored at or above the 50th percentile rank on standardized tests compared to ESL students who scored between the 10th and 18th percentile ranks (Nieto, 2002). "Teachers need to support the language that students bring to school, provide them with input from an additional code, and give them the opportunity to use the new code in a non-threatening, real communicative context" (Delpit, 1995, p. 53).

In the mathematics classroom, early childhood teachers can show the additive value of different languages by including the word names of the counting numbers (usually one to ten) in different languages such as Spanish, Swahili, and Chinese. For elementary- and middle-school students, lessons in numeration can include learning about ancient counting systems such as Babylon-ian, Egyptian, Mayan, and Roman number systems. Students may develop story problems using numeric scripts from different systems. Such lessons, as demonstrated in the Kay Tolliver series of videos (Foundation for Advance-ments in Science and Education (FASE), 1998), help students to improve their understanding of the base ten numeration while at the same time cele-brate the mathematical contributions of diverse people.

Use of multimedia to support mathematics learning

Children's literature books that incorporate multicultural aspects of mathe-matics may be used in the mathematics classroom. Texts such as *Moja Means One: Swahili Counting Book* (Feelings, 1971), *Two Ways to Count to Ten: A Liberian Folktale* (Dee, 1988), and *The Village of Round and Square Houses* (Grifalconi, 1986) are suggested. The content of the counting books are fairly obvious. In *The Village of Round and Square Houses*, traditions in the African village of Tos are described. Women lived in round houses, but men lived in square ones. Students can learn a great deal about measurement, area, and perimeter while building replicas of these village houses in the classroom.

I found in my own research that using real-world connections to involve students in a construction project improved student interest and motivation to learn mathematics. Not only did the construction project develop students' problem-solving skills and improve their knowledge of measurement and geometry, it provided a context to learn about power and social justice since architecture is one way of expressing power, prestige, and wealth. The project, which I called *The City*, was first implemented with urban students in Dallas, Texas, during my tenure as a mathematics teacher with the Dallas Independ-ent School District.

To support the project, I applied for and received a mini-grant from the Junior League of Dallas to purchase materials such as foam board, Popsicle sticks, hot glue sticks, hot glue guns, Exacto knives (for adult use only) and paint. Fourth graders were allowed to let their imaginations run wild as they designed and built a miniature community. Some students built schools and hospitals. Others built facsimiles of their own shotgun houses. In a shotgun house, the front and back doors are parallel and opposite to each other. Someone coined the phrase shotgun house because a gunshot could literally go through one door and out the other. Nevertheless, students took a great deal of pride in their constructions, bringing carpet pieces, floor tile, and wall-paper to school to improve their artifacts. Students literally ran down the hallway from science class to mathematics class asking, "Are we going to work on the project today?" To my surprise, teachers from other classrooms and Project SEED instructors (visiting professionals who taught a supplemental mathematics program at my school) (Phillips & Ebrahimi, 1993) offered to assist my students in building their structures and putting together model cars to line neighborhood streets. When the project was completed, students' artifacts were placed in the school's media center for all to enjoy.

In Prince George's County, Maryland, I repeated the project, which I called *Tale of Two Cities* (Leonard, 2004). Sixth-grade students conducted research about ancient cities and decided to build a replica of Rome. Students learned about ancient cultures by reading literature and watching videos about Pompeii and other cultures. Moreover, students used vivid images to design what they envisioned might be a city of the future. In addition to the materials described above, students used plywood and cardboard to make structures in the ancient city and plastic liter bottles and colored plastic wrap to create glasslike structures for a city of the future. Figure 7.1 depicts a model of a Roman coliseum that was created by two students. Such projects can easily be connected to African, Aztec, Caribbean, Chinese, Hawaiian or Native American cultures.

The affective impact of this project may be gauged by some of the comments students made during an interview. When asked which of three types of tasks they preferred among algebra (abstract), weather (integrated), and architecture (applied), three target students made the following remarks:

> Designing a city because maybe one of the things I do good is designing a city. You can make things that you want to do, and you can design it the way you want by using the right measurements.
> (African American male)

> Designing a city because it's more interesting. 'Cause if you want to be a builder when you grow up, then you have to learn that. You have to learn how to add, subtract, multiply, and divide for the building.
> (White female)

> Designing a city because it has a lot of angles, and it uses a lot of mathematics skills, and it could be something you want to do in the future.
> (Asian male)

Figure 7.1 Student artifact of the Roman coliseum.

All of these students preferred the architectural activity over abstract and science-integrated tasks. The African American male personalized the activity, stating that "perhaps he was good at designing a city." Moreover, the other two students linked the architectural activity with a future career. Thus, activities of this nature help students to develop a mathematics identity and have the potential to influence their career paths.

In addition to mathematical tasks, multicultural literature books may also be used to engage linguistically and culturally diverse students in mathematical discourse. Texts related to historical events or contemporary life are *Sadako* (Coerr, 1993), *First Day in Grapes* (Pérez, 2002), and *Harvesting Hope* (Krull, 2003). *Sadako* is a story about a Japanese girl's battle with Leukemia as a result of exposure to the atomic bomb during World War II. Origami activities and rate and time problems can be developed after reading the text. Critical discussion about the aftermath of war can also be facilitated with older students. *First Day in Grapes* is a story about a Latino boy named Chico. His parents are migrant farm workers, and the story describes Chico's life as a transient student in California. In third grade, Chico is confronted by a couple of bullies but uses his knowledge of mathematics to outsmart them and win their respect. A similar story is told about migrant farm life in *A Migrant Child's Dream: Farm Worker Adventures of Cholo, Vato, and Pano*. The story of Pano and his two dogs, Cholo and Vato, is available in English and Spanish (Silverman *et al.*, 2001). *Harvesting Hope* is the story of the life of political activist, Cesar Chavez, and his historic walk from Delano, California, to Sacramento, California, on behalf of migrant farm workers who suffered from backbreaking work and low wages. The movement became known as *Viva La Causa!* Numerous word problems may be written to accompany images like those shown in Figures 7.2 and 7.3. Examples of a few problems

Figure 7.2 Cesar Chavez organizes the National Farm Workers Association (source: Illustration by Francine Still Hicks).

are written below each figure. Specific lesson plans that use *Viva La Causa* as a theme may be found in Appendix C.

- Cesar Chavez organized the National Farm Workers Association to help fight for the rights of migrant farm workers. In 1965, Cesar and his followers organized a 250-mile march from Delano, California, to the state capital in Sacramento. It took 17 days for the marchers to reach Stockton, California. It is about 200 miles from Delano to Stockton. Find the average number of miles the people walked so far.
- Using the Internet, determine how much further it takes to walk from Stockton to Sacramento. If the people walk the same average number of miles it took to get from Delano to Stockton to get from Stockton to Sacramento, how many more days did it take to get to Sacramento?
- It takes about four hours to drive by car from Delano, California, to Sacramento, California. How much longer did it take Chavez and his followers to walk from Delano to Sacramento than to ride by car?
- Chavez's movement on behalf of migrant farm workers was non-violent. To bring attention to *La Causa*, Chavez would go on hunger strikes, refusing to eat food for many days. In 1993, Chavez went on a 36-day hunger strike. How many weeks did this hunger strike last?
- After helping to improve the wages and working conditions of migrant workers who harvested grapes, Chavez helped to organize a strike on behalf of lettuce workers in California. If he worked 12 hours a day, how many hours did Chavez work in a typical work week?

Figure 7.3 Gandhi and King's nonviolent influence on Chavez (source: Illustration by Francine Still Hicks).

Parental involvement

Parents of linguistically and culturally diverse students should be used as resources to help their children learn mathematics. De La Cruz (1999) helped to conduct a study of reform-based mathematics instruction called Children's Math Worlds Family Connection (CMWFC) among limited English-language students and their parents. Developed by researchers at Northwestern University for first-through third-grade students, CMWFC provided a model of successful approaches that helped meet the needs of Latina/o families (De La Cruz, 1999). First, researchers conducted a needs analysis to learn what Latina/o parents needed to help their children learn math. Second, all communication was written in both Spanish and English. Third, workshops were scheduled at times when parents were able to attend them. Fourth, a lending library was established for parents to check out videotapes, which were available in Spanish and English, whenever they needed to review how to implement the activities. Activity booklets contained tasks and games that parents and children could do together to reinforce the mathematics that was learned at school. Fifth, workshops were provided to help teachers understand how to be culturally responsive to parents. Results of the CMWFC study show 90% of the students scored at grade level on computation and 65% scored at grade level on problem solving. However, actual gains cannot be determined because the researchers did not report baseline scores.

In another study conducted by Strutchens (2002), African American parents participated in a program called *Mathematics: Application and Reasoning Skills* (MARS) that was designed to improve the mathematics achievement of their children through literature connections. Strutchens' (2002) research focused on how multicultural literature faired as a central component of a literature/mathematics program. Adult–child pairs completed and created mathematical problems as they read literature about different cultural groups. Facilitators in the program asked probing questions and concurrently taught parents how to ask their children mathematical questions at home. Participants responded favorably and wanted to continue beyond the program's planned six weeks. As a result of the program, parents and children became more engaged in mathematics. At home, parents talked about mathematics concepts as they applied to practical and culturally relevant situations more often, and both parents and children opened lines of communication and learned to work more collaboratively. Both the De La Cruz (1999) and Strutchens (2002) studies show that collaboration with parents is important in reversing the trend of underachievement among ethnically diverse students.

Fostering native language literacy in the mathematics classroom

Several studies that make connections to children's cultural heritage have been conducted in mathematics (Brenner, 1998; Gutstein, 2003; Gutstein *et al.*, 1997;

Lipka et al., 2005). Gutstein et al. (1997) describes one study of culturally relevant teaching in a Mexican American school community. The purpose of the study was to develop a three-part model of culturally relevant teaching (CRT). As previously described in Chapter 3, CRT is a pedagogy that imparts knowledge, skills, and attitudes (Ladson-Billings, 1994). CRT allows students to see their values, culture, or history embedded in curriculum and/or activities. Moreover, it empowers teachers and students to change society, challenging the status quo (Ladson-Billings, 1994). The three components of the Gutstein et al. study (1997) consisted of: (a) building on students' cultural and experiential knowledge; (b) developing tools of critical mathematical thinking; and (c) orientations to students' culture and experience.

Teachers in the study used the context of social activism, a form of culture that defines social and political relationships (Hollins, 1996), to make connections to mathematics. Gutstein et al. (1997) found that culturally relevant teaching existed in practice and was consistent with the goals described in the *Professional Standards for Teaching Mathematics* (NCTM, 1991). However, in order to understand what culturally relevant teaching meant in Mexican American classrooms, Gutstein et al. (1997) explored teachers' beliefs and educational practices as they related to the following:

- The role of culture in curriculum and pedagogy.
- Notions of cultural competence, bilingualism, and biculturalism.
- Perspectives on families and community.
- Relationships of students viewing knowledge critically to their role in society.
- Conceptions of knowledge and the role of the teacher in knowledge construction.

(p. 717)

In order to build on students' knowledge, teachers need to find out what students know as a starting point from which to scaffold (Gutstein et al., 1997). Some teachers in the study viewed students' informal mathematical knowledge as a way of integrating student culture into the curriculum. For example, in one class, students studied the names and meanings of mathematical concepts in both Spanish and English (Gutstein et al., 1997). In terms of critical thinking, the teachers in this study did not simply approach critical thinking about mathematics from the standpoint of helping students to learn mathematics, but their approaches empowered students as they learned how to question authority and promote democratic practices in the classroom (Gutstein et al., 1997). Cultivation of a learning environment where positive orientations toward students' culture and experience were allowed to thrive encouraged the development of personal and social agency among Mexican American students. It is not enough to teach mathematics and science literacy for literacy's sake; linking the content to issues of social justice and civil rights has been found to increase the participation of under-served and underrepresented students in mathematics classrooms (Gutstein, 2003; Leonard & Hill, in press).

In an intensive study of one teacher's work with third-grade Latina/o students, Hufferd-Ackles *et al.* (2004) developed a framework that can be used to help teachers establish a discourse community in their mathematics class-rooms. The case study took place in a Catholic school located in a working-class neighborhood in the Midwest. It described the growth of one teacher, Ms. Martinez, who began the year using a more traditional form of mathe-matics instruction and the changes that took place as she and her 25 students interacted in a math-talk learning community (Hufferd-Ackles *et al.*, 2004). The main principles in the framework include questioning and explaining mathematical thinking. Using a developmental trajectory that consisted of four levels (Level 0 to 3), the researchers examined changes over time in Ms. Martinez's classroom.

Results of the study found that Ms. Martinez's use of questioning techniques grew from Level 0 to Level 3 over the course of the year as discourse patterns shifted from the teacher as the primary source of student questioning to stu-dents asking questions of their peers. Another change in questioning patterns was less emphasis on "questioning to find answers to a focus on questions to uncover the mathematical thinking behind the answers" (Hufferd-Ackles *et al.*, 2004, p. 92). Student explanations of mathematical thinking also grew over time as short exchanges that focused on answers only (Level 0) became more elabo-rate as students became accustomed to communicating their thinking. Student explanations reached Level 2 in such cases, but students still required prompts, probing, and assistance to clarify their thoughts (Hufferd-Ackles *et al.*, 2004). In order to move to the highest level (Level 3), students had to learn to take on more responsibility in the classroom. However, shifts in power and authority are not easy for students and teachers who are not accustomed to such practices (Bernhard & Freire, 1999; Lee, 2003).

Gutstein (2003) conducted a teacher-research study on his class of Latina/o seventh and eighth graders, highlighting the difficulties and successes of his efforts to get students to think critically about mathematics and to use their mathematical knowledge to address issues of social justice. Learning mathematics within a social justice context allows students to develop sociopolitical consciousness or conscientização (Freire, 1982), which is a necessary tool to fight for equity and social justice (Gutstein, 2003). Teaching for social justice allows students to develop a sense of personal and social agency and positive social and cultural identities that validate their language and culture (Gutstein, 2003; Martin, 2000).

Gutstein's study (2003) took place in an urban school where the vast majority of students were Mexican American. Ninety-eight percent of the students were poor by federal subsidized lunch standards. Fifty percent were born as first generation U.S. citizens and the other 50% were immigrants. All of the students but one were bilingual in Spanish and English. In Gutstein's classroom, mathematics became the vehicle to question relations of power such as inequitable resources, disparate opportunities, and discrimination based on race, class, gender, and language. Some of the issues students investigated included SAT data, housing data, and international wealth. Two students reported the following analyses to the class:

> In the U.S. Bill Gates holds more money than anybody else, but if you divide the wealth by population, Bill would probably have an average amount of money and a homeless [person] would have an average amount of wealth.
>
> (Gutstein, 2003, p. 50)

> Our family makes somewhere in the neighborhood of $40,000. I heard that Michael Jordan makes about $1,000 for every minute he plays. So that means that in 40 minutes he makes our whole family's earnings. While my family works year round for that money.
>
> (Gutstein, 2003, p. 50)

In addition to learning mathematics for social justice, the students in Gutstein's class also developed mathematical power, which was demonstrated by their success on tests, quizzes, projects, and assignments. Some students invented their own algorithms for solving word problems and were able to communicate their mathematical thinking and rationale to the class. Most importantly, all students passed their eighth-grade standardized assessments and were promoted to ninth grade. These data show that culturally based curricula that is connected to social justice not only increases opportunities for students of color but *can* improve poor urban students' mathematical achievement (Gutstein, 2003). The following quote summarizes the importance of using such curricula:

> The challenge we now face is how to create a curriculum filled with responsible social and political issues that will help students understand the complexity of such problems, help them develop and understand the role of mathematics in their resolution, and allow them, at the same time, to develop mathematical power.
>
> (Romberg as cited in Gutstein, 2003, p. 44)

Reflections of a mathematics educator

When I reflect on my own pedagogy in mathematics methods and doctoral mathematics education courses, I think about how I can use lessons learned from teaching and research to emphasize the importance of valuing diverse students, their families and cultures, and the cultural capital they bring to the classroom. I present these reflections in two parts: (1) reflections on practice and (2) reflections on research. In the first part, I present and discuss lessons learned from teaching one of my graduate-level mathematics methods courses. Electronic discourse that occurred between my students and me in an online course (fall 2002) forms the basis of my reflections on practice. Classroom discourse that took place among second-grade Latina/o students in an urban school in Philadelphia forms the basis of my reflections on classroom research as it relates to culturally and linguistically diverse students.

Reflections on practice

After the class read an article about issues of culture in teaching mathematics by Malloy & Malloy (1998), the following discussion took place. Seventeen students in Cohort 2 entered an hour-long online chat room: 13 females (nine White, two African American, one Hispanic, one Asian); four males (four White). The dialogue that arose is presented below in Vignette 7.1. Out of these 17 students, 13 actively participated in the discussion that took place. Two students did not participate because they had technical difficulties, and the other two students chose not to participate in this particular discussion. In order to maintain anonymity, the students are identified as Student 1, Student 2, and so forth. I simply identify myself as JL.

Vignette 7.1

1	*JL:*	What is culture?
2	*Student 1:*	When I hear the word culture, I think of roles, norms, values that individuals hold.
3	*Student 2:*	Culture is the things that surround you your entire life, your family, your religion, basically everything.
4	*Student 3:*	Culture [is] the different values and standards and ways of doing things we learn from our parents and community as we grow up. I think that culture is not the same as ability and intelligence.
5	*Student 4:*	Culture also influences our morals and values.
6	*Student 5:*	Culture is a way of life passed down from the people who raise you.
7	*Student 6:*	I agree with Student 1—culture is a variety of things—it is your family, beliefs, morals, etc.
8	*Student 7:*	Culture is a person's past and present in a hereditary sense, kept within a family and a social group.
9	*Student 8:*	Culture is both your family background and the community in which you live.

10	*JL:*	What does culture have to do with math?
11	*Student 8:*	People bring their culture with them wherever they go, including the math classroom.
12	*Student 4:*	Teachers need to take into consideration children's culture, language, experience, etc.
13	*Student 2:*	Different cultures have to be studied to understand that everyone is different but equal in the same …
14	*Student 1:*	Not just the math classroom, in every classroom.
15	*Student 3:*	Math is affected by culture in a way more limited than say learning Standard English.
16	*Student 6:*	Culture can affect the way students learn, and it is important to keep that in mind when teaching any subject in any classroom.
17	*Student 7:*	Math plays a different role in different cultures, but it's always there, in every culture.
18	*Student 8:*	Student 1, yes, every classroom.
19	*Student 3:*	Math often demands precise answers. Many Asian students can do this math without any knowledge of English or American culture.
20	*JL:*	What does Malloy say about culture and mathematics learning?
21	*Student 10:*	Minority students are not benefiting from how American education works … It's dynamic!
22	*Student 7:*	Malloy says that the majority of students will learn math better if they can learn it within the context of their own culture.
23	*Student 3:*	Malloy says that culture is very important to math. I think culture may be important in motivating students, but not in their intrinsic aptitude for math.
24	*JL:*	Student 3, why do you think that many Asian students can do the math? Isn't this just another stereotype?
25	*Student 11:*	I'm Asian, and I can't stand math!
26	*Student 1:*	Ya [sic] know—a child's learning math can be affected by the way the teacher treats the child in the classroom, especially if he is not from a similar culture as the majority of the students.
27:	*Student 11:*	The only reason math is difficult for me is because I wasn't taught the right way.
28	*Student 5:*	Those stereotypes put pressure on Asian children.
29	*JL:*	Student 3, why do you think some children have an intrinsic aptitude and others do not?
30	*Student 3:*	There are always exceptions, but the authors speak of groups, in this case, African Americans, even if individuals do not always fit the group average.

31	*Student 12:*	I think our definition of "culture" is too broad.
32	*Student 4:*	There are so many stereotypes out there. The reality is to treat each child as an individual and to recognize some barriers such as culture.
33	*Student 8:*	Not only different cultural backgrounds, but different learning styles ... sometimes connected to culture ...
34	*Student 3:*	People are different. Not everyone has the ability to do math in the same way. There are obvious differences for everyone including children because we are not all identical.
35	*Student 1:*	Teachers need to disregard the cultural differences, I guess, and treat everyone similar.
36	*Student 10:*	The article sounds like nice over-arching reasoning to get students to do better in math, but this needs to reach administration people. Those who create the standards, ehhh?
37	*Student 7:*	Some people have the aptitude to understand math no matter how it is taught, no matter what their culture. Unfortunately, these kids are the minority, and most need the teaching to relate to their reality.
38	*Student 13:*	There needs to be some student input about learning and learning styles.
39	*Student 7:*	What I got from the Malloy article is that teacher research and reflection is going to be a large part of teaching math in the future.
40	*Student 14:*	I would have liked some concrete examples of how to implement culturally sensitive math.
41	*Student 13:*	I agree, Student 14.
42	*Student 7:*	Me, too, Student 14.

Vignette 7.1 was analyzed and coded for themes and patterns using the Constant-Comparative Method (Glaser & Strauss, 1967). The dialogue that emerged in this vignette reveals these prospective and beginning teachers' attitudes, perceptions, and stereotypes. When I asked these novice teachers what culture had to do with math, the responses were consistent with Gay's (2000) concept of caring [lines 12 & 16]. A caring teacher is one who "is sensitive to, emotionally invested in, and attentive to the needs and interests" of his/her students (Gay, 2000, pp. 47–48). In addition, caring demands action on the part of the teacher [line 13]. Student 2 realized that some effort on the part of the teacher is required to get to know his/her students, which concurs with Nieto's (2002) challenge for teachers to become "students of their students" (p. 217).

However, one student's remark reveals a common stereotype: "Many Asian students can do this math without any knowledge of English or American culture" [line 19]. The comment advances the stereotype that Asian students are naturally gifted in mathematics regardless of language and cultural barriers. Stereotypes that presuppose certain types of students always excel in a particular subject are just as damaging as beliefs that certain types of students are more likely to fail that subject. Moreover, such stereotypes may place a tremendous amount of pressure on students of a particular race or ethnic group [line 28]. Furthermore, as indicated by Student 11's response [line 25], these stereotypes may influence negative attitudes from members of a particular group about the subject they are supposed to excel in. As a mathematics educator, I became more aware of the negative aspects of positive stereotypes as a result of this online discussion.

Finally, when I prompted students to reflect on what Malloy had to say about culture and mathematics learning, I received several responses. Two responses dealt with the importance of using students' culture as a context for learning mathematics [lines 22 & 24]. Two students' comments focused on learning styles [lines 33 & 38]. Another comment revealed that some prospective and beginning teachers believed in the colorblind approach to diversity [line 35]. However, the colorblind approach has a tendency to marginalize students because it assumes "culture is a barrier" [line 32]. In other words, being different is viewed as a deficit. This view led one prospective teacher to state, "Teachers need to disregard … cultural differences" [line 35]. While the colorblind approach appears to be equitable, it is really detrimental. "Children made 'invisible' … become hard-pressed to see themselves worthy of notice" (Delpit, 1995, p. 177). Advocates of diversity pedagogy suggest that differences should be celebrated (Sheets, 2005).

In summary, the comments of Students 7 and 14 underscore the purpose for this text. Irvine (1992) acknowledges that limited research on effective pedagogy is partly responsible for teachers' inability to effectively teach students of color. While a great deal of emphasis has been placed on how to implement standards-based instruction, little has been done to prepare prospective teachers to utilize sociocultural and sociopolitical practices in their classrooms (Kitchen, 2007). Teacher research and reflection are a huge part of learning to teach mathematics. Concrete examples of culturally specific mathematics activities need to be studied and shared with other teachers in the field.

Since 2001, I have applied a social reconstructionist orientation in preparing preservice teachers to employ equitable and just practices in their classrooms (Leonard & Dantley, 2005). However, I have more recently come to believe that teachers also need to understand the sociopolitical aspect of teaching. "A sociopolitical context considers the issues of *power* and includes discussions of structured inequality based on stratification due to race, social class, gender, ethnicity, and other differences" (Nieto, 2002, p. 56). Helping prospective teachers become more aware of their own culture and how it influences their pedagogy is a necessary step to transformation (Nieto, 2000 & 2002; Price & Valli, 1998; Sleeter, 1997).

Reflections on classroom research

The following vignette was obtained from a portion of a transcribed mathematics lesson taught by a Latina/o teacher of 26 ELLs in an urban school in Philadelphia. The school had a special relationship with Temple University because it was a Professional Development School (PDS) (Leonard et al., 2004). The teacher was Puerto Rican, and many of the students were also Puerto Rican and bilingual. Only one student spoke very little English. In order to ascertain the mathematical needs of teachers and students in the PDS, I observed the Latina/o classroom in March 2002 as part of a pilot study. The warm-up problem, which came from the mathematics series, involved interpreting data and completing a bar graph. For anonymity the teacher is simply referred to as Ms. Lopez (pseudonym), and the students are referred to as Student 1, Student 2, etc.

Vignette 7.2

1	*Ms. Lopez:*	You're going to be reading the problem of the day. Go ahead, Student 1.
2	*Student 1:*	Make a bar graph from the data. Tally to show which flavor of ice cream is …
3	*Ms. Lopez:*	What do we have to do? Read it again. Student 2, what do they want us to do?
4	*Student 2:*	They want to know how many children like chocolate better than vanilla. Do they want us to show how many children like chocolate better than vanilla?
5	*Ms. Lopez:*	Yes. What do they want us to do, Student 3?
6	*Student 3:*	They want us to make a bar graph and show how many people chose chocolate rather than vanilla.
7	*Ms. Lopez:*	What do they want us to do, Student 4?
8	Inaudible.	
9	*Ms. Lopez:*	Student 3, can you come up and [show] us the words that tell us what we are going to do. Find the words that tell us what we're going to do.
10	*Student 3:*	[Goes to overhead and underlines the directions.]
11	*Ms. Lopez:*	Student 3 did an excellent job. She underlined the words that tell us what we have to do. Can you read the words she underlined?
12	*Students:*	Make a bar graph.
13	*Ms. Lopez:*	What do we have to do, Student 5?
14	*Student 5:*	Make a bar graph.
15	*Ms. Lopez:*	What do we have to do, Student 6?
16	*Student 6:*	Make a bar graph.

17	*Ms. Lopez:*	We have to make a bar graph. Look at the information, Student 7. Student 2.
18	*Student 2:*	How many kids like to play hide and go seek?
19	*Ms. Lopez:*	No, not play hide and go seek. You didn't read your information. Student 8.
20	*Student 8:*	Who likes different flavor?
21	*Ms. Lopez:*	What flavors do we have up there?
22	*Students:*	Chocolate and vanilla.
23	*Ms. Lopez:*	So we're going to take the information on the tally and we're going to change it into a bar graph. What information are we going to put on the bar graph? Before we do a tally, who can tell us how many children like chocolate ice cream?
24	*Students:*	Nine.
25	*Ms. Lopez:*	Yes, nine children liked chocolate. Who can tell us how many children like vanilla? Student 9.
26	*Student 9:*	Six.
27	*Ms. Lopez:*	Very good. So you read the tally very clearly. Now I'm going to set up a bar graph. I'm going to set it up for you and we're going to make it a vertical bar graph. We've been doing horizontal bar graphs, but we're going to do a vertical bar graph. Now to make it easier to read, I'm going to write the numbers right next to it. It would be a 1, 2 ... You can count with me ... 3, 4, 5, 6, 7, 8. Will this be enough?
28	*Students:*	No!
29	*Ms. Lopez:*	Why not? How many more should we have, Student 2?
30	*Student 2:*	One.
31	*Ms. Lopez:*	What shall we put in the first column?
32	*Students:*	Chocolate.
33	*Ms. Lopez:*	What shall we put in the second column?
34	*Students:*	Vanilla.
35	*Ms. Lopez:*	How many boxes do we need to color in the chocolate column? Student 2.
36	*Student 2:*	Nine.
37	*Ms Lopez:*	How many boxes in the vanilla column?
38	*Student 2:*	Six. [Goes to the overhead and colors in the bar.]
39	*Ms. Lopez:*	Good job, Student 2. Now do you want to come up and do vanilla, Student 10?
40	*Student 10:*	[Goes to overhead and completes the bar graph.]
41	*Ms. Lopez:*	Yes. Now what information were we going to put on our bar graph? Student 11.
42	*Student 11:*	And six people liked vanilla.
43	*Ms. Lopez:*	Good job. Now let's do our quick review.

An analysis of Vignette 7.2 shows that it follows the traditional IRE pattern of communication found in most U.S. classrooms (Cazden, 2001). However, some of the teaching strategies used by Ms. Lopez can serve as a model for teachers of Second Language Learners (L2). On two separate occasions, Ms. Lopez made sure the students understood the mathematical task [lines 3, 5, 7, 9, 11, 13, 15, & 23]. The initial directions to make a bar graph were given seven times. Moreover, she did not teach primarily by telling students what to do and asking them to repeat it. The students explained what it was they were supposed to do [lines 2, 4, 6, 10, 12, & 14].

Furthermore, Ms. Lopez involved 42% of the students in solving one mathematics problem. Students used complete sentences to respond to Ms. Lopez's queries 50% of the time. Three students went to the overhead to underline information or shade in the bars. However, Ms. Lopez called on Student 2 five times (four directly and one indirectly). It is unclear whether Student 2 needed additional practice, since he did have a miscue early on in the activity [lines 18 & 19] or whether he was one of the leaders in the class. It is possible that the teacher called on him more after the miscue to allow him to rebuild his self-esteem.

Ms. Lopez was explicit with the students about the task they were going to perform. When Student 2 asked a question about the task, her response was a resounding, "Yes." When he miscued, she was also explicit. Ms. Lopez not only said, "No," but elaborated on the cause of the miscue stating: "You didn't read your information" [line 19]. Getting and understanding the information is very important in linguistically and culturally diverse classrooms (Delpit, 1995; Nieto, 2002). Moreover, she focused on words that conveyed meaning as well as reading in this short exercise. Mathematics vocabulary was emphasized repeatedly throughout the activity: bar (15), graph (13), tally (4), vertical (2), and horizontal (1). Ms. Lopez also scaffolded the students' learning by drawing the graph that needed to be shaded on the overhead and involved the students by having them count along with her as she drew the graph.

The types of questions Ms. Lopez asked were also analyzed. She asked ten questions directly related to the graph [lines 21, 23, 25, 27, 29, 31, 33, 35, 37, & 41], but all of the responses except one were single-word answers. In addition to these lower-order questions, Ms. Lopez asked one higher-order question: "Why not?" However, she did not provide the wait time for students to answer the question. Allowing students to explain their mathematical reasoning helps children to develop mathematical power (Gutstein, 2003; Hufferd-Ackles *et al.*, 2004).

While Ms. Lopez's mathematics task was not culturally specific, it was culturally relevant since most of the students are familiar with ice cream and probably have a favorite. To personalize the activity for the students, Ms. Lopez could have surveyed the students to see what their favorite flavors of ice cream were and then allowed them to draw their own graph (with either vertical or horizontal bars) to show their work. Yet, Ms. Lopez's warm-up problem can be use as a model to show prospective teachers how to involve several students in an activity, ensure that students know what to do, engage children in verbal, auditory, and kinesthetic tasks, and build mathematics vocabulary. It can also be used to demonstrate the importance of questioning to help students develop mathematical thinking and reasoning. "Language is a tool for thought" (Sheets, 2005, p. 106), but mathematics can only become a universal language when everyone is empowered to understand it, use it to communicate mathematical meaning, and apply it in their everyday lives.

8
Race and achievement in mathematics

Our lives begin to end the day we become silent about things that matter.

Rev. Dr. Martin Luther King, Jr.

A historical perspective

The underachievement of students of color, African American students in particular, has a long history and continues to promote a great deal of debate. From a theory of lower intelligence such as that proposed in the *Bell Curve* (Herrnstein & Murray, 1994) to cultural deficit theory (Coleman, 1987; Jensen, 1969), some have tried to explain achievement differences in terms of what they believe is lacking among students of color. Others have examined social conditions such as poverty (Knapp, 1995; Kozol, 1995), inequitable school funding (Imazeki & Reschovsky, 2006; Kozol, 1991), and low teacher expectations (Irvine, 1991; Rist, 1970) as factors that contribute to under-achievement. In addition, Black scholars like Boykin & Toms (1985) describe the influence of cultural differences on Blacks' enculturation and assimilation in school. More recently, it has been argued that some African American students are disengaged and unmotivated to learn because of sociohistorical, community, school, and individual factors (Martin, 2000 & 2003; Ogbu, 2003). Needless to say, underachievement among students of color is complex and undeniably rooted in a system of inadequate schooling.

After slavery was abolished in 1863, public schools were established to educate Blacks throughout the South (Du Bois, 1903/1995). However, these *sharecropper* schools were inferior in terms of facilities and resources (Du Bois, 1903/1995; Moses & Cobb, 2001). When the renowned *Plessy* v. *Ferguson* case was brought forth to challenge segregation, the U.S. Supreme Court ruled in 1896 that separate but equal accommodations were constitutional. For 58 years, this ruling was applied to many aspects of American life to legally segregate Blacks from Whites. During that time period, most Blacks and Whites did not attend school together. It was not until the 1954 ruling of *Brown* v. *Board* that de facto segregation in schools was ruled unconstitutional.

The impact of *Brown* v. *Board* has been characterized in two waves (Tillman, 2004). During the first wave (1954–1963), attempts to integrate schools in the South were met with strong resistance by Whites (Fine, 2004). In 1957, the governor of Arkansas used the National Guard to block the Little Rock Nine from attending high school. In response, President Eisenhower sent federal troops to enforce court-ordered integration. In 1958, nine schools in four Virginia counties closed to avoid desegregation (Fine, 2004). In addition, Black schools were forced to close and Black administrators and teachers lost their jobs in droves (Tillman, 2004). These events created mistrust among African American parents who found it difficult to believe that school boards were acting in their children's best interest (Fine, 2004; Tillman, 2004). Nevertheless, the *Brown* decision brought an end to de jure apartheid in America's schools (Fine, 2004).

During the second wave (1964–present), reaction to *Brown* v. *Board* took on a different form. In response to the law, southern school districts published gaps in the test scores of Black and White students to justify their opposition to desegregation (Ogbu, 2003). The reaction of some Whites in the South and in the North was *white flight.* Urban public schools began to lose White students as White families moved to the suburbs or sent their children to private or religious schools (Fine, 2004). Instead of dismantling racial injustice and creating a system that provided quality education for advantaged and disadvantaged students alike, Black children were bused to White schools as a means to achieve racial integration (Fine, 2004).

Harmon (2002) described the experiences of gifted African American students who were bused to predominantly White schools in the Midwest during this time period. Two fourth-grade and four fifth-grade students were interviewed about their experiences. The African American students who were bused from urban Tacoma Elementary School to suburban Rocky Creek Elementary School, which was predominantly White, stated they were called names and harassed by White students on the bus as they rode to and from school. Moreover, these students reported disparate treatment by some teachers at Rocky Creek, stating "they won't teach us" (Harmon, 2002, p. 71).

The African Americans who participated in Harmon's study claimed they were placed in lower ability groups and given less challenging work compared to White students. African American students stated teachers at Rocky Creek did not explain concepts in a manner that they could understand. Moreover, these students claimed these teachers did not attempt to teach concepts in a culturally responsive way nor did they use visual or tactile methods of teaching during instruction (Harmon, 2002). African American students were simply told what to do and expected to sit still and follow directions. While their predominantly African American home school certainly had fewer resources and less modern facilities, the teachers at Tacoma cared for, accepted, and supported the children within a safe learning environment

(Harmon, 2002). Likewise, elders who were students in schools when the *Brown* decision was handed down reported their all-Black schools, while under funded, were "culture-rich, academically rigorous, and family-strong" (Fine, 2004, p. 504).

Such experiences lead one to ask: Were there any benefits to busing as a means of desegregation? One of the longest continuous voluntary school desegregation programs took place in Boston, Massachusetts (Schofield, 2001). The Metropolitan Council for Educational Opportunity (METCO) facilitated the enrollment of African American students from Boston schools in 32 suburban communities (Schofield, 2001). Eaton (2001), author of *The Other Boston Busing Story*, interviewed 65 adults about their experiences in the METCO program. Like the students at Rocky Creek, METCO students relived feelings of alienation and invisibleness when they were interviewed about their experiences (Schofield, 2001). However, some participants reported the METCO experience was valuable because it provided them with the opportunity to become familiar with "the world of power and privilege in the suburbs, which enabled them to overcome their fears of such settings and to make informed decisions" (Schofield, 2001, p. 386). In other words, these students were able to learn the dominant Discourses, which allow one to have greater access to people, power, prestige, money, and status (Gee, 1989).

Today, some believe schools are more segregated than they were prior to *Brown v. Board* (Fine, 2004; Tillman, 2004). More than 50 years later, the majority of African American children still attend racially and economically segregated schools. Public schools remain highly segregated along racial and social class lines because the neighborhoods that feed students to local schools remain highly segregated (Ogbu, 2003). Moreover, state and local policies that rely mostly on the use of property taxes to fund schools result in disparate school funding for property-poor segregated schools (Kozol, 1991).

I realized the depth of this disparity when I observed three early childhood classes in an affluent suburb in southern New Jersey on January 12, 2007. All three teachers observed were White. In the morning, I observed a first-grade teacher use a SMART board during a language arts lesson with 21 students (18 White, two Asian, and one African American). Clipart pictures of objects that contained the "sh" sound were shown on the SMART board. The teacher called on students to determine how to group the pictures based on where the sound occurred in a word: beginning, middle or end.

In the afternoon, I observed a kindergarten class of 17 students (11 White, three Asian, and three African American). The children went to the computer lab to engage in a computer-based reading activity. Each student put on a headset as two different stories were read aloud to them on the computer. Then they selected another feature of the program that allowed them to read the story for themselves. If the students needed help, they could click on the entire sentence or a specific word, and the computer would read the sentence or the word for the students.

Near the end of the day, another kindergarten teacher used an LCD projector to show a PowerPoint slideshow about Rev. Dr. Martin Luther King, Jr., since the following Monday would be the King holiday. She said, "Martin Luther King, Jr. was a great man who had a dream or idea that everyone should be treated fairly. He wanted students to be able to go to school wherever they wanted and for people to be able to shop wherever they wanted." At that juncture, I looked around the room of predominantly White middle-class kindergarten students and realized how much they still benefited from the current system of school funding and White privilege. The level of technology used at this school surpassed any that I had seen in North Philadelphia schools where mostly poor students of color attend. While what the teacher said about Dr. Martin Luther King's dream of racial equality and social justice was comforting, the truth is that everyone cannot go to school or shop where they want. Rapper Nelly was barred by security guards from shopping at Union Station in his home town of St. Louis because of his attire. The Union Station dress code, which bars customers wearing *do-rags* and other hip-hop attire from shopping in the mall, raises the question of whether such policies were adopted with the intention of preventing young Black males from shopping at exclusive malls (Benfer, 2002). Unfortunately, more than 40 years after Dr. King's *I Have a Dream* speech, parents of poor African American students have limited school choice, and their children attend apartheid schools where they are, for the most part, grossly underserved (Kozol, 2005).

Litigation such as *Edgewood* v. *Kirby* (1989) exposed the effect of inequitable school funding on the education of poor students in San Antonio, Texas (Imazeki & Reschovsky, 2006; Kozol, 1991). As a result, attention became focused on providing students with equal access to an *adequate* education. However, exactly what adequate means remains the subject of debate and litigation. Imazeki and Reschovsky (2006) examined the school funding issue in Texas to determine the impact of state funding policies on student achievement. Texas reformed its formula for funding schools in the 1990s with a plan that was dubbed "Robin Hood" (Imazeki & Reschovsky, 2006). In essence, less money was given to property-rich school districts while more money was given to property-poor districts. Although property-poor school districts began spending as much as $1,000 more per pupil, it was not enough to improve the educational performance of African American, Hispanic, and poor students (Imazeki & Reschovsky, 2006). Despite great strides to improve funding for Texas school districts, underfunded districts remain and are more likely to be large urban districts that consist of poor, minority, and Limited English Proficient students. Even if funding were equal, data imply that it will cost more than average to improve achievement in the lowest performing districts. "It is impossible to expect both equal outcomes *and* equal dollar allocations" (Imazeki & Reschovsky, 2006, p. 31). In November 2005, the Texas Supreme Court ruled in *Neeley* v. *West-Orange Cove* that the current funding system in Texas is unconstitutional (Imazeki & Reschovsky, 2006).

Although school funding is an important factor in the education of poor and minority students, what happens in urban classrooms is even more critical. No Child Left Behind (NCLB, 2001) legislation has spawned a great deal of rhetoric about "highly qualified" teachers and the importance of teacher quality on student achievement. However, policymakers and researchers are divided over exactly what highly qualified means and how to produce teachers who meet the standards of NCLB (Viadero, 2005). This policy underscores the importance of teachers' practice and subject-matter knowledge. Students in high-poverty schools are more likely to be taught by teachers who do not have sufficient knowledge of the subjects they teach (Haycock, 2001). Teacher practices in urban classrooms have a direct impact on student achievement in general and mathematics achievement in particular.

Haberman (1991) identified the following teacher practices, which he characterized as a basic urban style of teaching:

- Giving information
- Asking questions
- Giving directions
- Making assignments
- Monitoring seatwork
- Reviewing assignments
- Giving tests
- Reviewing tests
- Assigning homework
- Settling disputes
- Punishing non-compliance
- Marking papers
- Giving grades.

(p. 290)

While taken separately, Haberman (1991) admits these activities may not be deleterious. However, taken together and performed systematically to the exclusion of other activities, such as cooperative learning, inquiry-based instruction, and project-based learning, they constitute what Haberman (1991) calls the pedagogy of poverty. Teachers who attempt to go against the grain may be considered deviant and may even experience resistance from the students themselves, who may become accustomed to routine procedures and conceptualize learning as engagement in text-based activities (Haberman, 1991; Martin, 2000; Ogbu, 2003). Yet, such practices do not lead to higher academic achievement and stagnate the learning of above-average and gifted students (Haberman, 1991; Harmon, 2002).

Notions about the "achievement gap" continue to spark a great deal of debate. Cognitive, cultural, sociohistorical, community (roles of peers, parents, and community members), and institutional factors (school finance, school choice, roles of administrators and teachers) are reasons cited for underachievement among students of color (Boykin & Toms, 1985; Kozol, 1991; Martin, 2000; Ogbu, 2003). However, few research studies examine what students and parents themselves have to say about underachievement (Martin, 2000; Ogbu, 2003; Taylor, 2004). The next section synthesizes data and findings from two research studies that examine the perspectives of students and parents on underachievement in general. That section is then followed by data and findings from another research study on the perspectives of parents and students on underachievement in mathematics.

Perspectives on the achievement gap

While few researchers have conducted investigations that report what African American parents and students themselves think about the achievement gap (Ford, 1993; Martin, 2000; Ogbu, 2003), former teacher, administrator, and executive of two large urban school districts, Kay Lovelace Taylor (2004), presents a thoughtful treatise on the national achievement gap. She acknowledges that African Americans are performing below other ethnic groups on national assessments in reading and mathematics. Taylor (2004) offers an interesting approach, posing the following question to high-school students, graduate students, parents, and educators across the country: "What do you think is the number one reason African American children do not score as high as other ethnic groups?" (p. 2).

Taylor analyzed how high-school students, parents, and teachers responded to her question, noting both differences and similarities in their responses. As a result of these interviews, five barriers to academic success emerged: (1) student behaviors, (2) lack of parent and family support, (3) teacher behaviors, (4) school culture, and (5) community and environmental issues. Graduate students responded that students, teachers, and parents were to blame in part for the achievement gap. Teachers in the study were less willing to critically examine their role in the achievement gap and generally blamed parents and students for underachievement. Because student and parent perceptions are underreported in the literature, I have chosen to focus on Taylor's analysis of student and parent interviews.

African American students, ironically, "identified themselves as a part of the problem and the solution to poor academic achievement" (Taylor, 2004, p. 23). African American students identified lack of motivation, lack of focus, poor study habits, and simply not applying themselves as factors that contribute to their underachievement. Furthermore, peer pressure caused some students not to ask for directions or help in class even when they needed it from the teacher. Moreover, these high-school students believed their parents were too lax because they did not ask about homework, help with homework, or inquire about their grades. In addition, students faulted some teachers for giving unchallenging work and others for covering material at too fast a pace. Finally, students admitted they received mixed messages about school from their community. What students needed to survive on the streets was very different from what they were learning in school. Certain community elements sent students the message that achieving in school was synonymous with "acting White" while underachieving was considered "cool" (Taylor, 2004, p. 30).

The "acting White" concept is not new. Ogbu (1987 & 2003) suggests that internalization of the belief that Blacks are less intelligent than Whites translates into the belief that White students should succeed academically but Black students should not. As a result of internalized oppression (Ogbu, 2003), conflicting theories on school socialization and enculturation (Boykin & Toms, 1985; Gay, 2000; Stiff & Harvey, 1988), and the disconnect between African American culture and school culture (Banks, 2001; Diller, 1999), some African American students have come to believe that doing well in school is giving in to the status quo (Martin, 2000). The belief becomes even more of a dilemma when average, above average, and gifted African American students receive too little administrative and teacher support when they are harassed by underachieving peers (Martin, 2000).

Surprisingly, Taylor (2004) also found that parents held themselves responsible for African American students' underachievement. Parents noted lack of communication with their children as one problem. Some parents also stated they were ambivalent about helping their children with homework because they did not understand the subject matter or they had reading difficulties. Furthermore, several parents mentioned that they were often too tired to help their children after getting home from work and simply resigned the education of their children over to teachers (Williams & Leonard, 2004). In general, parents felt that society's low expectation of African American children was a huge part of the problem and believed lower expectations caused their children to have low self-esteem. Coupled with inadequate school resources and low teacher expectations, many of the parents who were interviewed were simply overwhelmed.

One parent shared his/her emotions after a parent conference: "You feel like you are failing in school all over again, even though you are there to talk about your child" (Taylor, 2004, p. 45). This comment is not only poignant but also very telling. Schools, by and large, have been failing to educate generations of African American students (Du Bois, 1903/1995). If the school has failed to educate the parent, how can the parent help the child? Moreover, how can either the parent or the child trust the educational system to do its job when it has failed so miserably in the past? Negative school experiences create a cycle of underachievement that is extremely difficult to break.

In a second study, Ogbu (2003) examined academic disengagement among African American students attending school in an affluent Ohio suburb. While parents of students in Shaker Heights were more likely to be involved in their children's education and to help them with homework, Ogbu (2003) found that African American students, as a whole, were still not performing up to their potential. School practices such as low teacher expectations, leveling, and disproportionate representations of Blacks in special education, reinforce the belief that Black students are not capable. The perception that Black students who perform well are "exceptional" continues to reinforce the stereotype that being Black and smart is abnormal (Ogbu, 2003, p. 85). A myriad of reasons was given by students for the "low-effort syndrome" described in the study (Ogbu, 2003, p. 17). Several reasons cited by students for their academic underperformance included: (1) lack of motivation; (2) norm of minimum effort; (3) "it's not cool" to work hard or show you are smart; (4) poor study habits; (5) poor teachers; and (6) boring or uninteresting courses.

Although the socioeconomic status of the students interviewed by Taylor (2004) and Ogbu (2003) was very different, student perceptions about low academic achievement overlap in both studies: lack of motivation, poor study habits, and the belief that underachieving was considered "cool" and achieving was considered "acting White". These perceptions reveal that underachievement among African American students is very complex. While one may be motivated by extrinsic rewards and study habits can be taught, how does one change African American student beliefs about academic success, especially in mathematics? Beliefs about achievement in general and mathematics achievement in particular, though influenced by external forces such as peers and community values, are intrinsic rather than extrinsic (Becker & Luthar, 2002; Ford, 1993; Martin, 2000). Therefore, an examination of African American students' mathematics identity and mathematics socialization add to the discussion about African American achievement.

Mathematics socialization and identity among African American students

Martin (2000) conducted a qualitative study on African American students' achievement and persistence in mathematics in Oakland, California. He used a multilevel framework to describe and analyze mathematics socialization and identity among African American students. He believed by investigating mathematics socialization and identity new understandings about success and failure among African American students in mathematics would explain their underachievement. Like Taylor (2004), Martin wanted to know why African American students, as a group, had low performance in mathematics. Martin (2000) asked the following question:

Why is it that despite increased demands for those who possess mathematics-related skills and knowledge, significant advances in educational theory, and calls for higher educational standards, African-Americans continue to experience their mathematics educations in ways that place them at or near the bottom on all measures of achievement and persistence?

(p. 9)

After interviewing four parents, Martin found that socioeconomic and educational experiences caused two participants to diminish the value of mathematical knowledge in their own and their children's lives. In the other two cases, parental experiences were a motivating factor to revisit obtaining mathematical knowledge for their own as well as their children's benefit. One African American male interviewee provides an alarming perception of mathematics education:

I only indulged myself in my studies to the degree that I was satisfied that I could do math up to multiplication and division of fractions and decimals and that was good enough for me for what I was going to do. I wasn't going to be doing any math. To be a laborer, all it's going to require is to run a piece of machinery.

(Martin, 2000, p. 42)

We don't have no industry out there and the industry that is out there, they're not targeting the Black community and saying, "If you go and get more math, then I can guarantee you this."

(Martin, 2000, p. 45)

I have hopes. My expectation is that (my son) will graduate from high school. If he doesn't, it's no big deal … My expectation for him is to probably be no worse than I was. Just to pass.

(Martin, 2000, p. 46)

Certainly, the norm of minimum effort and the low-expectation syndrome described by Ogbu (2003) is evident in the above parent's response to questions about his effort in school and his hopes for his son. However, the data also suggest that past discrimination and racism continue to have an impact on families as parental attitudes and values are often passed on to their children. The comment about industry providing incentives is an interesting one. The outsourcing of jobs overseas does not send marginalized communities the message that persons of color will be recruited to fill the high-tech jobs that largely go unfilled (Moses & Cobb, 2001). Moses and Cobb (2001) argue that a culture of mathematics literacy needs to operate in the African American community to the same extent as church culture does. But how to create that culture and provide support for African American students who choose to achieve and persist in mathematics without guaranteed employment is another dilemma.

Knowledge is power and mathematical literacy opens the door of opportunity. The demand for workers with high-tech skills is expected to be more than 1.3 million in this decade (Moses & Cobb, 2001). These jobs require knowledge of mathematics and technology. Employees in high-tech fields can earn 82% more than workers in other fields (Moses & Cobb, 2001). Industry needs to target diverse populations living in the U.S. with incentives to motivate them to achieve in mathematics and compete for the high-tech jobs that are available. Mathematics literacy and mathematics achievement lead to higher education and economic empowerment.

Martin's impetus for conducting a study about successful African American students' mathematics achievement was the paucity of such studies in the research literature (Brown & Boshamer, 2000; Leonard *et al.*, 2005; Malloy & Jones, 1998; Martin, 2000). Martin conducted a case study at Hillside School in Oakland. He observed middle-school teachers and students in three mathematics classrooms. The teachers were diverse in terms of ethnicity and gender. Two were identified as persons of color, and one was female. The curriculum used at the school during the time of the study was the *Algebra Project*. The reform-based curriculum included activities that required students to discuss, draw diagrams, and participate in cooperative learning.

Martin (2000) found that sometimes students did well and were highly engaged in the activities. However, on other occasions, students were off-task, stated they were bored, and apparently uninterested in the curriculum and materials. The comments of two students offer some insight:

> ... math is basically where you're adding things, and subtraction, and dividing. I don't think that in math you're drawing pictures. That's for art.
>
> (Carl, seventh grade) (Martin, 2000, p. 103)

> ... I like doing work out of the math book. I like doing math. I don't like writing.
>
> (Sheneka, seventh grade) (Martin, 2000, p. 103)

Despite the use of a reform-based curriculum, many students did not recognize it as mathematics. This dilemma points to the need for systematic curriculum reform at the elementary level (K—6). Unless all teachers of mathematics engage in reform-based activities, it will be difficult to change student conceptions of mathematics. Student achievement in mathematics does not occur within a vacuum. Curriculum, teacher behaviors, and teacher and student conceptions about mathematics must be in sync for significant change to occur.

In addition to making classroom observations, Martin interviewed 35 middle-school students. However, seven target students were selected for further study. Five of these students were female and two were male. Of this number, two were in seventh grade, three were in eighth grade, and two were in ninth grade. Their GPAs ranged from 3.33 to 4.0 during the year of the study. Some of the interesting themes and patterns that emerged across these interviews reveal startling facts about the students' mathematics socialization and identity.

In terms of mathematics socialization, all of the students believed learning mathematics was important and necessary to achieving their life goals. These views are illustrated in the students' responses to interview questions about learning math:

If I want to be a doctor or an engineer. It'd be good to already have [math] under your belt.
(Annette, eighth grade) (Martin, 2000, p. 144)

[Math] gets you into college. If you don't know it, you aren't going to be able to get a good job like computers or something. So, I feel I have to take it.
(Melody, ninth grade) (Martin, 2000, p. 155)

Jobs. You cannot go anywhere or do anything in this world without using math.
(Jasmine, seventh grade) (Martin, 2000, p. 160)

These students realized that knowing mathematics would not only help them gain access to higher education but that mathematics knowledge was extremely important in careers like medicine, engineering, and computer science. One student even realized that mathematics literacy was important to one's existence and survival. Such perspectives caused these students to excel and persist in mathematics.

Yet, while all of these students were high achievers, their experiences and perceptions about the school and their peers were not uniform. Lisa (eighth grade) and Paulette (ninth grade) described themselves are hardworking and intelligent. However, Annette (eighth grade) was competitive and wanted to be the best. Terrell (eighth grade) worked hard because he wanted to succeed, but he kept his grades up to continue playing hockey. Melody (ninth grade) and Carl (seventh grade) always liked school, but Melody was also motivated because she wanted a better life. Jasmine (seventh grade) was outgoing and confident in mathematics but found her mathematics class boring and unchallenging.

Other differences among these students were their perceptions about the school and underachieving students. In general, the girls were much more critical of the school and the students than the two males. Paulette believed the school was violent, and Melody would not recommend it to anyone. Lisa believed most of the students did not care about school, and Melody thought the kids were rowdy. Jasmine simply said, "They're bad" (Martin, 2000, p. 158). However, Carl was the most positive about the school stating, "I would describe it as good" (Martin, 2000, p. 162). Terrell admitted the school had a bad reputation but claimed, "The school is better than what people say it is" (Martin, 2000, p. 147). Carl and Terrell were critical of student behaviors but not the students themselves.

The children, I think they need better behavior ...
(Carl, seventh grade) (Martin, 2000, p. 162)

A lot of them care but it's just that a lot of them don't have that will to want to do it.
(Terrell, eighth grade) (Martin, 2000, p. 147)

Terrell's response shows his neutrality despite being criticized by some of his peers because he played hockey, which they claimed was a White sport. In fact, all seven of the target students reported that they experienced differential treatment by their peers. High-achieving students at the school in Oakland were often called geeks and nerds. Some of these students handled this situation by limiting their associations to other high-achieving students.

While all of their stories are different, these students demonstrated strength of character, resilience, and individual agency (Martin, 2000). Their dreams and aspirations were more powerful than negative peer pressure. Lisa's motivation was not only personal, but she wanted to become somebody successful in order to show others that African Americans were intelligent. Moreover, she wanted to give back to the community by becoming a teacher to show the next generation what they could become by her example. These students' comments suggest that development of mathematics socialization and identity are critical to success in mathematics.

Links to everyday mathematics

In order to help African American children develop mathematics socialization and identity, they must realize that mathematics may be found in many aspects of African American life and culture. Examples of mathematics and culture can be found in art. Mathematics and art can be integrated to help children observe different geometric patterns found in artifacts such as sculpture, paintings, prints, and posters (Chappell & Thompson, 2000; Leonard, 2001a). Students can use patterns and shapes to create their own tessellations (artistic patterns often found in tile and mosaics). These activities are not only fun but help students to develop and value their artistic talent while understanding the importance of mathematics.

Furthermore, nail salons, beauty shops, and barbershops are stable businesses that many students of color can identify with. Mathematics can be seen in patterns on sculptured nails, in hair braiding, and designer haircuts, respectively. The patterns and designs that are formed on sculptured nails and in hair styles can be examined from a geometric perspective. The list of prices found at these establishments provides teachers and parents with a source to develop culturally relevant mathematics problems for children to solve. For example, natural hair salons such as Duafe in Philadelphia offer a menu of ethnic hair styles: cornrows, coils, palm rolls, flat braids, two-strand twists, and locks. Teachers and parents can pose problems such as comparing the costs of maintaining a certain style over time and finding what percentage of a monthly budget is spent on hair care.

Mathematics can also be learned by participating in games like dominoes (Nasir, 2002), chess (Thomas-El, 2003), and sports. The game of dominoes, which appeals to both children and adults, is complex, and players must learn to handle addition and multiplication to keep track of scoring. The participants' identity as a participant in the game is shaped by the shared history and experience of all of the players (Nasir, 2002). Similar to those who call themselves ballers—men with high status, expensive possessions, or athletic ability—players develop an identity as they demonstrate their ability to challenge and compete with others (Nasir, 2002). Moreover, the game of chess requires the knowledge of the hierarchical roles of bishops, rooks, and knights as well as logic to win. The sport of track and field can also be used to help children learn mathematics. Students learn the value of decimals as they experience how tenths and hundredths of a second make the difference in winning or losing a race.

Conclusions and recommendations

After giving considerable thought to the work of Ladson-Billings (2006), Martin (2000), Ogbu (2003), Taylor (2004) and others, I believe two factors perpetuate underachievement among students of color: generational underachievement and institutional barriers to academic success. Generational underachievement is exacerbated by past discrimination and economic constraints. As a result of racial discrimination, Blacks living in the South received an inferior education that often culminated at the eighth grade (Du Bois, 1903/1995; Moses & Cobb, 2001). The cycle of underachievement and poverty for many African American and Latina/o families were tied to an agrarian lifestyle in the South and Southwestern U.S., respectively. In many African American and Latina/o families, children did not enroll in school until after the harvest (Borden & Kroeger, 2001; Krull, 2003; Pérez, 2002). Moreover, some Latina/o children had to attend several different schools because of migrant farming (Krull, 2003; Pérez, 2002). Such economic constraints have a definite impact on poor families. As a result, it has taken some families several generations to produce their first college graduate and to break the cycle of poverty.

In my immediate family, which is six generations removed from slavery, my grandmother only had a sixth-grade education. My mother dropped out of high school in twelfth grade. Both were single parents and had working-class jobs. For some students, poverty and negative school experiences have been limiting and debilitating, but for others, it has been a source of inspiration (Martin, 2000). Given the demographic variables associated with my childhood and upbringing in St. Louis, many researchers and policymakers would not have predicted my academic success. Other variables such as learning for the intrinsic value of learning, spiritual connectedness, motivation to exceed others' expectations, and family values contributed to my academic success. I believed that education was the key to my success and was the first in my immediate family to graduate with a college degree in 1981. I am still witnessing first generation college graduates among students of color in 2007. For some working-class African American and Hispanic families, it has taken more than a century to produce one college graduate. The legacy continues by maintaining strong educational values in the family, community, and social institutions.

The key to maintaining academic success after the cycle of underachievement has been broken is to shatter notions that equate academic success to "acting White" (Martin, 2000; Ogbu, 2003; Taylor, 2004). A legacy of high academic performance must become the norm, especially among first generation African American and Hispanic college graduates. In my immediate family there is a second generation of college graduates, having passed the legacy of academic success on to my two daughters. If we are able to pass the legacy on to a third generation, the cycle of poverty and underachievement may be broken for good. In order to shatter the notion that academic success is "not cool" or unattainable, children of color need to be exposed to young successful role models who look like them. Success breeds success.

In the African American community, positive role models may be found in Black sororities and fraternities such as Sigma Gamma Rho and Kappa Alpha Psi. In addition to these organizations, the Black Church has been a pillar in the African American community for generations, helping to instill strong education and family values, and can be even more proactive in the lives of African American children today. For example, Rev. Dr. Zan Wesley Holmes, Jr. established the pastor's report card review at St. Luke "Community" United Methodist Church in Dallas, Texas, when my children were growing up there. The program had a profound impact on my daughters long after we relocated to the East Coast. They continued to send Pastor Holmes copies of their report cards even when they were in college. From daycare centers to GED programs, the Black Church has supplemented education for children and adults for decades. As principal investigator of several community-based research studies, mathematics and science programs were implemented in several churches in Philadelphia, Pennsylvania. Funded by the National Science Foundation and the Office of Urban and Global Ministries of the United Methodist Church, more than 200 children have been impacted by these community-based projects. The Black Church can provide role models to promote the development of mathematics identity and socialization among African American students.

One of the greatest challenges to establishing a legacy is the American system of education itself. Institutional barriers such as apartheid schools must be dismantled (Kozol, 2005). First, we must find a way for students of color and poor students to gain access to the best schools in their community without regard to geographical boundaries (Kozol, 1991). Ideally, these schools should not be segregated but diverse in terms of race, ethnicity, language, and achievement variables. Second, the neediest students should have the most talented and culturally responsive teachers. Third, the curriculum, technology, and resources available to these students should be second to none.

Creating and maintaining a legacy of achievement requires a major overhaul of the current educational system and a substantial investment of capital: human, cultural, and social (Dance, 2002). Human capital refers to "the knowledge, skills, educational training, and other capabilities acquired by individuals that enhance economic productivity" (Dance, 2002, p. 72). Cultural capital may be interpreted as "the heritage or acquired linguistic codes, disposition, tastes, modes of thinking, and other types of knowledge or competences deemed legitimate by the dominant group or groups in society" (Dance, 2002, p. 74). Social capital is defined as the "resources that result from social relationships among individuals, families, communal groups, [and] social networks" (Dance, 2002, p. 72). I believe significant investment in the types of capital described above will help students become more successful in school and society in general. Thus, a legacy for academic and economic success can be established to benefit everyone.

In order to improve achievement and course-taking patterns among students of color in mathematics, curriculum must be meaningful and relevant to their lives, taught in interesting and sometimes non-traditional ways, valued in the community and seen as a means to economic success. When teachers incorporate the cultural identities that diverse students bring to school into the classroom, they create opportunities not only to learn important content but also to appreciate their rich cultural heritage, confronting notions that academic success is a White endeavor.

The bicultural identities of African American, Asian American, Native American, and Latina/o American students can be used as a springboard to engage these populations in culturally specific mathematics (Brenner, 1998; Gutstein *et al.*, 1997; Ladson-Billings, 1994; Lipka *et al.*, 2005). From the cradle to the schoolhouse door, from the pulpit to the pew, entire communities must be involved in helping to build mathematics identity among students of color, sending them the message that it is "cool" to be literate in mathematics. While these recommendations are no panacea, changing society's perceptions about who is expected to succeed, providing an infrastructure for all students to maximize their potential, and embracing the culture of all students is a humble beginning.

Appendix A
Research methods: Benjamin Banneker Project

Methodology

The exploratory study reported here involved three classes of fourth-grade students ($n = 73$) and their work on a culturally relevant computer-assisted task. We provided six teachers in three schools in Illinois, New York, and Pennsylvania with *Riding the Freedom Train* (Leonard & Leonard, 2003) computer software that provided students with a culturally relevant context to solve mathematics and science problems. The questions that guided this exploratory study were: (1) In what ways do students interact with a culturally relevant computer simulation? (2) How did the culturally relevant, computer-assisted software program impact student learning in mathematics and science? (3) What effect does the type of computer environment (lab or workstation) and prior instruction have on student outcomes?

The computer module was first field tested with African American students in a Philadelphia charter school to determine how well it could be implemented in classrooms and computer labs as well as to check the validity of the questions (Leonard *et al.*, 2005). The results of this field test determined that there were some flaws in the computer program. First, a clock that was used to advance the storyline did not allow some students enough time to answer a question before it advanced to the next one. To remedy the problem, the clock was removed from the program. In addition, students could easily move backward and forward in the program, which resulted in multiple opportunities to answer the same question and caused some students to skip a few problems. This feature prevented the research team from learning what some students actually knew. Therefore, the computer module was changed, allowing students to only go forward.

Furthermore, an answer was required for each question before students could advance the storyline. To assist students who may have difficulty understanding the questions, hints or scaffolds that suggested specific problem-solving strategies were provided to help students solve the problems. Each student was given three chances to solve the problems correctly before the program automatically advanced to the next item. The problems consisted of a mix of multiple choice and short answer items. The scaffold feature was used to allow the researchers to learn about student strategies, errors, and misconceptions since the software program had the ability to capture the responses the students entered during the computer-based task.

After making the aforementioned adjustments and adding two additional mathematics questions to balance the types of problems asked, a second field test was conducted at a charter school in New York. Then the module was implemented with one class of students in Illinois for comparative data.

Setting and participants

Six teachers in three different schools participated in the Banneker study. Participants included two fourth-grade teachers and their students ($n = 56$) in Pennsylvania, three teachers and their third- ($n = 44$) and fourth-grade students ($n = 22$) in New York, and one teacher and her students ($n = 21$) in Chicago.

Data collection

Quantitative and qualitative methods were used to collect the data in this study. Data sources included a unit plan, videotapes of lessons, teacher and student interviews, student work samples, and results of student input on the multimedia task. At the outset, students read multicultural texts about the Underground Railroad. Classes were videotaped and audiotaped as teachers used the books to help children learn about the Underground Railroad and the mathematics and science knowledge fugitive slaves needed to survive. Audiotapes of the teachers' lessons were systematically coded to find themes and patterns in the classroom discourse. The videotapes were used to triangulate and clarify the data obtained from the audiotapes as well as to observe teachers' and students' expressions during the lessons. Finally, teachers and students were interviewed using a standard protocol to determine what influence the computer module had on the learning context. These data were analyzed for themes and patterns.

After reading the texts and completing a series of lesson plans, students worked on the module in the computer lab. The computer program was able to archive all of the students' responses to the questions on the computer's hard drive. These files were saved to a floppy disk and opened with *Notepad*. Reports were generated and analyzed to determine the accuracy of students' responses. The reports allowed the research team to analyze patterns in students' answers, which revealed students' thinking about certain types of mathematics problems. The data also informed the researcher about the ability of multicultural texts and computer modules to engage students in discourse and problem solving.

Procedures

This study began with workshops to familiarize the teachers with a culturally specific computer software module called *Riding the Freedom Train* (Leonard

& Leonard, 2003), which was created with *Authorware* and *Flash MX*. The teachers and school administrator were introduced to the kinds of responses that could be embedded within the computer program as well as the kind of scaffolding it could support.

Teachers in Pennsylvania and New York were provided with three or four texts about the Underground Railroad to provide students with the background knowledge needed to successfully complete the computer module. Students in New York read *Sweet Clara's Freedom Quilt* (Hopkinson, 1993), *Minty: The Story of Young Harriet Tubman* (Schroeder, 1996), and *Aunt Harriet's Underground Railroad in the Sky* (Ringgold, 1992). Teachers in Pennsylvania read *Barefoot* (Edwards, 1997), *Sweet Clara's Freedom Quilt* (Hopkinson, 1993), *Minty: The Story of Young Harriet Tubman* (Schroeder, 1996), and *Freedom River* (Rappaport, 2000). The Illinois teacher did not read any of these books to students because she was the science teacher in a departmentalized setting. However, the students read several of the aforementioned texts in their language arts class. In New York and Philadelphia classrooms, reading lessons were audiotaped and videotaped as teachers read multicultural stories to their students. Likewise, literacy skills were embedded in the computer module as it told a story about travel on the Underground Railroad. Moreover, the module provided students with mathematics problems and science questions to complete as they advanced the storyline.

Teachers in New York and Pennsylvania implemented several lesson plans prior to the completion of the module in the computer lab. The unit included activities such as making a quilt, where concepts such as symmetry, area, and perimeter were introduced. In addition, connections were made to the Underground Railroad, since the quilt was often used as a map or a sign to identify safe houses where fugitive slaves could obtain food, clothing, and rest (Crafts, 2002).

After the unit was completed, the teachers in New York and Pennsylvania took the students to the computer lab to complete *Riding the Freedom Train* (Leonard & Leonard, 2003). Data were collected on two consecutive days at both sites. The computer module allowed the researcher to obtain information about students' learning and their ability to solve contextualized mathematics and science questions. Students used the hints or scaffolds only when needed. The data retrieved from the computer archives allowed the researcher to determine how many hints were needed for a student to solve each problem. This feature allowed the researcher to determine students' prior knowledge as well as the difficulty level of each problem. Moreover, the students' responses were used to determine how they were thinking about each problem and what strategies they used to solve the problems.

Appendix B
Interview protocol

1. How easy did you find it to work on the computer today?
2. How was working with the computer today different than usual?
3. Do you work with computers a lot?
4. What did you like most about working with computers at school today?
5. Was there anything you did not like about working with computers?
6. Was *Riding the Freedom Train* easy or difficult?
7. Was there anything you did not like about the software?
8. How well did you do answering the questions?
9. What did you learn about the Underground Railroad?
10. Did you learn anything else?

Appendix C
Culturally specific lesson plans (recommended for grades 3–5)

Underground Railroad Unit

Language Arts	Mathematics	Science	Social Studies
Read *Barefoot* to students. Introduce key science, math, and context vocabulary. Introduce students to the writing process and have them keep a journal pretending to be a fugitive slave.	Provide sample rate and distance problems for students to solve to understand the concept of traveling by foot on the Underground Railroad (i.e. Barefoot traveled eight hours per day. How far could he travel in five days?). Students will explain and show multiple ways to solve problems.	Students will learn about fresh water life and other animals that live in the marsh (i.e. heron, rabbits, deer, mosquitoes, and fireflies).	Students will watch segments (Oh, To Be Free; Slavery and Earliest Escapes) of the Underground Railroad documentary hosted by Alfre Woodard (Michaels, 1998).
Introduce new vocabulary; paired reading of *Minty*. Introduce students to character study; talk about Harriet Tubman's character traits; continue journaling.	Have students develop word problems around work (i.e. How much money could Minty earn in a week (five days) if she were paid $1.25 per hour for eight hours a day?). Students will also use data obtained from the Internet to graph high and low temperatures for the past week.	Students will learn about farm animals (chickens, roosters, horses, and cows) and river animals like the muskrat. Students will also learn about the weather, weather forecasting symbols, and discuss the best time of year to plan an escape on the Underground Railroad.	Students will watch three more segments of the Underground Railroad video (Abolition Now, The Angel of Philadelphia, and Great Escapes). They will develop a timeline of the history of U.S Slavery.
Introduce new vocabulary; paired reading of *Freedom River*. Introduce mosaics as an art extension. Continue journaling.	Have students develop wanted posters with rewards for capture. Discuss relative monetary values (place value). Discuss units of measurement. Have students measure the length of the classroom in feet.	Students will learn about the phases of the moon: full moon, quarter moon, crescent moon, gibbous moon, and new moon. They will also discuss how the moon was related to escape on the Underground Railroad. See	Students will watch three more segments of the Underground Railroad video (The Moses of her People, A Band of Angels, and Letters from Home). Students will also work on mapping skills (use URR route from Kentucky to Ohio). Make a

Introduce new vocabulary; paired reading of *Sweet Clara and the Freedom Quilt.* Complete graphic organizer on the quilt story and explain how to use a quilt as a map.	Help students understand the concept of fugitive slaves swimming a distance of 1,000 feet across the Ohio River to freedom?	www.eduref.org/cgi-bin/printlessons.cgi/Virtual/Lessons/Science/Astronomy/AST0201.html	collage that shows how a fugitive slave may have escaped.
	Introduce geometry terms such as area/perimeter. Students will create designs for a quilt patch. Students will measure the perimeter and area of their patch and find lines of symmetry if any. Allow students to discuss the meaning of symbols on quilts made by slaves, such as the star and a water jug. Then link each piece together to create a large classroom quilt.	Students learn about the constellations and how important the Big Dipper and the North Star was to fugitive slaves. Students will create a constellation using coordinates on a graph and identify six constellations. See www.eduref.org/cgi-bin/printlessons.cgi/Virtual/Lessons/Science/Astronomy/AST0200.html	Students will watch two more segments of the Underground Railroad video (Rebellion and Rescue, Free at Last!).
Read Nikki Giovanni's poem "Quilting the Blacked-eyed Pea: We're Going to Mars." In the poem, the journey of a slave from Africa to the U.S. is compared to a journey from Earth to Mars. Students may use journal notes to create a poem that tells a story about survival in space.	Students will graph data related to the Alka-Rocket activity to discuss the impact of using a quarter, half, and whole tablet and various amounts of water.	Show ten-minute clip of *Apollo 13* video to demonstrate how rockets take off for outer space. Have students design their own Alka Rocket. Explain how energy is transferred from Alka-Seltzer and water to gas to create lift off. See http://lunar.arc.nasa.gov/education/activities/active4.htm	Make a Family Tree. Students will interview an elder in their family to learn about their experiences with Civil Rights, citizenship, voting rights, etc. Students will write a report on the elder and share it with the class.

Blues highway

Language Arts/Reading	Mathematics	Science	Social Studies	Math/Science standards
1. Introduction of books. Teacher will do book talks about *ellington was not a Street* (readers needing extra support), *When Marian Sang* (independent readers), and *Bessie Smith and the Night Riders* (advanced readers). 2. Pre-reading activities (KWL chart) —Students will make predictions about the texts based on the titles/covers. 3. Writing: individual students will keep a journal/diary for one week to record life events.	1. Problem solving will be developed around the theme of the music industry: cost of making demo tapes; timing number of tracks and length of songs; calculating profits and royalties from hit records. 2. Students will learn about whole, half, quarter, and eighth notes while they learn to play the recorder.	1. Students will learn about the human ear and the sense of hearing. 2. Students will use Microcomputer-based Laboratory Sound (MBL) to collect waveforms on the following instruments: triangle, tambourine, harmonica, bongo, and maracas. 2. Students will compare and contrast the waveforms of each instrument. Students will work in groups, pairs, or individually, to write or create an original song (record on CD).	1. Students will watch the video *Standing in the Shadows of Motown— The Funk Brothers*. 2. Students will complete the lesson called *The Importance of Music* and learn about the accomplishments of Louis Armstrong and Bessie Smith. 3. Students will learn about the kinds of jobs Blacks were recruited to do and how Berry Gordy used the factory model to create the Motown music machine.	Mathematics: Number and Operations, Fractions and Decimals, Problem Solving, Communication, and Connections. Science: Science as Inquiry, Life Science, and Science in Personal and Social Perspectives.
1. Reading the texts: Teachers and students may read the texts in literature circles, paired readings, or independently.	1. Develop problems about the following: weekly wages that could be made in the 1920s as railroad workers and factory workers; develop	1. Students will learn about the automobile industry and its impact on African American migration from the South. 2. Students will use Tinker	1. Students will discuss the great migration after World War I to understand its importance as the biggest population shift in U.S. history.	Mathematics: Number and Operations, Algebra, Measurement, Geometry, Problem Solving, Communication, and Connections.

2. Response to text: Students will write double entry journals: quote excerpts from texts and personal comments.
3. Introduce vocabulary:—migration, Jim Crow, sod hut, pioneer, sharecropper, tenement, assembly line (word sort).
3. Writing:—Students will keep a journal about traveling from the South to the North.

a weekly budget for living in the city (rent, food, supplies), distance/rate problems of train trip from the South to the North.
2. Students will use their knowledge about measurement and geometry to design a city with townhouses and high rises for factory workers.

toys to create a model car to investigate speed by pushing the car down a ramp (FASE, 1998).
3. Students will record data and calculate speed in feet per second.
4. Students will redesign their model to try to improve speed.

2. Students will participate in discussion guide found at www.scholastic.com/dearamerica/parentteacher/guides/dearamerica/colordark.htm to talk about segregation and social injustice.

Science: Science as Inquiry and Science in Personal and Social Perspectives.

Viva La Causa!

1. Introduction of books. Teacher will do book talks about *First Day of Grapes* (readers needing extra support), *Harvesting Hope* (independent readers), and *Esperanza Rising* (advanced readers) http://nancykeane.com/booktalks/ryan_esperanza.htm

1. Use context of the books to develop problem solving around the following: adding the number of crates of grapes needed for a shipment to market; calculate how long it would take a family to make $1,000 if they made only 0.30 a day; distance/rate problems of freedom

1. Students will learn about the parts of a seed and what is needed for a plant to grow.
2. Students will plant lima beans in a classroom terrarium and observe and measure the growth of a lima bean over a two-week period to learn about the germination of seeds.

1. Discuss role models (St. Francis of Assisi, Gandhi, and Martin Luther King) of Cesar Chavez and why he thought nonviolence was the way to lead a protest.
2. Make the Eagle flag that symbolized the *La Causa* Movement.
3. Students will listen to

Mathematics: Number and Operations, Algebra, Measurement, Fractions and Decimals, Problem Solving, Communication, and Connections.

Science: Science as Inquiry, Life Science, and Science in Personal and Social Perspectives.

Language Arts/Reading	Mathematics	Science	Social Studies	Math/Science Standards
2. Pre-reading activities (pre-reading plan): Students will make predictions about the texts based on the titles/covers. 3. Writing: students will pretend to be on a freedom march and record journal entries (writing workshop). 1. Reading the texts: teachers and students may read the texts in literature circles, paired readings, or independently. 2. Response to texts: issues of social justice raised in the texts (reading logs). 3. Introduce vocabulary: drought, *La Causa*, migrant worker, nonviolence, National Farm Workers Association, short handled hoe, strike. 3. Writing (writing process): students will write a speech about use of nonviolence to achieve equality	walk from Delano to Sacramento. 1. Students will solve problems related to the farmers' strike to understand how much money the owners lost during the movement. 2. Students will use metric units to scale to build adobe houses (clay) to scale to replicate the Arizona/Mexican ranches that Cesar and Esperanza used to live on before the drought/Depression, respectively.	1. Students will learn about the importance of recycling and biodegradable objects. 2. Students will make a mini-landfill to learn about decomposition. They will observe the landfill for two weeks and record their observations in a journal. 3. Students will report their findings to the class using PowerPoint or other multimedia tools.	Spanish music, learn a Spanish song, and create a freedom song with a Latin beat (record on CD). 1. Select an appropriate video about Cesar Chavez or migrant farm workers. 2. Discuss the physical and emotional toll of walking across the state of California for human rights. 3. Discuss hunger strike as form of political action; ramification of hunger strike on individual and community.	Mathematics: Number and Operations, Measurement, Geometry, Problem Solving, Communication, and Connections. Science: Science as Inquiry and Science in Personal and Social Perspectives.

Mae Jemison/Bessie Coleman

Text-based lessons	Computer-based lessons	Math/science activities
Introduction of Books. Teacher will do a book talk about Mae Jemison (Braun, 2005). Pre-reading activities—Students will make predictions based on the cover and the title (anticipation guides). Teacher will read the text and present two math problems related to the story. Students will solve the problems in groups.	Students will select the first menu, which advances a storyline about Mae Jemison and presents them with ten to 12 new word problems (Level 2) to solve on the computer. Scaffolding and hints will be provided as well as calculator and manipulative tools.	Students will complete the Veggie Shuttle lesson in Mission Mathematics. They will simulate a Space Shuttle launch using an edible model. Students will compare the relative sizes of the Space Shuttle assembly to the external fuel tank, solid rocket boosters, and the orbiter and solve three to four word problems using these facts.
Students will read portions of Mae Jemison: A Space Biography (Yanuzzi, 1998) and solve five to six word problems related to the text. Students who finish early can create their own word problems. Students will be able to use hand-held calculators in order to focus on the process of problem solving. Strategies and solutions will be discussed.	Students will select the second menu, which advances a storyline about Mae Jemison and presents them with ten to 12 new word problems (Level 2) to solve on the computer. Scaffolding and hints will be provided as well as calculator and manipulative tools.	Students will watch a ten-minute video clip of Apollo 13 showing rocket lift off. Then they will complete Fizzy-Tablet Rockets lesson in Mission Mathematics. They will learn about Newton's Third Law of Motion, design a rocket, and watch the rocket launch. Data will be collected, compared, and represented in a graph.
Students will finish reading Mae Jemison text and solve five to six word problems related to the text. Students who finish early can create their own word problems. Students will be able to use hand-held calculators in order to focus on the process of problem solving. Strategies and solutions will be discussed.	Students will select the third menu, which advances a storyline about Mae Jemison and presents them with ten to 12 new word problems (Level 3) to solve on the computer. Scaffolding and hints will be provided as well as calculator and manipulative tools.	Students will continue to learn about rockets by completing the Protractor Rocket lesson in Mission Mathematics. Students will compare flight distances or rubber-band rockets when the launch angle and amount of force vary. They will also measure angles with a protractor and distances with a meter stick. They will collect, organize, analyze, and interpret data and find the range, median, and mean of a set of data.
Introduction of Books. Teacher will do a book talk about Nobody Owns the Sky, Fly High! and Story of Aviator Elizabeth	Introduction of Hypermedia. Teacher will review a demo version of the hypermedia module about Bessie Coleman to get children	Students will complete the Rescue and Mission lesson in Mission Mathematics. Activities include learning about life, gravity, drag, and thrust to

Text-based lessons	Computer-based lessons	Math/science activities
Coleman. Pre-reading activities—Students will make predictions about the texts based on the covers and the titles (anticipation guides). Read portions of *Talkin' About Bessie* and present two math problems related to the story. Students will work in groups to solve the problems.	familiar with logging in and using passwords. Children will be able to access four scenes, which will be read with voiceover technology. Each scene will also present students with four related story problems. Teacher will work with the students to help them solve problems and enter their responses on the computer.	understand aeronautics. Students will use spinners to play the game and learn probability as they learn these terms. Students will collect, organize, and interpret data as well as construct tally tables and bar graphs. They will also learn about probability to determine the likelihood or probability of success.
Students will read *Nobody Owns the Sky* independently, then they will work independently to solve five to six word problems related to the text. Students who finish early can create their own word problems. Students will be able to use hand-held calculators in order to focus on the process of problem solving. Strategies and solutions will be discussed.	Students will select the first menu, which advances a storyline about Bessie Coleman and presents them with ten to 12 word problems (Level 1) to solve on the computer. Scaffolding and hints will be provided as well as calculator and manipulative tools.	Students will use geometry and measurement skills to make their own kites (Indian, Box, or Diamond kite). The URL for the kite lesson is: www.aka.org.au/kites_in_the_classroom/plans.htm. Once the students finish their kites they will fly them and record data on how long their kite was able to stay in the air and estimate how high they think their kites flew.
Students will read *Fly High!* independently, then they will work independently to solve five to six word problems related to the text. Students who finish early can create their own word problems. Students will be able to use hand-held calculators in order to focus on the process of problem solving. Strategies and solutions will be discussed.	Students will select the second menu, which advances a storyline about Bessie Coleman and presents them with ten to 12 new word problems (Level 2) to solve on the computer. Scaffolding and hints will be provided as well as calculator and manipulative tools.	Students will complete the Air Show lesson in *Mission Mathematics*. Activities include making a paper airplane. Data will be gathered on how close the plane lands on a target, the number of flips it can make, how long it stays in the air, and how far it can fly. Students will record data and analyze data and complete a glyph to represent the data on their individual airplanes. Then the class will make a table from a sample of ten students' data and find the median score. A mapping activity will conclude the lesson as students learn how to use scale to determine distances.

Christa McAuliffe/Amelia Earhart

Text-based lessons	Computer-based lessons	Math/Science activities
Introduction of Books. Teacher will do a book talk about *Christa McAuliffe: A Space Biography* Pre-reading activities—Students will make predictions about the text based on the cover and the title (anticipation guides). Teacher will read portions of *text* and present two math problems related to the story. Students will work in groups to solve the problems.	Students will select the first menu, which advances a storyline about Christa McAuliffe and presents them with ten to 12 new word problems (Level 2) to solve on the computer. Scaffolding and hints will be provided as well as calculator and manipulative tools.	Students will complete the Veggie Shuttle lesson in *Mission Mathematics*. They will simulate a Space Shuttle launch using an edible model. Students will compare the relative sizes of the Space Shuttle assembly to the external fuel tank, solid rocket boosters, and the orbiter and solve three to four word problems using these facts.
Students will read portions of *Christa McAuliffe* story and solve five to six word problems related to the text. Students who finish early can create their own word problems. Students will be able to use hand-held calculators in order to focus on the process of problem solving. Strategies and solutions will be discussed.	Students will select the second menu, which advances a storyline about Christa McAuliffe and presents them with ten to 12 new word problems (Level 2) to solve on the computer. Scaffolding and hints will be provided as well as calculator and manipulative tools.	Students will watch a ten-minute video clip of *Apollo 13* showing rocket lift off. Then they will complete Fizzy-Tablet Rockets lesson in *Mission Mathematics*. They will learn about Newton's Third Law of Motion, design a rocket, and watch the rocket launch. Data will be collected, compared, and represented in a graph.
Students will finish reading *Christa McAuliffe* text and solve five to six word problems related to the text. Students who finish early can create their own word problems. Students will be able to use hand-held calculators in order to focus on the process of problem solving. Strategies and solutions will be discussed.	Students will select the third menu, which advances a storyline about Christa McAuliffe and presents them with ten to 12 new word problems (Level 3) to solve on the computer. Scaffolding and hints will be provided as well as calculator and manipulative tools.	Students will continue to learn about rockets by completing the Protractor Rocket lesson in *Mission Mathematics*. Students will compare flight distances or rubber-band rockets when the launch angle and amount of force vary. They will also measure angles with a protractor and distances with a meter stick. They collect, organize, analyze, and interpret data and find the range, median, and mean of a set of data.

Text-based lessons	Computer-based lessons	Math/Science activities
Introduction of Books. Teacher will do a book talk about *A Picture Book of Amelia Earhart, Amelia and Eleanor Go for a Ride,* and *Amelia Earhart: Pioneer of the Sky.* Pre-reading activities: students will make predictions about the texts based on the covers and the titles (anticipation guides). Teacher will read portions of *Amelia Earhart: Pioneer in the Sky* and present two math problems related to the story. Students will work in groups to solve the problems.	Introduction of Hypermedia. Teacher will review a demo version of the hypermedia module about Amelia Earhart to get children familiar with logging in and using passwords. Children will be able to access four scenes that include text, which will be read with voiceover technology. Each scene will also present students with four story problems related to the scenes. The teacher will work with the students to help them solve the problems and enter their responses on the computer.	Students will complete the Rescue and Mission lesson in *Mission Mathematics.* Activities include learning about life, gravity, drag, and thrust to understand aeronautics. Students will use spinners to play the game and learn probability as they learn these science terms. Students will collect, organize, and interpret data as well as construct tally tables and bar graphs. They will also learn about probability to determine the likelihood or probability of success.
Students will read *A Picture Book of Amelia Earhart* independently. Then they will work independently to solve five to six word problems related to the text. Strategies and solutions will be discussed. Students who finish early can create their own word problems. Students will use hand-held calculators in order to focus on the process of problem solving.	Students will select the first menu, which advances a storyline about Amelia Earhart and presents them with ten to 12 word problems (Level 1) to solve on the computer. Scaffolding and hints will be provided as well as calculator and manipulative tools.	Students will use geometry and measurement skills to make their own kites (Indian, Box, or Diamond kite). The URL for the kite lesson is: www.aka.org.au/kites_ in_the_classroom/plans.htm. Once the students finish their kites they will fly them and record data on how long their kite was able to stay in the air and estimate how high they think their kites flew.
Students will read *Amelia and Eleanor Go for a Ride* independently, then they will work independently to solve five to six word problems related to the text. Students who finish early can create their own word problems. Strategies and solutions will be discussed. Students will use hand-held calculators in order to focus on the process of problem solving.	Students will select the second menu, which advances a storyline about Amelia Earhart and presents them with ten to 12 new word problems (Level 2) to solve on the computer. Scaffolding and hints will be provided as well as calculator and manipulative tools.	Students will complete the Air Show lesson in *Mission Mathematics.* Activities include making a paper airplane. Data will be gathered on how close the plane lands on a target, the number of flips it can make, how long it stays in the air, and how far it can fly. Students will record and analyze data and complete a glyph to represent the data on their individual airplanes. Then the class will make a table from a sample of ten students' data and find the median score. A mapping activity will conclude the lesson as students learn how to use scale to determine distances.

Appendix D
Research methods: Space Links

Methodology

The purpose of the Space Links program was to influence the pedagogy of prospective teachers as well as impact diverse students in the School District of Philadelphia. The program provided participants with the following supports: (1) innovative curriculum; (2) professional development sessions; (3) informal community-based internship; and (4) formal externship. The first three supports were provided in Year 1 of the study. The last support, an externship at NASA GFSC, took place in Year 2 of the study. The research questions that guided the study in Year 2 were: (1) How did the interventions impact preservice and beginning teachers' self-efficacy and science pedagogy? (2) How did collaborations with NASA scientists advance prospective and beginning teachers' efficacy and their ability to teach inquiry-based space science lessons?

Participants and setting

Recruitment of preservice teachers began prior to the start of the study. The recruits were enrolled in a teacher certification program in the College of Education. At one northeastern university, information about the program was posted throughout the College of Education and announced in science and mathematics methods courses. Eleven females and one male were selected to participate in Space Links. The 12 participants selected for the study were diverse in terms of race (seven African American; two Asian American; three European American) and age (six traditional (ages 22–24)) and (six non-traditional (over 25)). In Year 1, nine participants worked with Pre-K–8 students in an informal science program at community-based sites. In Years 1 and 2, seven preservice teachers taught space or earth science lessons during student teaching. In Year 2, four of the 12 preservice teachers were selected by project staff to participate in the externship at NASA GSFC. However, only three of the participants returned to teach in the area after completing the externship. The other participant graduated and left the area to teach in a distant city within the same state where the college was located.

Procedures

There were four phases to the qualitative study: (1) community-based internships; (2) professional development sessions; (3) student teaching; and (4) externships. In Phase 1, the preservice teachers participated in a community-based science program. During this phase, preservice teachers worked with urban children ages three to 13. During Phase 2 of the study, preservice teachers were required to attend five half-day professional development sessions. The purpose of the professional development sessions was to enhance the preservice teachers' space science content knowledge and improve their self-efficacy prior to student teaching or induction. Phase 3 focused on the preservice teachers' formal student teaching experience, which was required by the College. Phase 4 of the study provided up to five preservice teachers with the opportunity to complete a summer externship at NASA GSFC. The purpose of the externship was to advance preservice teachers' science content knowledge and self-efficacy.

Data collection, data sources, and data analysis

In the early stages of the Space Links program, project staff made two visits to project sites to collect qualitative data. Data collection included videotaping preservice teachers' science lessons. Data were also collected through interviews with two groups of program participants: preservice teachers and student participants during the internship phase at community-based sites. In addition, the research team administered the Science Teacher Efficacy Belief Inventory (STEBI-B) (Enochs & Riggs, 1990) on a pre-post basis and used the Science Teaching Inquiry Rubric (STIR) (Bodzin & Beerer, 2003) to rate lessons.

Four primary sources of data were used to analyze the results of the Space Links study: (1) observations and field notes; (2) transcripts of preservice teachers' science teaching; (3) STIR scores; (4) STEBI-B scores; and (5) preservice teachers' interviews. The Constant-Comparative Method (Glaser & Strauss, 1967) was used to analyze transcripts and interview data. Because of the small sample size only descriptive statistics were used to analyze quantitative data.

Appendix E
Galaxy lab sheet

Identifying types of galaxies lab

Procedure:

1. In this lab, you will classify the different types of galaxies using the images provided.
2. Once you have identified a galaxy's type, mark an x in the appropriate column in the chart after each name.
3. After each galaxy has been classified, carefully answer each lab question on a separate sheet of paper. (Give detail!)

Galaxy name	Elliptical	Spiral	Irregular
Andromeda galaxy			
Bode's nebula (M81)			
M32			
M49			
M82			
Milky Way			
NGC 2–5			
NGC 1365			
NGC 6822			
Small magellanic cloud			
Sombrero galaxy			
Whirlpool galaxy (M51)			

Lab questions

1. What is a galaxy?
2. Describe the main distinguishing features of spiral, elliptical, and irregular galaxies.

3. What is a barred spiral galaxy? Could any of the galaxies be classified as barred spirals? Which ones?
4. How did you classify the Sombrero galaxy? Why? Be specific!
5. Why can't we see the spiral shape of the Milky Way when observing from the Earth?
6. Recent evidence indicates the Milky Way may be classified as what type of galaxy? Is this classification supported by the image?
7. Why are some galaxies classified as irregular?
8. What is a group of galaxies called?

Source: Chrystina Vandergast (Space Links participant).

Appendix F
Preservice teacher interview protocol

1. How user-friendly was the *Mission Mathematics* teachers' guide?
2. What problems (if any) did students have learning space science content at the churches or the schools?
3. How well did the curriculum address the science/mathematics needs of your students?
4. How do you feel that your knowledge of the subject has changed?
5. How did the space science curriculum fit into your school curriculum?
6. What are specific examples that you used in your student teaching experience to highlight earth or space science in your classroom?
7. Which of the instructional supports (i.e. professional development, internship, externship) did you find most helpful in developing your science content knowledge and teaching? What was least effective?
8. What content would you have liked more time/emphasis/information on during professional development sessions? (i.e. Do you feel prepared to teach the content?) Explain.
9. How will you use what you learned this year to help students to strengthen their science/mathematics knowledge and skills next year?
10. What was your overall impression of the Space Links project?

Riding the Freedom Train CD

Information about purchasing the Riding the Freedom Train CD may be obtained from the following URL: http://astro.temple.edu/~jleo/leonard/book.htm

References

Aikenhead, G. S. (1997). Towards a first nations cross-cultural science and technology curriculum. *Science Education, 81*, 217–238.

Aikenhead, G. S. (2001). Students' ease in crossing cultural borders in school science. *Science Education, 85*(2), 180–188.

Aikenhead, G. S. & Jegede, O. J. (1999). A cognitive explanation of a cultural phenomenon. *Journal of Research in Science Teaching, 36*(3), 269–287.

Ainsa, T. (1999). Success of using technology and manipulatives to introduce numerical problem solving skills in monolingual/bilingual early childhood classrooms. *Journal of Computers in Mathematics and Science Teaching, 18*(4), 361–369.

Albert, L. R. (2000). Lessons learned from the "Five Men Crew." In M. E. Strutchens, M. L. Johnson, & W. F. Tate (eds), *Changing the faces of mathematics: Perspectives on African Americans* (pp. 81–88). Reston, VA: NCTM.

Allexsaht-Snider, M. & Hart, L. (2001). Mathematics for all: How do we get there? *Theory Into Practice, 40*(2), 93–101.

Ambrose, R., Levi, L., & Fennema, E. (1997). The complexities of teaching for gender equity. In J. Trentacosta & M. J. Kennedy (eds), *Multicultural and gender equity in mathematics classrooms* (pp. 236–242). Reston, VA: NCTM.

Ameis, J. (2002). Stories invite children to solve mathematical problems. *Teaching Children Mathematics, 8*(5), 260–264.

American Association of University Women (1992). *How schools shortchange girls: The AAUW report: A study of major findings on girls and education.* Washington, DC: Author.

Anderson, A., Anderson, J., & Shapiro, J. (2004). Mathematical discourse in shared storybook reading. *Journal for Research in Mathematics Education, 35*(1), 5–33.

Anderson, J. R., Reder, L. M., & Simon, H. A. (2000, Summer). Applications and misapplications of cognitive psychology to mathematics education. *Texas Educational Review.* Retrieved on July 14, 2006 from: http://act-r.psy.cmu.edu/publications/pubinfo.php?id=146.

Apple, M. W. (1995). Taking power seriously: New directions in equity in mathematics education and beyond. In W. G. Secada, E. Fennema, & L. B. Adajian (eds), *New directions for equity in mathematics education* (pp. 329–348). New York: Cambridge University Press.

Apple, M. W. (2003). Freire and the politics of race in education. *International Journal of Leadership in Education, 6*(2), 107–118.

Ascher, M. (1991). *Ethnomathematics: A multicultural view of mathematical ideas.* Pacific Grove, CA: Brooks/Cole.

Avildsen, J. G. (Director) (1989). *Lean on me* [Film]. Burbank, CA: Warner Brothers.

Ball, D. L. (1993). With an eye on the mathematical horizon: Dilemmas of teaching elementary school mathematics. *The Elementary School Journal, 93*(4), 373–397.

Banks, J. A. (1974). Cultural pluralism and the schools. *Educational Leadership, 32*(3), 163–166.

Banks, J. A. (1993). The canon debate, knowledge construction, and multicultural education. *Educational Researcher, 22*, 4–14.

Banks, J. A. (2001). Citizenship education and diversity: Implications for teacher education. *Journal of Teacher Education, 52*(1), 5–6.

Baroody, A. J. & Coslick, R. T. (1998). *Fostering children's mathematical power: An investigative approach to k-8 mathematics instruction.* Mahwah, NJ: Lawrence Erlbaum.

Becker, B. E. & Luthar, S. S. (2002). Socio-emotional factors affecting achievement outcomes among disadvantaged students: Closing the achievement gap. *Educational Psychologist, 37*(4), 197–214.

Bernhard, J. K. & Freire, M. (1999). What is my child learning at elementary school? Culturally

191

contested issues between teachers and Latin American families. *Canadian Ethnic Studies, 31*, 72–94.

Beerer, K. & Bodzin, A. (2004). How to develop inquiring minds. District implements inquiry-based science instruction. *Journal of Staff Development, 25*(4), 43–47.

Benfer, A. (2002). Policing gangsta fashion. Retrieved on January 13, 2007 from: http://archive.salon.com/mwt/feature/2002/05/29/nelly/print.html

Bodzin, A. & Beerer, K. (2003). The validation of the science teacher inquiry rubric. *Journal of Elementary Science Education, 15*(2), 39–49.

Bollin, G. G. & Finkel, J. (1995). White racial identity as a barrier to understanding diversity: A study of prospective teachers. *Equity & Excellence in Education, 28*(1), 25–30.

Borden, L. & Kroeger, M. K. (2001). *Fly High! The story of Bessie Coleman*. New York: Margaret K. McElderry Books.

Bourdieu, P. (1973). Cultural reproduction and social reproduction. In R. Brown (ed.), *Knowledge, education and cultural changes* (pp. 56–69). London: Tavistock.

Box Office Mojo (2007). Retrieved on January 17, 2007 from http://boxofficemojo.com/about/adjuster.htm

Boykin, A. W. & Toms, F. D. (1985). Black child socialization: A conceptual framework. In H. McAdoo & J. McAdoo (eds), *Black children: Social, educational, and parental environments* (pp. 33–51). Beverly Hills, CA: Sage.

Bransford, J., Brown, A., & Cocking, R. (2000). *How people learn*. Expanded edition. Washington, DC: National Research Council.

Braun, E. (2005). *Mae Jemison*. Rocheport, MO: Pebbles Books.

Brayboy, B. M. (2005). Toward a tribal critical race theory in education. *The Urban Review, 37*(5), 425–446.

Brenner, M. E. (1998). Adding cognition to the formula for culturally relevant instruction in mathematics. *Anthropology & Education Quarterly, 29*(2), 214–244.

Brown v. Board of Education, 347 U.S. 483 (1954).

Brown, F. & Boshamer, C. C. (2000). Using computer-assisted instruction to teach mathematics: A study. *The Journal of the National Alliance of Black School Educators, 4*(1), 62–71.

Buerk, D. (1985). The voices of women making meaning in mathematics. *Journal of Education, 167*(3), 59–70.

Bumiller, E. (1998, June 30). Six generations of strong women: History leaves mark on Elizabeth Cady Stanton's line. *New York Times*, p. B1, B6.

Campbell, P. B. (1989). So what do we do with the poor, nonwhite, female: Issues of gender, race, and social class in mathematics and equity. *Peabody Journal of Education, 66*(2), 95–111.

Campbell, P. B. (1995). Redefining the "girl problem in mathematics." In W. G. Secada, E. Fennema, & L. B. Adajian (eds), *New directions for equity in mathematics education* (pp. 225–241). New York: Cambridge University Press.

Campbell, P. F. & Johnson, M. L. (1995). How primary students think and learn. In I. Carl (ed.), *Prospects for school mathematics: 75 years of progress* (pp. 21–42). Reston, VA: National Council of Teachers of Mathematics.

Carey, D. A., Fennema, E., Carpenter, T. P., & Franke, M. L. (1995). Equity and mathematics education. In W. G. Secada, E. Fennema, & L. B. Adajian (eds), *New directions for equity in mathematics education* (pp. 93–125). New York: Cambridge University Press.

Carpenter, T. P. & Lehrer, R. (1999). Teaching and learning mathematics with understanding. In E. Fennema & T. Romberg (eds), *Mathematics classrooms that promote understanding* (pp. 19–32). Mahweh, NJ: Lawrence Erlbaum.

Carpenter, T. P., Ansell, E., Franke, M. L., Fennema, E., & Weisbeck, L. (1993). Models of problem solving: A study of kindergarten children's problem solving processes. *Journal for Research in Mathematics Education, 24*(5), 428–441.

Carpenter, T. P., Fennema, E., & Franke, M. L. (1992, April). *Cognitively guided instruction: Building the primary mathematics curriculum on children's informal mathematical knowledge*. Paper presented at the Annual Meeting of the American Educational Research Association, San Francisco.

Carpenter, T. P., Fennema, E., Franke, M. L., Levi, L., & Empson, S. B. (1999). *Children's Mathematics: Cognitively Guided Instruction*. Portsmouth, NH: Heinemann.

Carraher, T. N., Carraher, D. W., & Schielmann, A. D. (1987). Written and oral mathematics. *Journal for Research in Mathematics Education, 18*(2), 83–97.

Cathcart, W. G., Pothier, Y. M., Vance, J. H., & Bezuk, N. S. (2006). *Learning mathematics in elementary and middle school* (4th ed.). Columbus, OH: Pearson Merrill Prentice Hall.

Cazden, C. B. (2001). *Classroom discourse: The language of teaching and learning* (2nd ed.). Portsmouth, NH: Heinemann Educational Books, Inc.

Celedón-Pattichis, S. (2007). The Young Women's Leadership School case study. In R. Kitchen, J. Depree, S. Celedón-Pattichis, & J. Brinkerhoff, (eds), *Mathematics education at highly effective schools that serve the poor: Strategies for change* (pp. 131–145). Mahwah, NJ: Lawrence Erlbaum.

Chappell, M. F. & Thompson, D. R. (2000). Fostering multicultural connections in mathematics through media. In M. E. Strutchens, M. L. Johnson, & W. F. Tate (eds), *Changing the faces of mathematics: perspective on African Americans* (pp. 135–150). Reston, VA: NCTM.

Chen, Z. (1999). Schema induction in children's analytical problem solving. *Journal of Educational Psychology, 91*, 703–715.

Child Poverty Fact Sheet. (2001). New York: National Center for Children in Poverty, Columbia University.

Christmann, E. & Badgett, J. (1999). A comparative analysis of the effects of computer-assisted instruction on student achievement in differing science and demographic areas. *Journal of Computers in Mathematics and Science Teaching, 18*(2), 135–143.

Cobb, P., Wood, T., Yackel, E., & McNeal, B. (1992). Characteristics of classroom mathematics traditions: An interactional analysis. *American Educational Research Journal, 29*(3), 573–604.

Coerr, E. (1993). *Sadako and the thousand paper cranes.* New York: G. P. Putnam's Sons.

Cole, M. (1992). Culture in development. In M. H. Borenstein & M. E. Lamb (eds), *Developmental psychology: An advanced textbook* (3rd ed.) (pp. 731–789). Mahweh, NJ: Lawrence Erlbaum.

Coleman, J. (1987). Families and schools. *Educational Researcher, 16*(6), 32–38.

College Board (2005). 2005 College-bound seniors: Total group profile report. Retrieved on August 12, 2006 from: http://www.collegeboard.com/prod_downloads/about/news_info/cbsenior/yr2005/2005-college-bound-seniors.pdf

Cone, J. H. (1990). *A black theology of liberation* (20th anniversary ed.). Maryknoll, NY: Orbis. (Original work published 1970.)

Cooper, P. (2002). Does race matter?: A comparison of effective black and white teachers of African American students. In J. J. Irvine (ed.), *In search of wholeness: African American teachers and their specific classroom practices* (pp. 47–63). New York: Palgrave.

Costa, V. B. (1995). When science is "another world": Relationships between worlds of family, friends, schools, and science. *Science Education, 79*, 313–333.

Crafts, H. (2002). *A bondwoman's narrative,* H. L. Gates, Jr. (ed.). New York: Warner.

Craig, D. V. (1999). Science and technology: A great combination. *Science and Children, 36*(4), 28–32.

Crespo, S. (2003). Learning to pose mathematical problems: Exploring changes in preservice teachers' practices. *Educational Studies in Mathematics 52*, 243–270.

Crews, T., Biswas, G., Goldman, S., & Bransford, J. (1997). Anchored Interactive Learning Environments. *International Journal of Artificial Intelligence in Education, 8*, 142–178.

Czerniak, C. M. & Schriver, M. (1994). An examination of preservice science teachers' beliefs. *Journal of Science Teacher Education, 5*(3), 77–86.

D'Ambrosio, U. (1985). *Socio-cultural bases for mathematics education.* Cumpinas, Brazil: UNICAMP Centro de Producoes.

Dance, L. J. (2002). *Tough fronts: The impact of street culture on schooling.* New York: Routledge.

Davis, R. B., Maher, C., & Noddings, N. E. (1990). Constructivist views on the teaching and learning of mathematics. *Journal for Research in Mathematics Education, Monograph Series Number 4.* Reston, VA: National Council of Teachers of Mathematics.

Dee, R. (1988). *Two ways to count to ten: A Liberian folktale.* New York: Henry Holt & Co.

De La Cruz, Y. (1999). Reversing the trend: Latino families in real partnership with schools. *Teaching Children Mathematics, 5*(5), 296–300.

Delgado, R. (1995) (ed.) *Critical race theory: The cutting edge.* Philadelphia: Temple University Press.

Delpit, L. (1995). *Other people's children: Cultural conflict in the classroom.* New York: The New Press.

Demi (1997). *One grain of rice: A mathematical folktale.* New York: Scholastic Press.

Demmert, Jr., W. G. & Towner, J. C. (2003). A review of the research literature on the influences of culturally based education on the academic performance of Native American students. Retrieved on July 6, 2006 from: http://www.nwrel.org/nwreport/2003-03/index.html

Diller, D. (1999). Opening the dialogue: Using culture as a tool in teaching young African American children. *Reading Teacher, 52,* 820–827.

Diller, J. V. & Moule, J. (2005). *Cultural competence: A primer for educators.* Canada: Thompson Wadsworth.

Dixson, A. D. & Rousseau, C. K. (2005). And we are still not saved: Critical race theory in education ten years later. *Race Ethnicity and Education, 8*(1), 7–27.

Dossey, J. A., Giordano, F., McCrone, S., & Weir, M. D. (2002). *Mathematics methods and modeling for today's mathematics classroom: A contemporary approach to teaching grade 7–12.* Pacific Grove, CA: Thomson Learning.

Du Bois, W. E. B. (1903/1995). *The souls of black folk.* New York: New American Library. (Reprint: original work published 1903.)

Duncan, G. A. (2005). Critical race ethnography in education: Narrative, inequality and the problem of epistemology. *Race Ethnicity and Education, 8*(1), 93–114.

Eaton, S. E. (2001). *The other Boston busing story: What's won and lost across the boundary lines.* New Haven, CN: Yale University Press.

Ebby, C. B. (2000). Learning to teach mathematics differently: The interaction between coursework and fieldwork for preservice teachers. *Journal of Mathematics Teacher Education, 3*(1), 69–97.

Edelson, D. C. (2001). Learning-for-Use: A framework for the design of technology-supported inquiry activities. *Journal of Research in Science Teaching, 38*(3), 335–385.

Edgewood Independent School District v. Kirby, 777 SW2d 391 (1989).

Edwards, P. D. (1997). *Barefoot: Escape on the Underground Railroad.* New York: HarperCollins.

El Nasser, H. (2006, May 10). U.S. born Hispanics propel growth: Census finds immigration is not biggest factor in boom. *USA Today,* p. A1.

Enochs, L. & Riggs, I. (1990). Further development of an elementary Science Teaching Efficacy Belief Instrument: A preservice elementary scale. *School Science and Mathematics, 90*(8), 694–706.

Entwisle, D. R. & Alexander, K. L. (1992). Summer setback: Race, poverty, school composition, and mathematics achievement in the first two years of school. *American Sociological Review, 57,* 72–84.

Ertmer, P. A., Addison, P., Lane, M., Ross, E., & Woods, D. (1999). Examining teachers' beliefs about the role of technology in the elementary classroom. *Journal of Research on Computing in Education, 32*(1), 54–73.

Feelings, M. (1971). *Moja means one: Swahili counting book.* New York: Puffin Pied Piper Books.

Fennema, E. (1974). Mathematics learning and the sexes: A review. *Journal for Research in Mathematics Education, 5*(3), 126–139.

Fennema, E. & Sherman, J. (1976). Fennema-Sherman Mathematics Attitude Scales: Instruments designed to measure attitudes toward the learning of mathematics by females and males. *Journal for Research in Mathematics Education, 7*(5), 324–326.

Fennema, E., Franke, M. L., & Carpenter, T. P. (1993). Using children's mathematical knowledge in instruction. *American Educational Research Journal, 30*(3), 555–583.

Fine, M. (2004). The power of the *Brown v. Board of Education* decision: Theorizing threats to sustainability. *American Psychologist, 59*(6), 502–510.

Flam, F. (2006, August 25). Earth to Pluto: You're outta here. *The Philadelphia Inquirer,* A1 & A10.

Ford, D. Y. (1993). Black students' achievement orientation as a function of perceived family orientation and demographic variables. *Journal of Negro Education, 62*(1), 47–66.

Foundations for the Advancements in Science and Education Productions (1998). *The Kay Tolliver Files.* Los Angeles, CA: FASE Productions.

Franke, M. L. & Kazemi, E. (2001). Learning to teach mathematics: Developing a focus on students' mathematical thinking. *Theory into Practice, 40*(2), 102–109.

Freire, P. (1982). *Pedagogy of the oppressed.* Harmondsworth: Penguin.

Fuchs, L. S., Fuchs, D., Prentice, K., Hamlett, C. L., Finelli, R., & Courey, S. J. (2004). Enhancing mathematical problem solving among third-grade students with schema-based instruction. *Journal of Educational Psychology, 96*(4), 635–647.

Fullan, M. (2000). The three stories of education reform. *Phi Delta Kappan, 81*(8), 581–584.

Garofalo, J. & Sharp, B. D. (2003). Teaching fractions using a simulated sharing activity. *Learning and Leading with Technology, 30*(7), 36–41.

Gay, G. (2000). *Culturally responsive teaching: Theory, practice and research.* New York: Teachers College Press.

Geary, D. C. (1996). *Children's mathematical development: Research and applications.* Washington, DC: American Psychological Association.

Gee, J. P. (1989). Literacy, discourse, and linguistics: Introduction. *Journal of Education, 171*(1), 5–17.

Glaser, B. G. & Strauss, A. L. (1967). *The discovery of grounded theory: Strategies for qualitative research.* Chicago: Aldine.

Grifalconi, A. (1986). *The village of round and square houses.* Boston: Little, Brown & Co.

Grimes, N. (2002). *Talkin' about Bessie: The story of aviator Elizabeth Coleman.* New York: Scholastic.

Guberman, S. R. (2005). Cultural aspects of young children's mathematics knowledge. Retrieved May 10, 2005, from: http://spot.colorado.edu/~gubermas.NCTM_paper.htm

Guha, S. (2006). Using mathematics strategies in early childhood education as a basis for culturally responsive teaching in India. *International Journal of Early Years Education, 14*(1), 15–30.

Guitérrez, R. (2002). Enabling the practice of mathematics teachers in context: Toward a new equity research agenda. *Mathematical Thinking and Learning, 4*(2&3), 145–187.

Gutstein, E. (2003). Teaching and learning mathematics for social justice in an urban, Latino school. *Journal for Research in Mathematics Education, 34*(1), 37–73.

Gutstein, E., Lipman, P., Hernandez, R., & de los Reyes, R. (1997). Culturally relevant mathematics teaching in a Mexican American context. *Journal for Research in Mathematics Education, 28*(6), 709–737.

Haberman, M. (1991). The pedagogy of poverty versus good teaching. *Phi Delta Kappan, 73,* 290–294.

Hamza, H. M. & Blake-Stalker, A. (2005). *Addressing diversity in teacher education programmes: Syllabi analysis and faculty resources and needs assessment survey.* Paper presented at the 2005 Annual Conference of the American Educational Research Association, Montreal, Quebec.

Hanna, G. (2003). Reaching gender equity in mathematics education. *The Educational Forum, 67,* 204–214.

Harmon, D. (2002). They won't teach me: The voices of gifted African-American inner-city students. *Roeper Review, 24*(2), 68–75.

Hatfield, M. M., Edwards, N. T., Bitter, G. G., & Morrow, J. (2000). *Mathematics methods for elementary and middle school teachers* (4th edition). New York: John Wiley & Sons, Inc.

Haycock, K. (2001). Closing the achievement gap. *Educational Leadership, 58*(6), 6–11.

Hennessy, S. (1993). Situated cognition and cognitive apprenticeship: Implications for classroom learning. *Studies in Science Education, 22,* 1–41.

Herrnstein, R. J. & Murray, C. (1994). *The bell curve: Intelligence and class structure in American life.* New York: Free Press.

Hill, J. R. & Hannafin, M. J. (2001). Teaching and learning in digital environments: The resurgence of resource-based learning. *Educational Technology Research and Development, 49*(3), 37–52.

Hollins, E. R. (1996). *Culture in school learning: Revealing the deep meaning.* Mahwah, NJ: Lawrence Erlbaum.

Hopkinson, D. (1993). *Sweet Clara and the freedom quilt.* New York: Random House.

Hopkinson, D. (2002). *Under the quilt of night.* New York: Simon & Schuster.

Hort, L. (1991). *How many stars in the sky?* New York: Tambourine Books.

Howard, T. C. (2003). Culturally relevant pedagogy: Ingredients for critical teacher reflection. *Theory into Practice, 42*(3), 195–202.

Hufferd-Ackles, K., Fuson, K. C., & Sherin, M. G. (2004). Describing levels and components of a math-talk learning community. *Journal for Research in Mathematics Education, 35*(2), 81–116.

Hurricane exposes issues of class, race [Editorial] (2005, September 2). *USA Today*, A20.

Imazeki, J. & Reschovsky, A. (2006). *The legacy of Rodriguez: Three decades of school finance reform in Texas.* Paper presented at the Earl Warren Institute on Race, Ethnicity, and Diversity, University of California Berkeley, April 27–28, 2006.

Irvine, J. J. (1991). *Black students and school failure: Policies, practices, and prescriptions.* Westport, NY: Praeger.

Irvine, J. J. (1992). Making teacher education culturally responsive. In M. E. Dilworth (ed.), *Diversity in teacher education: New expectations* (pp. 79–92). San Francisco: Jossey-Bass.

Irvine, J. J. (2002). African American teachers' culturally specific pedagogy. In J. J. Irvine (ed.), *In search of wholeness: African American teachers and their specific classroom practices* (pp. 139–146). New York: Palgrave.

Jacobs, J. E. & Becker, J. R. (1997). In J. Trentacosta & M. J. Kennedy (eds), *Multicultural and gender equity in mathematics classrooms* (pp. 107–114). Reston, VA: NCTM.

Jeffrey, L. S. (1998). *Christa McAuliffe: A space biography.* Berkeley Heights, NJ: Enslow Publishers.

Jegede, O. J. & Olajide, J. O. (1995). Wait time, classroom discourse, and the influence of sociocultural factors in science teaching. *Science Education, 79*(3), 233–249.

Jensen, A. R. (1969). How much can we boost IQ and scholastic achievement? *Harvard Educational Review, 39*, 1–123.

Jordan, N. C., Levine, S.C., & Huttenlocher, J. (1994). Development of calculation abilities in middle- and low-income children after formal instruction in school. *Journal of Applied Developmental Psychology, 15*, 233–240.

Kahan, J. A., Cooper, D. A., & Bethea, K. A. (2003). The role of mathematics teachers' content knowledge in their teaching: A framework for research applied to a study of student teachers. *Journal of Mathematics Teacher Education, 6*(3), 223–252.

Kazemi, E. & Stipek, D. (2001). Promoting conceptual thinking in four upper-elementary mathematics classrooms. *The Elementary School Journal, 102*(1), 59–80.

Keats, E. J. (1962). *The snowy day.* New York: The Viking Press.

Kerkman, D. D. & Siegler, R. S. (1993). Individual differences and adaptive flexibility in lower-income children's strategy choices. *Learning and Individual Differences, 5*(2), 113–136.

Kinard, B. & Bitter, G. G. (1997). Multicultural mathematics and technology: The Hispanic Math Project. *Computers in the Schools, 13*(1/2), 77–88.

Kitchen, R. (2007). An overview of schooling in high-poverty communities. In R. Kitchen, J. Depree, S. Celedón-Pattichis, & J. Brinkerhoff (eds), *Mathematics education at highly effective schools that serve the poor: Strategies for change* (pp. 1–19). Mahwah, NJ: Lawrence Erlbaum.

Kitchen, R., Depree, J., Celedón-Pattichis, S., & Brinkerhoff, J. (2007). *Mathematics education at highly effective schools that serve the poor: Strategies for change.* Mahwah, NJ: Lawrence Erlbaum.

Knapp, M. (1995). *Teaching for meaning in high-poverty classrooms.* New York: Teachers College Press.

Kozol, J. (1991). *Savage inequalities.* New York: Crown.

Kozol, J. (1995). *Amazing Grace: The lives of children and the conscience of a nation.* New York: Crown.

Kozol, J. (2005). *The shame of the nation: The restoration of apartheid schooling in America.* New York: Crown.

Krull, K. (2003). *Harvesting hope: The story of Cesar Chavez.* New York: Harcourt.

Ku, H. & Sullivan, H. J. (2001). *Effects of personalized instruction on mathematics word problems in Taiwan.* Paper presented at the 24th National Convention of the Association for Educational Communications and Technology, Atlanta, GA.

Ladson-Billings, G. (1994). *The dreamkeepers: Successful teachers of African American children.* San Francisco: Jossey-Bass.

Ladson-Billings, G. (1995). Toward a theory of culturally relevant pedagogy. *American Educational Research Journal, 32* (3), 465–491.

Ladson-Billings, G. (1997). It doesn't add up: African American students' mathematics achievement. *Journal for Research in Mathematics Education, 28*(6), 697–708.

Ladson-Billings, G. (1998). Just what is critical race theory and what's it doing in a *nice* field like education? *Qualitative Studies in Education, 11*(1), 7–24.

Ladson-Billings, G. (2006). From the achievement gap to the education debt: Understanding achievement in U.S. schools. *Educational Researcher, 35*(7), 3–12.

Land, S. M. & Hannifin, M. J. (1996). A conceptual framework for the development of theories-in-action with open-ended learning environments. *Educational Technology Research and Development, 44,* 37–53.

Lave, J. (1988). *Cognition in practice: Mind, mathematics, and culture in everyday life.* Cambridge: Cambridge University Press.

Lave, J. & Wenger, E. (1991). *Situated learning: Legitimate peripheral participation.* Cambridge, England: Cambridge University Press.

Leder, G. C. (1992). Mathematics and gender: Changing perspectives. In D. A. Grous (ed.), *Handbook of research in mathematics teaching and learning* (pp. 597–622). New York: Macmillan.

Leder, G. C. & Forgasz, H. J. (1997). Single-sex classes in a coeducational high school: Highlighting parents' perspectives. *Mathematics Education Research Journal, 9,* 274–291.

Lee, C. D. (2001). Is October Brown Chinese? A cultural modeling activity system for underachieving students. *American Educational Research Journal, 38*(1), 97–142.

Lee, H. & Songer, N. B. (2003). Making authentic science accessible to students. *International Journal of Science Education, 25*(8), 923–948.

Lee, O. (2003). Equity for linguistically and culturally diverse students in science education: A research agenda. *Teachers College Record, 105*(3), 465–489.

Lehman, J. R. (1994). Integrating science and mathematics: Perceptions of preservice teachers and practicing elementary teachers. *School Science and Mathematics, 94*(2), 58–64.

Leonard, J. (2000). Let's talk about the weather: Lessons learned in facilitating mathematical discourse. *Mathematics Teaching in the Middle School, 5*(8), 518–523.

Leonard, J. (2001a). Integrating art and mathematics: Using art to teach math concepts. *The Journal of the New England League of Middle Schools, 14*(1), 36–39.

Leonard, J. (2001b). How group composition influenced the achievement of sixth-grade mathematics students. *Mathematical Thinking and Learning, 3*(2&3), 175–199.

Leonard, J. (2002a). The case of a first-year charter school. *Urban Education, 37*(2), 217–238.

Leonard, J. (2002b). Taking science dialogue by storm. *Science and Children, 39*(4), 31–35.

Leonard, J. (2004). Integrating mathematics, social studies, and language arts with "A Tale of Two Cities." *Middle School Journal, 35*(3), 35–40.

Leonard, J. & Campbell, L. L. (2004). Using the stock market for relevance in teaching number sense. *Mathematics Teaching in the Middle School, 9*(6), 294–299.

Leonard, J. & Dantley, S. J. (2005). Breaking through the ice: Dealing with issues of diversity in mathematics and science education courses. In A. J. Rodriguez & R. Kitchen (eds), *Preparing prospective mathematics and science teachers to teach for diversity: Promising strategies for transformative action* (pp. 87–117). Mahwah, NJ: Lawrence Erlbaum.

Leonard, J. & Guha, S. (2002). Creating cultural relevance in teaching and learning mathematics. *Teaching Children Mathematics, 9*(3), 114–118.

Leonard, J. & Hill, M. L. (in press). Using multimedia to engage African-American children in classroom discourse. *Journal of Black Studies.*

Leonard, J. & Leonard, D. (2003). Interactive Journeys in Mathematics and Science: Riding the Freedom Train (Book Companion Edition) [Computer Software]. Ann Arbor: Renaissance Micro, Inc.

Leonard, J., Boakes, N., & Oakley, J. E. (2005). *Balancing self-efficacy and conflict in teaching science inquiry: A case study of preservice teachers' field experiences.* Paper presented at the Annual Meeting of the American Educational Research Association, Montreal, Quebec.

Leonard, J., Davis, J. E., & Sidler, J. L. (2005). Cultural relevance and computer-assisted instruction. *Journal of Research on Technology in Education, 37*(3), 259–280.

Leonard, J., Taylor, K., Sanford-De Shields, J., & Spearman, P. (2004). Professional development schools revisited: Reform, authentic partnerships and new visions. *Urban Education, 39*(5), 561–583.

Lesh, R., Post, T., & Behr, M. (1987). Representations and translations among representations in mathematics learning and problem solving. In C. Javier (ed.), *Problems of representation in the teaching and learning of mathematics* (pp. 33–40). Hillsdale, NJ: Lawrence Erlbaum.

Lester, F., Garofalo, J., & Kroll, D. (1989). *The role of metacognition in mathematical problem solving: A study of two grade seven classes* (Report No. NSF-MDR 85–50346). Washington, DC: National Science Foundation.

Lindbergh, R. (1998). *Nobody owns the sky.* Cambridge, MA: Candlewick.

Linn, M. C. & Hsi, S. (2000). *Computers, teachers, peers: Science learning partners.* Mahweh, NJ: Lawrence Erlbaum Associates, Inc.

Lipka, J. & Adams, B. (2002). *Improving Alaska Native rural and urban students' mathematical understanding of perimeter and area.* Unpublished manuscript. Alaska School Research Fund.

Lipka, J., Hogan, M. P., Webster, J. P., Yanez, E., Adams, B., Clark, S., & Lacy, D. (2005). Math in a cultural context: Two case studies of a successful culturally based math project. *Anthropology in Education Quarterly, 36*(4), 367–385.

Lo, J. J. & Wheatley, G. H. (1994). Learning opportunities and negotiating social norms in mathematics class discussions. *Educational Studies in Mathematics, 37*, 145–164.

Longo, J. P. (1993). National mathematics standards and communicative competence: A sociolinguistic analysis of institutionalized and emergent forms of classroom discourse (Doctoral dissertation, The American University, 1993). *Dissertation Abstracts International, A: 55/11*, 3440.

Lowell, S. (1992). *The three little javelinas.* Hong Kong: Rising Moon.

Lubienski, S. T. (2000). Problem solving as a means toward mathematics for all: An exploratory look through a class lens. *Journal for Research in Mathematics Education, 31*(4), 454–482.

McNeal, B. (1995). Learning not to think in a textbook-based mathematics class. *Journal of Mathematical Behavior, 14*, 205–234.

Malloy, C. & Jones, G. (1998). An investigation of African American students' mathematical problem solving. *Journal for Research in Mathematics Education, 29*(2), 143–163.

Malloy, C. E. & Malloy, W. M. (1998). Issues of culture in mathematics teaching and learning. *The Urban Review, 30*(3), 245–257.

Manoucherhri, A. (1999). Computers and school mathematics reform: Implications for mathematics teacher education. *Journal of Computers in Mathematics and Science Teaching, 18*(1), 31–48.

Martin, D. B. (2000). *Mathematics success and failure among African American youth: The roles of sociohistorical context, community forces, school influence, and individual agency.* Mahweh, NJ: Lawrence Erlbaum.

Martin, D. B. (2003). Hidden assumptions and unaddressed questions in *Mathematics for All* rhetoric. *The Mathematics Educator, 13*(2), 7–21.

Mayer, R. E. & Hagerty, M. (1996). In R. J. Sternberg & T. Ben-Zeev (eds), *The nature of mathematical thinking* (pp. 29–53). Mahweh, NJ: Lawrence Erlbaum.

Mellado, V. (1998). The classroom practice of preservice teachers and their conceptions of teaching and learning science. *Science Education, 82*(2), 197–214.

Mendez, P. (1989). *The black snowman.* New York: Scholastic.

Menéndez, R. (Director) (1988). *Stand and deliver* [Film]. Burbank, CA: Warner Brothers.

Mensher, G. B. (1994). A Harriet Tubman celebration: Here's how we do this annual mixed-age project. *Young Children, 50*(1), 64–69.

Meringolo, J. (2006). *Gender differences in mathematics achievement and mathematics attitude through participation in athletics.* (Doctoral dissertation, Temple University, 2006.)

Michaels, S. (Producer) (1998). *Underground Railroad.* New York: A & E Home Video.

Montecinos, C. & Nielson, L. E. (1997). Gender and cohort differences in university students' decisions to become elementary teacher education majors. *Journal of Teacher Education, 48*(1), 47–54.

Morrison, T. (1992). *Playing in the dark: Whiteness and the literacy imagination.* Cambridge, MA: Harvard University Press.

Moses, R. P. & Cobb, Jr., C. E. (2001). *Radical equations: Math literacy and civil rights.* Boston: Beacon Press.

Mulryan, C. M. (1995). Fifth and sixth graders: Involvement and participation in cooperative small groups in mathematics. *The Elementary School Journal, 95*(4), 297–310.

Musgrove, M. (2001). *The spider weaver.* New York: Blue Sky Press.

Nasir, N. S. (2002). Identity, goals and learning: Mathematics in cultural practice. *Mathematical Thinking and Learning, 4*(2&3), 211–245.

Nasir, N. S. (2005). Individual cognitive structuring and the sociocultural context: Strategy shifts in the game of dominoes. *The Journal of the Learning Sciences, 14*(1), 5–34.

National Center for Children in Poverty (1999). *One in four: America's youngest poor.* New York: Columbia School of Public Health.

(NCES) National Center for Educational Statistics. (2005). *The nation's report card.* Retrieved October 18, 2005, from: http://nces.ed.gov/nationsreportcard/ltt/results2004/age_9_math_pref_table.asp

(NCES) National Center for Educational Statistics. (2006). *The nation's report card.* Retrieved August 12, 2006, from: http://nces.ed.gov/nationsreportcard/nrc/reading_math_2005/s0017.asp?printver=

National Council of Teachers of Mathematics (1989). *Curriculum and evaluation standards for school mathematics.* Reston, VA: Author.

National Council of Teachers of Mathematics (1991). *Professional standards for teaching mathematics.* Reston, VA: Author.

National Council of Teachers of Mathematics. (1997). *Mission mathematics K-6.* Reston, VA: Author.

National Council of Teachers of Mathematics. (2000). *Principles and standards for school mathematics.* Reston, VA: Author.

National Science Foundation (1996). Women, minorities, and persons with disabilities in science and engineering: 1996 (National Science Foundation Publication No. 96–311). Arlington, VA: Author.

(NSTA) National Science Teachers Association (2005). TIMSS 2003: Eighth-grade performance up, fourth-grade scores flat. *NSTA Reports, 16*(4), 1, 4.

Newell, M. (Director) (2003). *Mona Lisa Smile* [Film]. Culver City, CA: Columbia Pictures.

Nieto, S. (2000). Placing equity front and center: Some thoughts on transforming teacher education for a new century. *Journal of Teacher Education, 51*(3), 180–187.

Nieto, S. (2002). *Language, culture, and teaching: Critical perspectives for a new century.* Mahwah, NJ: Lawrence Erlbaum.

No child left behind: Reauthorization of the Elementary and Secondary Education Act of 2001 (2001). A report to the nation and the Secretary of Education, U.S. Department of Education, President Bush Initiative.

Nosek, B. A., Banaji, M. R., & Greenwald, A. G. (2002). Math = Male, Me = Female, Therefore Math ≠ Me. *Journal of Personality and Social Psychology, 83*(1), 44–59.

Núñez, R., Edwards, L. D., & Matos, J. F. (1999). Embodied cognition as grounding for situatedness and context in mathematics education. *Educational Studies in Mathematics, 39,* 45–65.

Oakes, J. (1990). Opportunities, achievement, and choice: Women and minority students in science and mathematics. In C. B. Cazden (ed.), *Review of research in education* (vol. 16, pp. 153–222). Washington, DC: American Educational Research Association.

O'Connor, M. C. & Michaels, S. (1993). Aligning academic task and participation status through revoicing: Analysis of a classroom discourse strategy. *Anthropology and Education Quarterly, 24*(4), 318–335.

Ogbu, J. U. (1987). Variability in minority school performance: A problem in search of an explanation. In E. Jacob & C. J. Jordan (eds), *Minority education: Anthropological perspectives* (pp. 83–111). Norwood, NJ: Ablex.

Ogbu, J. U. (2003). *Black American students in an affluent suburb: A study of academic disengagement.* Mahweh, NJ: Lawrence Erlbaum.

Oloko, B. A. (1994). Children's street work in urban Nigeria: Dilemma of modernizing tradition. In P. M. Greenfield & R. R. Cocking (eds), *Cross-cultural roots of minority child development* (pp. 197–224). Hillsdale, NJ: Lawrence Erlbaum.

Olsen, L. (1997). *Made in America: Immigrant Students in Our Public Schools.* New York: The New Press.

Page, M. S. (2002). Technology-enriched classrooms: Effects on students of low socioeconomic status. *Journal of Research on Technology in Education, 34*(4), 389–409.

Parker, L. H. & Rennie, L. F. (2002). Teachers' implementation of gender-inclusive instructional strategies in single-sex and mixed-sex science classrooms. *International Journal of Science Education, 24*(9), 881–987.

Patton, M. Q. (1990). Qualitative evaluation and research methods (2nd ed.). Newbury Park, CA: Sage.

Paznokas, L. S. (2003). Teaching mathematics through cultural quilting. *Teaching Children Mathematics, 9*(5), 250–255.

Peréz, L. K. (2002). *First day in grapes.* New York: Lee & Low Books.

Peterson, P. L., Fennema, E., Carpenter, T. P., & Loef, M. (1989). Teachers' pedagogical content beliefs in mathematics. *Cognition and Instruction, 6*(1), 1–40.

Phillips, S. & Ebrahimi, H. (1993). Equation for success: Project SEED. In NCTM (ed.), *Reaching all students with mathematics* (pp. 59–74). Reston, VA: The Council.

Phuntsog, N. (1995). Teacher educators' perceptions of the importance of multicultural education in the preparation of elementary teachers. *Equity & Excellence in Education, 28*(1), 10–14.

Piaget, J. (1965). *The child's conception of number.* New York: Norton.

Piaget, J. (1972). Development and learning. In C.S. Lavatelli & F. Stendler (eds), *Readings in child behavior and development* (3rd ed., pp. 38–46). New York: Harcourt.

Plessy v. Ferguson, 163 U.S. 537 (1896).

Polya, G. (1945). *How to solve it.* New York: Doubleday.

Price, J. & Valli, L. (1998). Institutional support for diversity in prospective teacher education. *Theory into Practice, 37*(2), 114–120.

Prince George's County (n.d.). Prince George's County Fun Facts. Retrieved on January 21, 2007 from: www.goprincegeorgescounty.com/subsites/visitors/kids4.htm

Public Broadcasting System. (n.d.) People and events: Harriet Tubman. Retrieved on January 25, 2007 from: www.pbs.org/wgbh/aia/part4/4p1535.html

Quintero, E. P. (2004). *Problem posing with multicultural children's literature: Developing critical early childhood curricula.* New York: Peter Lang.

Rappaport, D. (2000). *Freedom river.* New York: Hyperion.

Reisman, F. K. & Kauffman, S. H. (1980). *Teaching mathematics to children with special needs.* Columbus, OH: Charles E. Merrill.

Remillard, J. (2000). Prerequisites for learning to teach mathematics for all students. In W. G. Secada (ed.), *The changing faces of mathematics: Perspectives on multiculturalism and gender equity* (pp. 125–136). Reston, VA: NCTM.

Rey, H. A. (1982). *Find the constellations.* New York: Houghton Mifflin.

Ringgold, F. (1992). *Aunt Harriet's Underground Railroad in the Sky.* New York: Crown.

Ringgold, F. (2002). *Cassie's word quilt.* New York: Knopf.

Rist, R. (1970). Student social class and teacher expectations: The self-fulfilling prophecy in ghetto education. *Harvard Educational Review, 40,* 411–451.

Roberts, B. C. (2004). *Jazzy Miz Mozetta.* New York: Farrar Straus Giroux.

Robinson, R. (2000). *The debt: What America owes to Blacks.* New York: Dutton Books.

Rousseau, C. & Tate, W. F. (2003). No time like the present: Reflecting on equity in school mathematics. *Theory into Practice, 42*(3), 210–216.

Ryan, P. M. (1999). *Amelia and Eleanor go for a ride.* New York: Scholastic Press.

Ryan, P. M. (2002). *When Marian sang.* New York: Scholastic Press.

Salomon, G., Perkins, D. N., & Globerson, T. (1991). Partners in cognition: Extending human intelligence with intelligent technologies. *Educational Researcher, 20,* 2–9.

Saxe, G. (1991). *Culture and cognitive development: Studies in understanding mathematics.* Hillsdale, NJ: Lawrence Erlbaum.

Saxe, G. (1999). Cognition, development, and cultural practices. In E. Turiel (ed.), *Culture and development: New directions in child psychology* (pp. 19–36). San Francisco, CA: Jossey-Bass.

Saxe, G., Dawson, V., Fall, R., & Howard, S. (1996). Culture and children's mathematical thinking. In R. J. Sternberg & T. Ben-Zeev (eds), *The nature of mathematical thinking* (pp. 119–144). Mahweh, NJ: Lawrence Erlbaum.

Schifter, D. & Fosnot, C. T. (1993). *Reconstructing mathematics education*. New York: Teachers College Press.

Schofield, J. W. (2001). Inside desegregated schools: Understanding how and why they influence students. *American Journal of Education, 109*, 383–390.

Schroeder, A. (1996). *Minty: The story of young Harriet Tubman*. New York: Dial.

Secada, W. G. (1992). Race, ethnicity, social class, language and achievement in mathematics. In D. A. Grouws (ed.), *Handbook of research on mathematics teaching and learning* (pp. 623–660). New York: Macmillan.

Shange, N. (2004). ellington was not a street. New York: Simon & Schuster.

Sheets, R. H. (2005). *Diversity pedagogy: Examining the role of culture in the teaching-learning process*. Boston: Allyn and Bacon.

Sherin, M. G. (2002). When teaching becomes learning. *Cognition and Instruction, 20*(2), 119–150.

Silver, E. A., Smith, M. S., & Nelson, B. S. (1995). The QUASAR Project: Equity concerns meet mathematics education. In W. G. Secada, E. Fennema, & L. B. Adajian (eds), *New directions for equity in mathematics education* (pp. 9–56). New York: Cambridge University Press.

Silverman, F. L., Strawser, A. B., Strohauer, D. L., & Manzano, N. N. (2001). On the road with Cholo, Vato, and Pano. *Teaching Children Mathematics, 7*(6), 330–333.

Sleeter, C. E. (1997). Mathematics, multicultural education, and professional development. *Journal for Research in Mathematics Education, 28*(6), 680–969.

Solano-Flores, G. & Trumbull, E. (2003, March). Examining language in context: The need for new research and practice paradigms in the testing of English-language learners. *Educational Researcher, 32*(2), 3–13.

Soloway, E., Guzdial, M., & Hay, K. E. (1994, April). Learner-centered design: The challenge for HCL in the 21st century. *Interactions*, 37–48.

Spielberg, S. (Director). (1985). *The Color Purple* [Film]. Burbank, CA: Warner Brothers.

Stauffacher, S. (2006). *Bessie Smith and the night riders*. New York: G. P. Putnam's Sons.

Steele, M. M. & Steele, J. W. (1999). DISCOVER: An interactive tutoring system for teaching students with learning difficulties to solve word problems. *Journal of Computers in Mathematics and Science Teaching, 18*(4), 351–359.

Steffe, L. P. & Kieren, T. (1994). Radical constructivism and mathematics education. *Journal for Research in Mathematics Education, 26*(5), 711–733.

Stein, M. K., Grover, B. W., & and Henningsen, M. (1996). Building student capacity for mathematical thinking and reasoning: An analysis of mathematical tasks used in reform classrooms. *American Educational Research Journal, 33*, 455–488.

Stiff, L. & Harvey, W. B. (1988). On the education of black children in mathematics. *Journal of Black Studies, 19*(2), 190–203.

Strutchens, M. E. (2002). Multicultural literature as a context for problem solving: Children and parents learning together. *Teaching Children Mathematics, 8*(8), 448–454.

Strutchens, M., Lubienski, S. T., & McGraw, R. (2006). A closer look at gender in NAEP mathematics achievement and affect data: Intersections with achievement, race/ethnicity and socioeconomic status. *Journal for Research in Mathematics Education, 37*(2), 129–150.

Swain, C. & Pearson, T. (2003). Educators and technology standards: Influencing the digital divide. *Journal of Research on Technology in Education, 34*(3), 326–333.

Talbot, A. (2004). Quilt square math. Retrieved May 23, 2005, from: http://teacher.scholastic.com/products/instructor/jan04_quiltmath.htm

Tartre, L. A. & Fennema, E. (1995). Mathematics achievement and gender: A longitudinal study of selected cognitive and affective variables [Grades 6–12]. *Educational Studies in Mathematics, 28*, 199–217.

Tate, W. F. (1994). Race, retrenchment, and the reform of school mathematics. *Phi Delta Kappan, 75*(6), 477–484.

Tate, W. F. (1995). Returning to the root: A culturally relevant approach to mathematics pedagogy. *Theory into Practice, 34*(3), 166–173.

Tate, W. F. (1997). Race-Ethnicity, SES, gender, and language deficiency trends in mathematics achievement: An update. *Journal for Research in Mathematics Education, 28*(6), 652–679.

Taylor, K. L (2004). *Through their eyes: A strategic response to the national achievement gap.* Philadelphia: Research for Better Schools.

Tharp, R. G. (1982). The effective instruction of comprehension: Results and description of the Kamehameha Early Education Program. *Reading Research Quarterly, 14*(4), 503–527.

ThinkExist. (2006). Harriet Tubman quotes. Retrieved on January 25, 2007 from: http://thinkexist.com/quotes/harriet_tubman/

Thomas-El, S. (2003). *I choose to stay: A black teacher refuses to desert the inner city.* New York: Kensington Press.

Tillman, L. C. (2004). (Un)intended consequences?: The impact of the *Brown* v. *Board of Education* decision on the employment status of black educators. *Education and Urban Society, 36*(3), 280–303.

Tompert, A. (1997). *Grandfather Tang's story.* New York: Crown.

Two Blacks on Discovery launch [Editorial] (2006, December 25). *Jet 110*(25), 64.

U.S. Department of Commerce (n.d.). Current Populations Report. Retrieved May 18, 2005, from: www.census.gov/prod/1/pop/p25–1130/p251130b.pdf

Vale, C. M. & Leder, G. C. (2004). Student views of computer-based mathematics in the middle years: Does gender make a difference? *Educational Studies in Mathematics, 56,* 287–312.

Van Dusen, L. M. & Worthen, B. R. (2000). Can integrated instructional technology transform the classroom? *Educational Leadership, 52*(2), 28–22.

van Garderen, D. & Montague, M. (2003). Visual–spatial representations, mathematical problem solving, and students of varying abilities. *Learning Disabilities Research & Practice, 18*(4), 246–254.

Viadero, D. (2005). Transition mathematics project. Retrieved August 12, 2005 from: http://www.transitionmathproject.org/marketingarticle.asp

Villasenor, Jr., A. & Kepner, Jr., H. S. (1993). Arithmetic from a problem-solving perspective: An urban implementation. *Journal for Research in Mathematics Education, 24*(1), 62–69.

Vygotsky, L. (1978). *Mind in society: The development of higher psychological processes.* Cambridge, MA: Harvard University Press.

Vygotsky, L. (1986). *Thought and language.* Cambridge, MA: MIT Press.

Weiss, I., Banilow, R., McMahon, C., & Smith, S. (2001). Report of the 2000 National Survey of Science and Mathematics Education. Chapel Hill, NC: Horizon Research, Inc.

Wenglinsky, H. (1998). *Does it compute? The relationship between educational technology and student achievement in mathematics.* Princeton, NJ: Educational Testing Service.

Williams, S. R. & Baxter, J. A. (1996). Dilemmas of discourse-oriented teaching in one middle school mathematics classroom. *The Elementary School Journal, 97*(1), 21–38.

Williams, Y. M. & Leonard, J. (2004, April). *Charter school reform as rational choice: An analysis of African American parents' perceptions of charter schools located in residentially segregated inner-city communities.* Paper presented at the Annual Meeting of the American Educational Research Association, San Diego, CA.

Wood, T. (1999). Creating a context for argumentation in mathematics class. *Journal for Research in Mathematics Education, 30*(2), 171–191.

Wood, T. (2001). Teaching differently: Creating opportunities for learning mathematics. *Theory into Practice, 40*(2), 110–117.

Wright, R. J. (1994). A study of the numerical development of 5-year-olds and 6-year-olds. *Educational Studies in Mathematics, 26*(1), 25–44.

Yanuzzi, D. A. (1998). *Mae Jemison: A Space Biography.* Berkeley Heights, NJ: Enslow Publishers.

Index

Figures are indicated by **bold** page numbers, tables by *italics*.